LIFE IN THE LAW

ANSWERING GOD'S INTERROGATORIES

EDITED BY
GALEN L. FLETCHER and JANE H. WISE

J. REUBEN CLARK LAW SOCIETY
BRIGHAM YOUNG UNIVERSITY LAW SCHOOL
PROVO, UTAH

For David Blatt and Ed Hunter,
for first showing me the path
to a faithful life in the law — GLF

To Joseph and Lorraine
for a love of law and reading — JHW

Opinions expressed in this publication are the opinions of the authors, and their views should not necessarily be attributed to The Church of Jesus Christ of Latter-day Saints, Brigham Young University, the J. Reuben Clark Law Society or the Brigham Young University Law School.

Prepared for publication by BYU Studies, 403 CB, Brigham Young University, PO Box 24098, Provo, Utah 84602. To contact the J. Reuben Clark Law School, the J. Reuben Clark Law Society, write to 341 JRCB, Brigham Young University, PO Box 28000, Provo, Utah 84602.

Library of Congress Cataloging-in-Publication Data

Life in the law : answering God's interrogatories / edited by Galen L. Fletcher and Jane H. Wise.
    p. cm.
        ISBN 0-8425-2575-0 (alk. paper)
    1. Practice of law—United States—Moral and ethical aspects. 2. Legal ethics—United States. 3. Religion and law—United States. I. Fletcher, Galen L., 1961– II. Wise, Jane H., 1951–
    KF298 .L54 2002
    342.73'0852--dc21

2002011706

Printed in the United States of America
10 9 8 7 6 5 4 3 2

Contents

UNTO WHAT WERE YE ORDAINED? (D&C 50:13)

WHAT THINK YE OF CHRIST? (Matthew 22:42)

Preface

H. Reese Hansen

This book contains a prized collection of exceptional essays by thoughtful men and women who have examined things that matter most in both their professional and private lives. Most of these pieces were first published in the *Clark Memorandum*, the J. Reuben Clark Law School alumni magazine. A few are from other sources. All of them address important questions about the experience of being a Christian attorney.

Elder Marlin K. Jensen's 1997 talk introduced the idea of "answering God's interrogatories." Eventually, God will ask every professional several penetrating questions. The articles in the first section of this book ask, *"Adam, Where Art Thou?"* and speak to the concepts of balance, purpose, priorities, and preparation. The next section, *"What is Property Unto Me?"* looks at materialism, economic issues, greed, and integrity. The third group considers what a faithful lawyer does, focuses on service to others, and ponders *"Unto What Were [We] Ordained?"* The final section, *"What Think Ye of Christ?"* examines our duty and devotion to God, asking about our relationship to the master Advocate of us all, Jesus Christ. These essays point to the questions He asks of each of us in this life (and will equally ask us in the next) concerning what we've made of our lives in mortality. The authors explore their own choices in addressing these pivotal questions through instructive circumstances and people they have encountered along life's way.

My hope is that *Answering God's Interrogatories* will influence the ways in which all professionals think about themselves in terms of eternal values, and that by so doing, well-trained men and women will shape a life in the law that is both deeply satisfying and genuinely worthy.

H. Reese Hansen received his J.D. from the University of Utah in 1972 and served as Dean of the J. Reuben Clark Law School at Brigham Young University in Provo, Utah, 1989–2004.

Answering God's Interrogatories

Marlin K. Jensen

Trying to combine both religion and law, I have bravely entitled my remarks "Answering God's Interrogatories." I'm quite certain I would not know what an interrogatory was if I hadn't gone to law school. For those of you who are uninitiated, I wish to point out that interrogatories are questions—usually in writing—that parties to lawsuits ask each other for discovering what the opposing party's case is all about. More simply, the word *interrogatory* means a question. And for a long time, as I've read the scriptures, I've been impressed that one way God teaches us is through the questions he asks. We often call these rhetorical questions, which are questions asked for effect—for teaching effect, usually—with no answer expected. It's obvious that a Heavenly Father who knows all doesn't have much to discover, but we, his children, certainly do.

"Adam, Where Art Thou?"

It appears that this business of interrogatories began very early as Adam and Eve got into a little difficulty in the Garden of Eden. In calling Adam to account, God asked, "Adam, where art thou?" (Genesis 3:9). I've thought a lot about that question, and I don't think the Lord asked it because he didn't know where Adam was! He obviously wanted Adam to think about where he was and possibly about where he ought to be.

On this watershed day in your lives, may I ask you graduates to consider for a moment where you are? Is there a better way to determine that than by using gospel reference points—those eternal truths that are constant and sure?

Where are you, for example, concerning faith? Is it stronger and more evident in your life than when you began your legal education? It would be

1

a sad day if what you lost during your law school experience was far more important than what you've gained.

Where are you with prayer? Are you like my associate in the Quorums of Seventy who, when the opening hymn was announced in our weekly meeting as "Ere You Left Your Room This Morning, Did You Think to Pray?" winked at me and jokingly said, "Well, I thought about it!" How would we feel if we thought President Hinckley didn't say his daily prayers? Aren't our loved ones entitled to the same expectation on our part?

Where are you concerning the scriptures—God's word? Does section 76 of the Doctrine and Covenants mean more to you than and is it as well understood as section 501(c)(3) of the Internal Revenue Code? Remember that 25 years from today section 76 will remain unamended and in force. We can hardly offer the same assurances for section 501(c)(3)!

Where are you with reference to your spouse, if you are married, and to your family members? Several years ago I had the experience of interviewing 30 or so men in an effort to call a new stake president in central Utah. Among those interviewed were two brothers serving on the high council. When we asked the first one for three men he could recommend we consider, he told us that when his brother and he had been helping their widowed mother that morning with yard work, the thought occurred to him that his brother was the best man, the kindest man in the stake, and ought to become the new stake president. His brother was his only recommendation! When that brother came in next for his interview, his answer to our question was essentially the same. He recommended the first brother! As I drove home the next day I couldn't help wondering what my brothers would have said about me in that situation—or what my wife and children might have said.

I think there are many other implications of God asking where we are. One that has meaning for me is best described in Joseph Smith's History, verse 29. Joseph records that he retired to bed for the night and then, he says, "I betook myself to prayer and supplication to Almighty God for for- giveness of all my sins and follies." Then he makes this interesting statement: "And also for a manifestation to me, that I might know of my state and standing before him." In a sense, isn't that the question God was posing to Adam? "Where are you, Adam? Where have you been? Where are you going? What is your state and standing before me?" As I've thought about it, I don't know that there is a more profitable question for us to ask, especially in our prayers. If we really are brave, maybe we'd even ask that of our spouse or a close friend. I did that not long ago. I said, "Honey, how am I doing?" Kathy said, "Well, I think you're nicer than you used to be." I suppose you'd have to know what a scoundrel I was to appreciate how far I've come. Sometimes you can get that kind of feedback from people who really love you.

But getting feedback from God is even more helpful; and could there be a higher purpose for personal revelation than to have God answer our prayers and reveal to us where we lack—where we really are, so to speak? Then we can go to work on ourselves and our deficiencies and really do some good!

"What Is Property unto Me?"

A second helpful interrogatory posed by God is contained in section 117 of the Doctrine and Covenants. This is a verse directed to the Church land agents who were purchasing Church property in Missouri. The Lord says to them, "Let them repent of all their sins, and of all their covetous desires, before me, saith the Lord." The question is then asked: "For what is property unto me? saith the Lord" (v. 4). What a useful question for those of you poised to become generators of legal fees!

Then, as he often does when he asks these questions—or poses these interrogatories—the Lord provides the answer. He says:

> Have I not the fowls of heaven, and also the fish of the sea, and the beasts of the mountains? Have I not made the earth? Do I not hold the destinies of all the armies of the nations of the earth?

> Therefore, will I not make solitary places to bud and to blossom, and to bring forth in abundance? saith the Lord.

> Is there not room enough on the mountains of Adam-ondi-Ahman, and on the plains of Olaha Shinehah [that little valley that stretches out in front of Spring Hill], or the land where Adam dwelt, that you should covet that which is but a drop [That's what property is unto our Lord: a drop!] and neglect the more weighty matters? (D&C 117:6–8)

What are the weightier matters? He mentions some of them in the book of Matthew: judgment, mercy, faith. These are attributes a good lawyer can't afford to neglect.

Some years ago I was invited to lunch with a young man who was a bishop in a humble area of Salt Lake City. He was also a well-known corporate attorney and had a good job making probably somewhere between $90,000 and $100,000 a year. During the luncheon, in a very thoughtless way, I said to him, "When will you and your family be moving from your current home?" He looked at me with a surprised and hurt look on his face and said, "Why do you ask?" I said, "Well, I just assumed that as well as you're doing, you'd be moving soon to a more prosperous part of our city." He responded, "On the contrary. My wife and I have made a very conscious decision to live where we live and to share the surplus that we have with those around us who really need it." Boy, did I beat a hasty retreat! Here was someone who really did believe that property doesn't mean much to the Lord, who was planning his life and acting accordingly.

Isn't our best answer to God's interrogatories given by how we live? That would be our best response. So let me pose a hypothetical case or two. If we really felt about property the way the Lord defines it—that it's but a drop and that there are far more weighty matters—then if we were trying to make a decision about material things, wouldn't our feelings about this subject influence that decision? For example, let's say you were fortunate enough to inherit $25,000 from a grandmother who just passed away and had something to bequeath to you, because she did something you struggle to do—save. If you received such a sum, would you spend the entire amount on the new car you've wanted for so long? Or would you buy a reliable used car from your neighbor for $8,000 and use the excess funds helping those around you who are struggling financially and have many unmet needs? Or let's say you are making a decision about building a home and would like the very best and finest for your family. Would you build one you could reasonably afford for $110,000, or would you build a more palatial one for $225,000 and spend the next 30 years working 12-hour days, possibly requiring the help of a working spouse, to pay for it? This is obviously an interrogatory with very practical implications for our lives.

"Unto What Were Ye Ordained?"

This next interrogatory comes from section 50 of the Doctrine and Covenants. "Wherefore, I the Lord ask you this question—unto what were ye ordained?" (v. 13). Now you sisters may think this doesn't apply to you, but it does. In a sense we have all been foreordained. And what was that foreordination? In verse 14 the Lord answers his own question again: "To preach my gospel by the Spirit, even the Comforter which was sent forth to teach the truth." This brings to mind the Abrahamic covenant. All of us have covenanted with God. As we become partakers of the gospel and receive the wonderful blessings that are part of Abraham's covenant, we enter into a serious obligation—even a burden—to become an agent people for God. Our covenant is to share the gospel so the families of this earth will come to know about Christ and his plan for our lives.

William J. Cameron has written beautifully about this idea.

A man will rise and demand, "By what right does God choose one race of people above another?" I like that form of the question. It is much better than asking by what right God degrades one people beneath another, although that is implied. God's grading is always upward. If He raises up a nation, it is that other nations may be raised up through its ministry. If He exalts a great man, an apostle of liberty, or science, or faith, it is that He might raise a degraded people to a better condition. The Divine selection [of which we are the beneficiaries] is not a prize, a compliment paid to the man or the race—it is a burden imposed. To appoint a chosen people is not a pandering to the racial vanity of a "superior people;" it is a yoke bound upon the necks of those who are chosen for a special service.[1]

We are such a covenant people, and I think it's very helpful to constantly ask ourselves the question "Unto what were [we] ordained?" Can you see the implications this has, for instance, for our duty to spread the gospel?

For example, I've just been amazed by the experiences I've had when flying. I usually sit in an aisle seat and introduce myself to my seatmate. I ask him about himself, hoping that he'll ask me about myself and that somehow out of that a gospel conversation will ensue. Often, over the past eight years, the Lord has helped me find a way to share the gospel. It's a rare weekend that I come back not having made a contact that I can follow up on in some way—a referral or sending a book or something. When I'm in those situations, I just have a little prayer in my heart: "Father, I don't know if this person will be receptive, but I do know that maybe he'll never have a better chance to meet a Latter-day Saint and to hear a little bit about the gospel. Please help me find a way to share it."

In the back of my mind I'm thinking that this is my burden, my opportunity, and my obligation as a member of God's covenant people. That's what I was ordained to do. This is what all of us are ordained to do. So, again, God's interrogatory can be very helpful by working itself out in practical ways. I hope considerations such as these have had some impact on your postgraduate planning.

"What Think Ye of Christ?"

Finally, I share my favorite interrogatory. Christ posed it to the Pharisees in Matthew 22:42. You'll recognize it. He said to them simply, "What think ye of Christ? whose Son is he?" I constantly ask myself, What do I think of him? Am I truly Christian? I've always said to my wife, "I'm the theologian, honey, you're the Christian." Is being a Christian more than just theology? Isn't it really something that has to do with our behavior? Are we Christians? We've all recently read about a young man in Tennessee who was a member of the Federation of Christian Athletes. He was selected to receive his high school's FCA Male Athlete of the Year award and then was denied the award because, as a member of our Church, he was not considered a Christian.[2] Are we Christian? What and who defines that?

In a 1951 conference talk, President McKay said, "What you sincerely in your heart think of Christ will determine what you are, will largely determine what your acts will be."[3] That is a beautiful and sobering thought, relating directly to the interrogatory "What think [we] of Christ?" In our lives, how can we demonstrate what we think of him?

One way would be to repent more continuously. We recently served a mission in New York. One day, in an interview with a missionary, something happened that let me know what he thought of Christ. He had been on his mission 15 months, and that morning during our interview he asked, "Do you have a little extra time?" And I said, "Sure." He said, "Well, I'm going to do something today that I really should have done almost two years ago, but I didn't have the faith in Christ to do it."

Then he poured out his heart about a transgression that occurred long before his mission call. His first pre-mission interview was with his bishop, who also happened to be his father (a complicating factor). He was not able to tell his father what he had done. Adam had that same problem, remember? I think that might be why God asked, "Where art thou?" Well, God knew where Adam was. He was hiding. That's what most of us do when we disobey God. And when that doesn't work, we often do just what Adam did. We blame someone. "The woman, she . . ." And then Eve's response, "The serpent, he . . ." It is so easy and natural to excuse our weaknesses this way.

But on that morning this young elder was ready to level with the Lord. So, in deep humility he said, "I didn't feel this way two years ago, but I know now that there is no way around what I'm going to do." He quoted the scripture "By this shall ye know if a man hath repented of his sins; behold, he will confess them and forsake them" (D&C 58:43). Then he said, "There are things more important than finishing my mission, and one of them is to have my sins forgiven. I know I've got to confess to get this started, so here goes." And out it came. Oh, how I loved him. I cried with him, and I knew that his faith in Christ was to the level described by the Book of Mormon as "faith unto repentance" (Alma 34:15). There are levels of faith, and when we've only got a "particle of faith" (Alma 32:27) we don't do what this young missionary did. But when our faith grows to the level of "faith unto repentance," then in our minds and in our hearts we say, "I really believe that the Atonement works and that there is no other way." Then we bring ourselves into compliance and pay the price and claim the blessings.

What did this young missionary think of Christ? It was clear. He knew Christ was his Redeemer. He knew there was no other way, and he was willing to be completely submissive to the processes of repentance.

What else would we do if we really thought the way we should about Christ? I think we would be very charitable in our treatment of others. The quality of our daily relationships with others is the best indication of what we think about Christ. Elder Marvin J. Ashton said once that how we treat others is the best measure of how we're doing in our efforts to come unto Christ.[4] In our quest to come unto him, how we relate daily with our family and with our associates gives the best evidence about how we really feel about the Savior.

Can you imagine what a difference it will make if you practice law with Christ and his teachings in your heart and on your mind each day? I actively practiced for 20 years and received some wonderful financial rewards. My most memorable fees, though, are the banana cream pies I used to bill and receive from the widows of our ward for services rendered!

I'll end here, though God has posed many other interrogatories. "Did I not speak peace to your mind concerning the matter? What greater witness can you have than from God?" (D&C 6:23). "What manner of men ought ye to be?" (3 Nephi 27:27). "Many are called and few are chosen. And why are they not chosen?" (D&C 121:34). I hope you can value these and many other questions. They merit our contemplation. More than that, they merit our faithful response in the way we live our lives.

The use of such interrogatories by a loving and wise Heavenly Father guides us. The technique enables him to raise relevant issues, to encourage our thoughtful analysis of them, and then to leave us to the exercise of our agency to act. It sounds almost lawyerlike; but I would prefer to describe the process as godlike, because through it we may become more like him. Wouldn't that be a wonderful outcome of a life in the law?

God bless you all to succeed on those terms—his terms! In the name of Jesus Christ. Amen.

This convocation address was given April 25, 1997, when Elder Jensen's son, Matthew, graduated from the BYU Law School. Reprinted from "Where Art Thou? Answering God's Interrogatories," Clark Memorandum, Fall 1997, 2-7.

Marlin K. Jensen received his J.D. from the University of Utah in 1970. He is currently a member of the First Quorum of the Seventy of The Church of Jesus Christ of Latter-day Saints.

Notes

1. William J. Cameron, *The Covenant People* (Merrimac, MA: Destiny Publishers, 1966), 8.

2. "'Christian' Athletic Group Denies Award to Mormon," *Deseret News*, 26 April 1996, B1. See also "Christian Group Apologizes for Way It Handled LDS Incident," *Deseret News*, 27 April 1996, B12.

3. David O. McKay, "Highest of All Ideals," *Conference Report*, April 1951, 93–94, as quoted in *Gospel Ideals* (Salt Lake City: Improvement Era, 1953), 34.

4. Marvin J. Ashton, "The Tongue Can Be a Sharp Sword," *Ensign*, May 1992, 20.

ADAM, WHERE ART THOU?

And the Lord God called unto Adam,
and said unto him, Where art thou?
(Genesis 3:9)

Balance

Robert L. Backman

My dear young brothers and sisters, this is a privilege for me to be here among you. It brings back so many fond memories and some not-so-fond days in law school. I saw some of you come in with young children, and I thought back to my days in law school. I had three children by the time I was through with law school. I guess I attribute the loss of my hair to that.

I will never forget, as we finished our law school, we started exam week, and my wife was seriously ill. She was so ill that I thought she was dying. The night before exams started, we had to get the ambulance to come for her, because she was hemorrhaging. I piled into the ambulance with her and my law books, went up to the hospital, and wondered all night whether she was going to live or die. I had to go up the next morning and start my exams. When we finished our exams that week, I broke out in hives from head to toe. That was my introduction to the practice of law.

It has been a most pleasant and wonderful career. I commend all of you who are seeking to become legal scholars and practitioners and promise you a rich and wonderful adventure ahead of you. I want you to know that law school is worth it, and the light at the end of the tunnel becomes brighter as you go along. The wonderful experiences you have when you can share your knowledge and understanding of the law and what this great country is built upon will redound to your benefit often, believe me.

I am honored to be here with you. I am honored to be here with my younger brother [Professor James Backman]. Unfortunately, I haven't been able to spend much time with him since he was plucked away from the law practice by Dean Rex Lee many years ago. I am also grateful to be here with Scott Cameron, who was a member of our firm when I was called to be a General Authority of the Church. So I feel I am among friends. Also, Dean Reese Hansen and my brother came down here to BYU the same year; I have known him for a long time and admired him. I want you to know how fortunate you are to have the people who are teaching you in the Law School.

I wonder what I could say to you that could be worthwhile. I hope you will let an old man talk a little bit about his own experiences, some things I think might be important for you as you embark upon this great adventure that lies ahead of you.

There is only one short verse in all the Bible that describes the 18 years of the Savior's life—the years between his visit in the temple with the rabbis as a boy of 12 and the beginning of his ministry at the age of 30—but that one verse gives us a marvelous pattern to follow in obtaining a rich, happy, fulfilling life: "And Jesus increased in wisdom and stature, and in favour with God and man" (Luke 2:52). I take that to mean that Jesus Christ grew mentally, physically, spiritually, and socially. On the threshold of your adult life as you are, it is an appropriate time, it seems to me, for you to ponder what you are doing, what you can do to achieve that kind of balance in your lives.

How vital such balance is was shown by the man who was driving a huge truck full of lumber. The truck had a powerful motor with plenty of horsepower, the frame was well built, and it held all the lumber that could be stacked on its mighty bed. But a strange thing happened to that truck as it pulled out toward the street. Just as the rear wheel dipped into the gutter, the entire front end of the truck reared up off the ground. The heavy load of lumber on the truck bed teetered slowly toward the ground. It was an odd sight to see the driver sitting in the cab frantically turning the front wheels back and forth but unable to steer his vehicle. The power was still there, but he couldn't do anything with it. He lost control, not because of the size of the load of lumber or the lack of power in the vehicle, but because the load was simply misplaced.

Sometimes, like the load of lumber, our lives get out of balance. Before we know it, our load controls us. We lose the ability to steer and to direct our lives. The remedy is to grow mentally, physically, socially, and spiritually—to become well-rounded squares, so to speak.

In our own dispensation, the Lord gave us this direction:

Teach ye diligently and my grace shall attend you, that you may be instructed more perfectly in theory, in principle, in doctrine, in the law of the gospel, in all things that pertain unto the kingdom of God, that are expedient for you to understand;

Of things both in heaven and in the earth, and under the earth; things which have been, things which are, things which must shortly come to pass; things which are at home, things which are abroad; the wars and the perplexities of the nations, and the judgments which are on the land; and a knowledge also of countries and of kingdoms—[And this interesting verse:]

That ye may be prepared in all things when I shall send you again to magnify the calling whereunto I have called you, and the mission with which I have commissioned you (D&C 88:78–80).

Abbreviating that challenging passage of scripture, the Lord has told us to keep balance in our lives by being instructed in all things, "that ye may be prepared . . . to magnify the calling whereunto I have called you." None of you here knows what life has in store, its length, its breadth, what experiences lie ahead of you. Looking back on my own life, I marvel at the rich adventure I've enjoyed, and I thank God for the balance I've been able to maintain.

I well remember my first day in law school at the University of Utah, as the dean (Dean Leary, a frightening man, a long, spare man, with less hair than I have, a very ruddy complexion, and small glasses that he wore on the end of his nose) looked at us, a class of new law students, and thundered, "The law is a jealous mistress! You will have no time for anything else. It must be first in your life."

I resolved then that I was going to prove him wrong, and I did. I am grateful for my education. I thoroughly enjoyed my law practice, but I enjoyed it because of other interests I maintained. I love my family; I recognize at this stage in my life they really are my wealth, and little else counts.

When I was a boy of 12, my dad was called to be the president of the South African Mission. We left our home in Salt Lake City and journeyed out to that far-off land. We stopped in London to wait for a ship to take us down the west coast of Africa to our home in Capetown. While we were there we attended a testimony meeting in a branch in south London. To give you some idea of how long ago it was, the missionary who escorted us was one Gordon B. Hinckley, who was then serving as a missionary in England. During that meeting, my father stood to bear his testimony and said something very important. He said, "When you come right down to it there are only two things in life that really count: the gospel of Jesus Christ and your family."

You know, young friends, the older I get, the more I realize the truth in what my dad was saying. It is hard for me to separate my family from the gospel, the gospel from my family. They're so held in esteem by me. I love my family.

I have served my community. Jim mentioned the fact that I have been active in Scouting. I have had some very rich experiences just out of that little bit of service. I challenge you to find ways to serve that way.

I will never forget when I came back from serving as a mission president in the Northwestern States Mission. I was trying to get back into my law practice and trying to get my life back in order when I received a telephone call from the chair of a political party in the state of Utah, asking me to run for the state legislature. I said, "No, I don't want to do that. I have been away for three years; I've got to put things back in order, and I need some time for myself." I continued with one excuse after another.

He finally stopped me and said, "Yes, you have done all of that, but what have you done for your community lately?" I couldn't answer very well. So I enjoyed four wonderful years in the House of Representatives in this state—an experience I would wish on any of you because of the genius of this government of ours that I love so much.

I have had many callings in the Church. I lamented every release I received, because I thoroughly enjoyed every assignment. I challenge you to do the same.

I try to keep myself physically fit. I walk regularly; I play squash and golf. I have attempted to be a well-rounded square. It has paid rich dividends, dividends beyond my imagination. The challenge I extend to you, my young friends, is for you to maintain balance in your life—to keep growing mentally, physically, socially, and spiritually.

To grow mentally, of course, is to increase in wisdom as Christ did. What opportunities lie ahead of you if you take advantage of your educational blessings here at Brigham Young University! I am so grateful to live in a land and at a time when all of us can have an education. I am so grateful for the gospel, which encourages us to learn, study, grow, magnify, increase, expand, and progress forever. Isn't that a glorious idea to think about? Consider the impact these inspired statements have on us as members of God's Church: "The glory of God is intelligence" (D&C 93:36). "It is impossible for a man to be saved in ignorance" (D&C 131:6). Man can be saved no faster than he gains knowledge.[1]

Brigham Young told us how important our mental development is:

> I tell you in a few words what I understand "Mormonism" to be. . . .
>
> It embraces every fact there is in the heavens and in the heaven of heavens— every fact there is upon the surface of the earth, in the bowels of the earth, and in the starry heavens; in fine, it embraces all truth there is in all the eternities of the Gods. . . .
>
> "Mormonism" embraces all truth that is revealed and that is unrevealed, whether religious, political, scientific, or philosophical.[2]

God expects us to use our minds, to stretch our intellect, to think. Some people would rather die than think, and many do. I envy you; the years are ahead of you. There are so many frontiers yet to be conquered by you. Think of the vistas that are open for you: the exploration of space, computers, medical advances, transportation, communication, social and moral revolutions, the expansion of God's church, the search for truth—all the challenges facing the world and mankind. What a time to be alive!

In 1972, after landing on an area of the moon named for René Descartes (the 17th century mathematician and philosopher), astronaut

John W. Young chose a quotation from Descartes to summarize the meaning of that space flight. Listen to his words: "There is nothing so removed from us as to lie beyond our reach or so hidden that we cannot discover it." Isn't that exciting?

Yes, my young brothers and sisters, I urge you to soak up all the education you can in this singular learning environment. Stretch your minds and skills as far as you can, but beware. Heed the counsel given to us by the prophet Nephi:

> O that cunning plan of the evil one! O the vainness, and the frailties, and the foolishness of men! When they are learned they think they are wise, and they hearken not unto the counsel of God, for they set it aside, supposing they know of themselves, wherefore, their wisdom is foolishness and it profiteth them not. And they shall perish.
>
> But to be learned is good if they hearken unto the counsels of God (2 Nephi 9:28–29).

I can give you no better advice than that given to Henry Eyring, the famous scientist, by his father, as Henry left the farm to attend his freshman year at the University of Arizona. His father said:

> So you're going to Tucson to study science, eh? Well now, that's what you want to do, isn't it? I don't know much about science, son, but I know quite a bit about some other things. I do know the Lord spoke to the Prophet and that the gospel is true. I know our gospel teaches truth regardless of its source. Now, I've tried to tell you the way things look to me, and perhaps sometimes I've told you things that don't exactly jibe with the truth. If I have, just discard those things. In this Church you don't have to believe anything that isn't true. If you want to be a scientist, son, you hit it just as hard as you can. You're going to hear some things up there that don't exactly jibe with what you have learned in Sunday School, but don't worry about it. Just keep an open mind and truth will eventually work its way to the surface. I don't worry about how much you learn. Study all the science you can, and remember your prayers and don't profane and live in such a way that you will feel comfortable in the company of good people, then mother and I will feel good about your going. Don't you worry about the gospel, son. It will stand the test of all truth.[3]

Develop physically, increase in stature as Christ did. Unfortunately, our worldly way of life is gradually and quietly, but steadily, robbing us of physical health and robust fitness—cars, TV, spectator sports, rich foods, drinking, smoking, drugs, immorality, emphasis on luxury, hedonism, and the doctrine that pleasure is the highest good. Someone described our lifestyle as GIGO (garbage in, garbage out). How grateful I am for the Word of Wisdom. Practicing its saving principles has been a real blessing in my life. I assure you that the Lord was speaking to us when he gave the glorious promise contained in the 89th section of the Doctrine and Covenants, which we often overlook as we talk about the Word of Wisdom:

And all saints who remember to keep and do these sayings, walking in obedience to the commandments, shall receive health in their navel and marrow to
their bones;

And shall find wisdom and great treasures of knowledge, even hidden treasures;

And shall run and not be weary, and shall walk and not faint.

And I, the Lord, give unto them a promise, that the destroying angel shall pass
by them, as the children of Israel, and not slay them (D&C 89:18–21).

Please remember that these bodies of ours are the tabernacles of our
spirits, which have come to us from God. As we care for them, bridle our
passions, appetites, and thoughts, and take control of our lives, we will
experience the promises God has made to us. We will achieve a balance that
would be lacking without our self-discipline. How I pray that you great
young people will be modern Daniels, as you develop physically by living
the Word of Wisdom in all of its aspects and experience the promises God
has made to you in return.

Notice how our physical development influences our mental growth
and our social and our spiritual progress. Grow socially; increase in favor
with man. I love these words of John Donne:

No man is an island, entire of itself; every man is a piece of the continent, a
part of the main; if a clod be washed away by the sea, Europe is the less, as well
as if a promontory were, as well as if a manor of thy friends or of thine own
were; any man's death diminishes me, because I am involved in mankind; and
therefore never send to know for whom the bell tolls; it tolls for thee.[4]

We live in a society. The better adjusted we are to our society the happier
we are going to be. If we are to have a better society, it will not be assembled
in think tanks or by computers; it will be fashioned in the hearts of men; it
will be found in seven simple words, "Thou shalt love thy neighbor as
thyself" (D&C 59:6). That is a surefire formula for happiness, believe me.
The Lord says, "Thou shalt love," not "Thou shalt *try* to love." Can love be
commanded? Can we force ourselves to love? Someone asked me, "How
can you love a neighbor you just don't like?" The key is, how do we express
love to ourselves?

We have a deep and continuing desire to stay alive, to stay well, to
avoid hurt or physical danger. We want to have friends, to develop our
capacity. We want to enjoy beauty. We want to be secure financially. We
want to know who we are, where we came from, and where we are going.
When we supply these and other basic wants, we do it because we love
ourselves. Now, if we love our fellowman, friend or enemy, we develop
within ourselves a desire to help them realize the same things we want for
ourselves. This desire for others can be willed; it can be developed; it can be
commanded. What it takes is getting to know them and accepting them as

our brothers and sisters, with the same divine potential to become like our Father in Heaven that you and I have.

I love the words of Will Rogers: "I never hated a man I knew." We best show our love for our neighbor by serving him. It's no accident that the primary role of the priesthood of God is to serve our fellowman, and it's no accident that we are happiest when we are serving. I don't hesitate to tell you that your happiness will be commensurate with the service you render. So find ways to serve and be happy. There is no better place for service than in The Church of Jesus Christ of Latter-day Saints. How badly God needs faithful young men and women who know who they are, where they came from, why they are here, and where they are going. The Church is just gathering steam, my young friends, and in your lifetime you will experience some of the greatest events in the world's history. Don't let anyone sell the future short. You are going to be there.

Many years ago, I was called by President Harold B. Lee to be the president of the Aaronic Priesthood MIA. When he called me, he issued me a challenge that I never have gotten out of my mind. He said, "Bob, I challenge you to present a program to prepare this generation of youth to meet the Savior when he comes."

Wow! You think of that. I don't know whether he meant that in our lifetime we would see that great historical event for which we are all waiting. I do know that you and I can prepare for that event, whether we are here or not. We will have that opportunity of meeting our Lord and Savior. I challenge you to be where the Lord can find you, and many wonderful opportunities for service will lie ahead, and you will grow socially. One word of warning: we are to be *in* the world but not *of* the world.

When we become worldly, carnal, sensual, and devilish, we lose that important balance that is vital to our well-being. We find ourselves in monkey traps.

When I lived in South Africa, I remember hearing about how natives trapped monkeys. They simply took coconuts, knocked the tops off, and hollowed them out, with a hole in the top large enough for a monkey to get his paw in. Then they anchored the coconuts to the ground and put a peanut in the bottom of each one. The monkeys would smell those peanuts and, loving them as they do, would reach in and grab the peanuts. They would take the peanuts in their paws, but with doubled-up fists they couldn't get their paws out of the holes. All the natives had to do was pick up those monkeys and put them into gunnysacks. They would bite and kick and scream and yell, but they would not let go of the peanuts, even to save their lives.

Do you know anyone who is caught in a monkey trap, who is worshiping false gods: position, fame, wealth, approval, success?

Success. I recently read Viktor Frankl's *Man's Search for Meaning*, a tremendous book written by a man who suffered through the Holocaust, saw his family killed in the ovens, and yet came out of it with a marvelous philosophy of life. Listen to what he says about this matter of success.

> Don't aim at success—the more you aim at it and make it a target, the more you are going to miss it. For success, like happiness, cannot be pursued; it must ensue, and it only does so as the unintended side-effect of one's personal dedication to a cause greater than oneself or as the by-product of one's surrender to a person other than oneself. Happiness must happen, and the same holds for success: you have to let it happen by not caring about it. I want you to listen to what your conscience commands you to do and go on to carry it out to the best of your knowledge. Then you will live to see in the long run— in the long run, I say—success will follow you precisely because you had forgotten to think about it.[5]

Isn't that an interesting comment, from a man who really did discover the secret of happiness? Remember that God has commanded us, "Thou shalt have no other gods before me" (Exodus 20:3).

I pray that you will grow spiritually, in favor with God. Carol Lynn Pearson and Scott Whitaker wrote a beautiful poem concerning that:

> O Man, ascending on your self-built step of steel,
>
> Raising hands in praise of your own bright artistry,
>
> Looking at your world through the audacious glass of newly conquered space
>
> With never a thought for tomorrow's consequences,
>
> Letting the material things of this world
>
> Shut out your view of a better one,
>
> Forever scurrying in a frenzy to acquire more than your neighbor,
>
> Neglecting the spiritual while perfecting the physical,
>
> Waving a worded banner of Utopian hopes,
>
> Never learning from the same words carved on the stones
>
> Of every century since words and stones and centuries began,
>
> Looking in vain for happiness that constantly eludes,
>
> Devising monuments to your own greatness;
>
> O man, ascending on your self-built step of steel.
>
> You forget the true purpose of life until too late,
>
> Until the harvest is past, the summer is ended, and
>
> Death, the stranger, is at your door.

Blessed with testimonies of the gospel of Jesus Christ, you and I understand the purpose of life and our eternal goals. Contrast that with the understanding of your friends outside the Church, who do not have a testimony of the gospel. That blessed testimony, my brothers and sisters, gives us the proper perspective and the motivation as we grow mentally, physically, and socially, and in favor with God. We have the truth, and we practice virtue. That sets us apart from the rest of the world, which tries to find truth without getting virtue. Yes, we want you to get an education, to achieve academic excellence in the context of Latter-day Saint values. There is no end in the progress of a man or a woman who seeks the truth. President Harold B. Lee, in a talk to seminary teachers several years ago, said: "Drive your testimony deep into the rock like a stake, tie the rope of faith to it, and play it out as far as you can. When you feel yourself slipping, pull back into the stake, your testimony of the gospel of Jesus Christ."

The Lord declared to us, "Seek ye first the kingdom of God, and his righteousness; and all these things shall be added unto you" (Matthew 6:33). All these things—God was speaking of all that he has. The blessings are unlimited for those who are faithful and true. The prophet Alma counseled his son Helaman in these words:

> O, remember, my son, and learn wisdom in thy youth; yea, learn in thy youth to keep the commandments of God.
>
> Yea, and cry unto God for all thy support; yea, let all thy doings be unto the Lord, and whithersoever thou goest let it be in the Lord; yea, let all thy thoughts be directed unto the Lord; yea, let the affections of thy heart be placed upon the Lord forever.
>
> Counsel with the Lord in all thy doings, and he will direct thee for good; yea, when thou liest down at night lie down unto the Lord, that he may watch over you in your sleep; and when thou risest in the morning let thy heart be full of thanks unto God; and if ye do these things, ye shall be lifted up at the last day (Alma 37:35–37).

Can you apply that to your studies here at the Law School? If you do these things, you will then study along with your law the holy scriptures, the principles of the gospel of Jesus Christ. You will pray earnestly and sincerely from the heart, seeking guidance for your life, building your faith in God, understanding your relationship to him. You will fast purposefully, thoughtfully, prayerfully, and regularly. You will live his holy principles and commandments, which is really the true test of your faith. You will respond to calls to serve in his kingdom, experiencing the joy that comes from such service. You will sustain and follow your leaders, confident that they are inspired in their callings. You will bear witness of the gospel through your words and actions, sharing the truth with your fellowman. You will seek his Holy Spirit knowing that the things of God are only understood by the Spirit of God. You will be honest, true, chaste, benevolent, virtuous, doing good to all men. You will love your neighbors as yourself, even those you don't like. You will continue to seek anything virtuous, lovely, or of good report, or praiseworthy. You will be a devoted Latter-day Saint throughout your life.

My young brothers and sisters, our victory over Satan is dependent upon our being taught the gospel of Jesus Christ, in experiencing those gospel principles in our lives, in developing firm, unshakable testimonies, in showing that the gospel is the solution to our problems and the problems of the world. As one of your leaders who loves you dearly, I challenge you to find the anchor that will bless you forever, to maintain the balance in your individual lives that will lead to rich, full years of service and happiness here and the glorious promise of eternal lives and exaltation hereafter.

I will never forget when I was in your shoes. I came to law school fresh out of the army after the Second World War. I had been away from my studies for a long, long time. I resolved as I was aboard the troop ship on my way home from the war that I was going to concentrate all my efforts on my law studies. I came home with that intention and believed what Dean Leary later said to me when I went to law school, that the law was a jealous mistress and I would have no time for anything else. With the savings I had from being overseas, not spending any money while I was in combat, my wife and I bought a little house. One of the first things I did was to go to downtown Salt Lake City to find a job so we could sustain ourselves. I boarded the bus, because we didn't have a car, and rode downtown. Wouldn't you know it? A man sat next to me on the bus who turned out to be the bishop of our ward. Before I got off that bus, I was the deacons quorum adviser of that ward. Gone were all my good intentions to concentrate on the law only.

I'm so grateful for that bishop; I'm so grateful for the direction of my Lord and Savior. I'm so grateful he saved me from an unbalanced life and gave me a rich assurance that life can be beautiful. You can make a good living; you can enjoy the blessings of the law; and you can enjoy the blessings of a great society and service to your fellowman. I still keep that balance of which the Lord spoke to all of us. My young friends, will you accept the challenge to be instructed in all things, that you may be prepared to magnify the calling whereunto God has called you? I assure you he has. Sitting in front of me are the future leaders of this Church and of this and other communities: political leaders, business leaders, lawyers of note, jurists, and great citizens of this nation. God bless you to experience life to the fullest, by keeping the balance that will assure you that you are a son or a daughter of God, that he loves you, knows you, and knows the experiences you need to come back into his presence. He will grant you those adventures if you place yourself in his care, seeking first things first, and maintaining a balance in your life.

Remember what the scriptures said, "And Jesus increased in wisdom and stature, and in favour with God and man." I could wish nothing better for each of you at this stage in your life. I love you as brothers and sisters in the gospel of Jesus Christ. I pray his blessings upon each of you and all you undertake to do. As difficult as it may seem, I want you to know right now you are as much alive as you will ever be. So enjoy every day what you are doing. Make the most of it, and let the Lord reach out and touch you, bless you, and enlarge you with the capacity to do all he asks you to do.

This fireside address was given at the BYU Law School on March 24, 1991. Reprinted from the Clark Memorandum, *Fall 1991, 12–19.*

Robert L. Backman received his LL.B. from the University of Utah in 1949. He served as a member of the First Quorum of the Seventy 1978–92 and was named an emeritus General Authority in 1992.

Notes

1. *Teachings of the Prophet Joseph Smith* (Salt Lake City: Deseret Book, 1976), 217.

2. *Journal of Discourses,* 9:149.

3. *The Search for Truth in Science and Religion* (Salt Lake City: The Church of Jesus Christ of Latter-day Saints, 1961), 13–14.

4. John Donne, *Devotions upon Emergent Occasions* (1624), no. 17.

5. Viktor Frankl, *Man's Search for Meaning* (New York: Washington Square Press, 1985), 16–17.

Unmeasured Factors of Success

John K. Carmack

The year was 1956. I was in Seoul, Korea, serving in the Adjutant General Corps of the Eighth Army Headquarters. My closest friend at the time was David Gardner, then in dangerous army intelligence work along the coasts of China, but housed in Seoul. We were both struggling to decide what to do with our careers when we left the army. He was considering real estate as a career, and I, city management. But in the back of my mind law school was still a possibility, and I had applied to UCLA School of Law as insurance against a change of mind. We spent many nights in the library talking, thinking, browsing, and considering our options.

David chose the road into academics and university administration. You know him as the former president of both the University of Utah and the University of California. I chose law school. We still laugh when we recall David's reaction to my suggestion that he go back to graduate school. He rejoined with, "Carmack, I'm just not the academic type." I have never regretted my own decision, although it isn't the only road I could have taken.

For centuries lawyers have been maligned and their role in society misunderstood. For example, in the year 1790, the town of Watertown issued this annual report:

> Our inhabitants now comprise some 525, of whom two are blacksmiths, one is a doctor, three are storekeepers, and one is an innkeeper. We have no lawyer amongst us, for which latter fact we take no credit to ourselves, but give thanks to almighty God.

I visit with you tonight from the perspective of one whose legal career has been satisfying, rewarding, and in most ways very ordinary. My career as a lawyer is probably over, although its benefits for me and my family continue.

Perhaps this helps me see law school in the context of life and to observe and report some unmeasured factors affecting success.

At this point in your lives, due to the extraordinary pressure and competitive environment of law school, many of you probably wonder if the profession or some other field of endeavor will be satisfying and rewarding.

If you are not in the top of your class, you may even wonder if you will have opportunities to prove your worth. It doesn't take a mathematical genius, however, to figure that 90 percent of us are not in the top 10 percent in class standing, and that will be true with 90 percent of those with whom we interview and compete. But in a profession where class standing is considered much too seriously, one's standing can be of concern and damaging to one's self-esteem.

Remember the fact that you are all achievers: qualified, bright, and energetic people. Most of us are just common folks, as President Gordon B. Hinckley once described himself. In time you will find that it is fine to be a simple, hardworking, garden-variety person, not accustomed to walking in the elite corridors of life.

Tonight I will share some convictions, concepts, and principles as a kind of road map to remember in the days and years after law school. During my years of law practice, I noticed that certain people rose to the top in their work. Class standing and LSAT scores were not good predictors of whom they would be. Their rise had more to do with habits, abilities, characteristics not readily apparent, and good choices along the way. Almost any graduate of a good law school has useful writing and analytical skills. These are important, but other factors matter even more. Raw intellectual talent counts for much and is a wonderful gift, but other things seem to make even more difference.

May I draw an analogy from success in basketball? I've noticed that John Stockton of the Utah Jazz, who started in the NBA the year I arrived in Salt Lake City, has risen steadily to the top. In those early days most observers thought he was lucky to have a chance to play in the NBA. Other players seemed to have more physical ability and raw talent, although Stockton was not deficient in those things. Somehow he has surpassed most of them. His place in basketball history is now certain. He holds the all-time record for assists and steals and is high in other important categories. Like Cal Ripken in baseball, he has been almost indestructible and steady, playing nearly every game since arriving on the NBA scene. He is a perennial all-star performer and has been selected for his second Olympic Dream Team. Years ago many observers thought Kevin Johnson would be Stockton's superior. He was and is a superb and talented player with extraordinary athletic gifts, but somehow Stockton has risen to the top year in and year out. Why?

Likewise, new players in the NBA like Jason Kidd are highly touted, but a wise observer will say, "Let's wait and see. Will he maintain his intensity, fit in well with his team, play in such an unselfish way that he makes others better, improve year by year, avoid burnout and injuries, and maintain a steady personal life?"

Since I am using basketball as an example, consider the case of John Wooden, who may have been the finest college basketball coach of all time. From the beginning he was a good coach with a fine grasp of the game, but he gradually developed into a great coach. How did he do it? One way was the practice of his own aphorism: "It is what you learn after you know it all that counts."

Great corporate lawyers, such as you have observed in President James E. Faust and President Howard W. Hunter, develop wise and wonderful perspectives and instincts applicable to everything they do. The French financier and international organizer Jean Monnet once noted that American corporate lawyers "seemed peculiarly able to understand at once the consequences of unprecedented situations and immediately to set about devising new and practical ways of dealing with them."

Trial lawyers may not always be the greatest analysts or legal drafters, but they develop their unique skills and abilities through hard work and practical education during years of trial experience. They learn the fine art of preparing, presenting, persuading, dramatizing, and convincing. An excellent lawyer, John W. Davis, once observed:

> True, we build no bridges. We raise no towers. We construct no engines. We paint no pictures—unless as amateurs for our own principal amusement. There is little of all that we do which the eye of man can see. But we smooth out difficulties; we relieve stress; we correct mistakes; we take up other men's burdens and by our efforts we make possible the peaceful life of men in a peaceful state.[1]

You can't measure all these skills and this knowledge in an LSAT test or discover them through examining law school grades, as important as those may be. Don't you sometimes have a vague feeling that we may be excluding the best possible lawyers from the profession by our emphasis on classroom performance and aptitude tests? But since we don't yet know how to measure the other less tangible aptitudes, we are left with our imperfect system. For those embarking on a legal career, these seemingly unmeasurable things, when added to our outwardly visible academic performance, can take us to the top like a John Stockton or a John Wooden.

What these intangibles are is important to know; social science is just beginning to discover and analyze these other factors. For example, Richard Herrnstein and Charles Murray, who wrote *The Bell Curve,* giving much credence to the concepts embodied in the notion of IQ, concluded:

Perhaps a freshman with an SAT math score of 500 had better not have his heart set on being a mathematician, but if instead he wants to run his own business, become a U.S. Senator or make a million dollars, he should not set aside his dreams. . . . The link between test scores and those achievements is dwarfed by the totality of other characteristics that he brings to life.[2]

In his groundbreaking book *Emotional Intelligence,* Daniel Goleman identifies some of those overlooked and hard-to-measure characteristics that bring success as "being able to motivate oneself and persist in the face of frustrations, to control impulse and delay gratification, to regulate one's moods and keep distress from swamping the ability to think, to empathize, and to hope."[3]

Years ago Stewart Grow, who as a political science professor and prelaw adviser guided many future lawyers such as Elder Dallin H. Oaks, called these intangible factors "mugginess." I think he meant to convey the idea of hanging in there and having mental and emotional toughness. Coach Vince Lombardi of the Green Bay Packers often emphasized that "mental toughness is essential to success."

Live with Integrity

What are some ingredients important to your success? I will start with perhaps the most important one, difficult as it is to predict or measure. This ingredient is essential for success in almost all human endeavors, certainly for businessmen and lawyers, which most of you will be. In his excellent little book *The Effective Executive,* Peter Drucker put his finger on this intangible as follows:

> By themselves character and integrity do not accomplish anything. But their absence faults everything else. Here, therefore, is the one area where weakness is a disqualification in itself rather than a limitation in performance capacity and strength.[4]

Integrity involves the concept of a whole and integrated person, all of his or her parts acting harmoniously, honestly, and completely. The decisions of such a person are honest and wise, their effect on the lives of others carefully considered.

Let me use an incident from David Gardner's career as an example of integrity in action. It not only illustrates the point but has a happy ending.

When David had served as University of Utah president for about five years, the Board of Regents of the University of California conducted a search for a new president of that statewide university system. David, having previously served as a vice president of the university, was nominated by several influential people. Early in the process I visited with a regent with whom I served on a board of directors in southern California. I told him of my friendship with David, who I recommended highly. My friend was on the search committee and took an interest in David's qualifications.

One night my friend called to ask me if I could locate David. It seemed that the committee had narrowed the candidates to three, and my friend said he had the votes to select David. With some distress, however, he reported that David had refused the position, and he then pleaded, "Would you please call him and get him to change his mind?"

I reached David late in the evening at his home in Salt Lake City and explained that my friend had the votes to appoint him president of the University of California. He answered, "Carmack, you know that I grew up in sight of the University of California in Berkeley. It would be the highest honor I could imagine as an educator to be president of the university, but I am in the middle of important matters here that will take a few years to complete. I am certain that the university would understand and let me go, but there would always be a feeling that I had left in the middle of vital matters. And that wouldn't be right. I can't do that and live with myself."

I better understood then why David had enjoyed such an excellent reputation in his field. I called my friend, who sadly accepted David's declination. The regents appointed another fine educator, who served about five years and then resigned. Perhaps remembering David's integrity, the regents nominated him again, and this time he accepted, serving with distinction.

In the field of law, where one is entrusted with people's lives and fortunes, integrity takes on heightened importance. The exigencies of the moment sometimes persuade some of our number to thrust aside their integrity to achieve some seemingly desirable goal. The great English lawyer and jurist Thomas More refused to take an oath supporting King Henry VIII because the king's cause was wrong and corrupt. In *A Man for All Seasons*, More's daughter Margaret and his wife visited him in prison where he awaited execution. Margaret asked him to "say the words of the oath and in your heart think otherwise." More explained, "When a man takes an oath, Meg, he's holding his own self in his own hands. Like water. *(He cups his hands.)* And if he opens his fingers *then*—he needn't hope to find himself again. Some men aren't capable of this, but I'd be loathe to think your father one of them."[5]

There are many such women and men. Most of my fellow lawyers had integrity, belying their reputation otherwise. David Kennedy, former head of international affairs for the Church, taught us a valuable lesson in his article "Personal Integrity" as he described his reaction to an offer tendered him by Continental Bank chair Walter Cummings. Kennedy's reply to the offer to become Continental Bank board chair was to explain that his priorities were home, Church, and work—in that order. He said he must speak to Lenora and the family before giving his answer.

It became quite clear that I should accept the position. I could and would continue my family and Church responsibilities [as counselor in the Chicago Stake presidency] as well as the work of the bank, in that order. And I would neglect none of them. But I felt an obligation to explain my priorities to Mr. Cummings.

Notice how David Kennedy clarified his priorities clearly and up front. Cummings not only agreed to the conditions but said that his own priorities (he was a devout Catholic) were the same.[6] Kennedy, who incidentally was a law school graduate, went on to become a national figure, taking Continental Bank to the forefront in international banking and becoming U.S. secretary of the treasury.

Integrity is the one essential characteristic without which all other characteristics fall.

Manage Your Career Wisely

For want of a better label, I will call the second concept simply successfully managing your career. Robert Frost, we remember, wrote of two roads and taking the one less traveled by. He concluded his poem with the words "And that has made all the difference."[7]

In deciding what road to take, we need to know something about ourselves and be honest in our personal evaluation. When you look in the mirror, what do you see? Do you see a whole person or a lawyer? I think we are all merely people with complex talents and abilities—the products of homes and churches and deeply held beliefs. We have studied many subjects in school, experienced a variety of challenges, and have strengths and weaknesses. A part of our education is a brief three-year stint in law school.

Where your career will take you and what contribution you will make in life has much more to do with things other than your law school training, although that is an important era of your lives. Your deepest interests, beliefs, and talents will assert themselves as time goes by. The decisions you make along the way will be critical. They will be the keys in successfully managing your career.

I have a friend who dropped out of law school for financial reasons. With his talent he would have made an excellent lawyer. Surely he could have found a way to complete his education, but he didn't. Having multiple talents, he went another direction. Although he was rising rapidly in that field, he then switched to a third field. Wisely he stayed with his new work for many years, rising to a high level of competence and developing a fine reputation. Seeing other opportunities on the horizon, however, he made another series of abrupt about-faces that eventually led to a dead end.

My friend is a fine person, and maybe it wasn't so important that he take the right road, but my honest feeling is that his decisions resulted in achieving much less. Today he deeply regrets his failure to manage his career wisely and successfully.

How will you manage your career? You will leave BYU with an excellent general education. I doubt that we could have a better general education than law school affords. You will have tools and skills and potential opportunities in law practice, government, education, or business. Along the way you will face two roads, perhaps several times. The roads you take will make all the difference. Since you are unique, which of the roads is right for you will be something only you can discover.

One significant help is the advice of family and good friends. In deciding which road to travel, I always counseled with my best friend in prayer. But my own earthly father, a successful, self-educated small businessman who loved his work, gave me excellent guidance and helped steer me away from mistakes three or four times. I made it a point to seek and obtain his feelings when I faced two roads. In one sense, his advice was uneducated because of his limited schooling opportunities, but that advice always seemed visionary and practical. I find President Hinckley to be a similar type of person. One can trust his advice because he is such a wise and experienced man besides being a man of God. We need such people, and they are available.

We all need vision and perspective in making decisions. In a speech to the Harvard class of 1913, Oliver Wendell Holmes said:

> I learned in the regiment and in the class the conclusion, at least, of what I think the best service that we can do for our country and for ourselves: *to see so far as one may,* and to feel the great forces that are behind every detail . . . to hammer out as compact and solid a piece of work as one can, to try to make it first rate, and to leave it unadvertised.[8]

In seeing where you fit into the future, you will also need to assess your strengths in making choices. Don't doubt yourselves, but also don't overestimate yourselves. You can know—if you are honest—if something is within your capability and competence level. Peter Drucker said, "There is no such thing as a 'good man.' Good for what? is the question."[9]

Be careful not to jump at a job simply because it promises to be lucrative. Assess the fit of the job with your strengths and your vision of the future. Avoid changing compulsively from one pathway to another. It takes many years to grow a tree. Keep focused on long-term objectives. Build stability into your career management and be conscious of who you are. Ask yourself if your best strengths are analytical thinking and writing? Or are you a more creative and expressive person? Are your best skills those of dealing with people? Perhaps you are a potential driving executive. Be realistic. I've advised more than one friend to stop pointing out his or her own weaknesses. We all have them, but so what? Our humility can be shown in other healthy ways.

What you truly are will come out in time. The more you know yourself and manage your career wisely, the more excitement and joy you will feel in what you do. Some of the unmeasured strengths that bring success to a lawyer include

- personal and family stability
- ability to work steadily and hard
- skills in understanding and getting along with people
- ability to size up situations
- being street-smart, i.e., learning from experience and having common sense
- ability to think procedurally about tasks
- ability to communicate on the level of common people

Grow with Your Work

Having first emphasized integrity as the one essential ingredient of a successful career, followed by the advice just concluded to manage your career wisely, I turn to my third and last suggestion. This is simply to grow as your career unfolds. Actually, I would give the same advice to everyone, even those who, like my daughters, may not have full-time careers. My oldest daughter is a full-time mother of five who graduated from this law school. She is an excellent mother who tries to grow with the times in that role as well as keep up as much as possible in the things she studied while attending the university.

If we fail to grow by developing new knowledge and skills and keeping up, we are destined to become professionally irrelevant. Growing with your work is critical. If you do, you will find in time that you have surpassed most of your colleagues. Though you start with an excellent education, most of what you will need to know and the skills you will need you have yet to learn. Master the details and skills required by your chosen work. Beyond such mastery you will discover the rarefied level of the unwritten laws of your field, or, as Coach Wooden said, "What you learn when you know it all."

In the process you have to avoid burnout, discouragement, and the temptation to quit and drop out. Common sense, balance, and the right priorities between home, church, and work will help you avoid these failures, as David Kennedy's example teaches us. And you need to serve your church and your community in the process. I've kept handy this 1944 statement by George Wharton Pepper. From the vantage point of a brilliant legal career, he said:

> I estimate that through the year about half of the whole amount of my activity has been gratuitous nonlegal service to the church, to the university, to the profession, to the community, and to individuals; and that of the other half, which represents my legal work, about a quarter has been done without charge.[10]

Lawyers do much work without fee, and rightly so. Once I asked President John K. Edmunds, who presided over the Chicago Stake while practicing law, how he handled Church members who had no idea of the value or cost of his legal services. He told me of doing hours of legal work for a sister who had no idea of its value. Though he decided to do it freely, she insisted on paying the fair value of his services. He agreed to accept what she felt was fair. When she reached in her purse and handed him a 50-cent piece, he gravely reached in his pocket and handed her a quarter in change.

The profession has an immense capacity to absorb problems. I would estimate that during 20 years of law practice I spent my time similarly to Pepper's. Great achievements require diligence, taking risks intelligently, and sometimes working around the clock. The standards and competition are high in our work. Yet people grow by courageously taking responsibility and discharging it. We should not shy away from our challenges.

I discovered that there is help from above. I have settled or solved more than one lawsuit or problem based on dreams, intuition, and the whisperings of the still small voice.

I now have a second career: my calling in Church leadership. The Church calling probably fits my own interests and background well at this stage in my life. You may want to establish a goal of serving your church and community after a certain age.

Another good friend, Judge Clifford Wallace, left a fine career as a trial lawyer to become a federal judge. There his skills, honed in years of Church leadership, have brought him to the top of his second profession as a judicial administrator, presiding judge, and twice a United States Supreme Court finalist. I feel his success has been due more to his leadership ability than his pure legal talent—in which he was not in the least deficient. He has grown, developed, and worked exceptionally hard. His emotional IQ has been a great asset.

Yes, I have found much of value in our profession. John J. McCloy, prominent in many international legal and leadership capacities, captured my feelings well when he said:

> [The lawyer] has learned to gauge human emotions and to make due allowance for them, for in his practice he has seen them flare and subside; his training has taught him the practical necessity at least of assessing the other side's point of view if not of conceding its merit; it has similarly given him the ability to judge what are the important and the less significant facts of a situation. I think that practice in explaining matters clearly and concisely and in drafting documents which are to be read and understood by others, sometimes others at a far removed point of time as in the case of a will or deed, also has an important use in these situations. . . . The lawyer who has faced the give and take of the courtroom, who has debated before the appellate court with lawyers of equal skill and resourcefulness, or who has run the

gamut of conferences with counsel for opposing sides has usually had a rich background with which to face [the negative comments] of public life.[11]

Remember my third point: grow with your work. When President Franklin D. Roosevelt visited the 91-year-old Justice Oliver Wendell Holmes, he found him reading Plato's *Republic* in his study. When he asked why on earth he was doing that, Holmes replied, "I'm reading to improve my mind."

Having made my three points—anchor your career with integrity, manage it wisely, and grow with it—I add a few feelings about how my law training relates to my service as a General Authority. In this calling I try to think of myself as a General Authority who once was a lawyer rather than a lawyer who is a General Authority. The experience of having practiced in a small law firm in western Los Angeles has enriched my Church service. But I don't think of myself as a Church lawyer any more than Elder Russell Nelson thinks of himself as a Church doctor.

My wife and I spent four years in Asia meeting with government officials in 23 countries including India, Pakistan, Vietnam, Cambodia, China, and Mongolia. The legal skills of drafting documents, negotiating agreements, handling legal and political procedures, and general advocacy were useful there.

During similar U.S. assignments, I have given testimony before the California legislature, the Los Angeles County Board of Supervisors, and the United States Congress. I have worked in anti-pornography legislative matters and served on executive committees of the Religious Alliance Against Pornography and the National Coalition Against Pornography.

I have served on the Salt Lake Chamber of Commerce Board of Governors and the Redevelopment Agency Advisory Board and have worked on issues such as school prayer in Utah. I have submitted to interviews with newspaper and television reporters.

To say that those three years of law training have benefited me in this calling is an understatement. I would add, however, that the two years I served as a young missionary have benefited me even more, and the years as a Church leader were critical in preparing me. I believe my three years as a mission president were equivalent in practical education to my three years in law school. A combination of all life experiences contributes to what we bring to our work.

During your journey I hope you will find balance that will keep you healthy physically, mentally, and spiritually. If you are wise, you will place your family and core beliefs in the center. Your career requires a large segment of your time, but many have grown and achieved professionally without upsetting the needed balance. There is time for all these things if you use time properly.

This fireside address was given at the BYU Law School on March 10, 1996. Reprinted from the Clark Memorandum, *Spring 1997, 32–38.*

John K. Carmack received his LL.B. from the University of California, Los Angeles in 1961. He served as a member of the First Quorum of the Seventy 1984–2001 and was named an emeritus General Authority in 2001. He is currently the managing director of the Church's Perpetual Education Fund.

Notes

1. John W. Davis, Address, New York, 16 March 1946, in 1 *Record of the Association of the Bar of the City of New York* 101, 102 (1946), as quoted in Fred R. Shapiro, *The Oxford Dictionary of American Legal Quotations* (New York: Oxford University Press, 1993), 273.

2. Richard J. Herrnstein and Charles A. Murray, *The Bell Curve: Intelligence and Class Structure in American Life* (New York: Free Press, 1994), 66.

3. Daniel Goleman, *Emotional Intelligence* (New York: Bantam Books, 1995), 34.

4. Peter Ferdinand Drucker, *The Effective Executive* (New York: Harper & Row, 1967), 89.

5. Robert Bolt, *A Man for All Seasons* (New York: Random House, 1962), 81 (emphasis in original).

6. David M. Kennedy, "Personal Integrity," *Ensign*, December 1979, 17–18.

7. Robert Frost, *The Road Not Taken* (New York: Holt, Rinehart and Winston, 1971), 13.

8. Oliver Wendell Holmes, Jr., "The Class of '61: At the Fiftieth Anniversary of Graduation, June 28, 1911," in *The Collected Works of Justice Holmes*, ed. Sheldon M. Novick (Chicago: University of Chicago Press, 1995), 3:504 (emphasis added).

9. Drucker, 74.

10. George Wharton Pepper, *Philadelphia Lawyer: An Autobiography* (Philadelphia: J. B. Lippincott Company, 1944), 384.

11. John J. McCloy, "The Extracurricular Lawyer," 15 *Washington & Lee Law Review* 171, 182–183 (1958); see also John J. McCloy, "Reflections on the Lawyer as a Public Servant," *Washington University Law Quarterly* 307–314 (1977).

The Study and Practice of the Laws of Men in Light of the Laws of God

James E. Faust

I am humbled by the presence of some of the distinguished members of the Law School faculty. As you would suppose, they are carefully chosen, even invited to this faculty, not only on the basis of what they know, but what they are. This faculty is competent and unique. Sister Faust and I have been grateful for and impressed by what this faculty has been able to do for two of our sons.

At the beginning I apologize to you because I will be drawing from my own experience. This is the risk you take when you invite an old, broken-down lawyer to speak to law students about the law. Even those who do not "suffer fools gladly" have to put up with such reminiscing in these circumstances (1 Cor. 11:19). Someone paraphrased General McArthur's statement, "Old soldiers never die, they just fade away," to "Old lawyers never die, they just lose their appeal."

I hope that what I say of a personal nature will not be too subtle. President Hugh B. Brown told us of a lawyer who received an unfavorable ruling from the bench in one of Canada's dominion courts. He reacted by turning his back on the judge. The judge asked: "Are you trying to show your contempt for this court?" The lawyer answered: "No, my Lord, I am trying to disguise it."

Some time ago, Dean Bruce Hafen invited me to speak to you concerning a fundamental purpose for establishing the J. Reuben Clark Law School at Brigham Young University. My great respect for this school, as well as my gratitude for our system of law, encourages me to do so. My mentor, Dean Wm. H. Leary, a devout Catholic, taught us that a fundamental purpose of going to law school was to learn to think straight. He also taught us that our fundamental rights came from God himself.

I wish to address a principle that President Marion G. Romney announced at the dedication of the J. Reuben Clark Law School. This principle is that students at this school should study the laws of man in the light of the laws of God. I should like to enlarge this to the study and practice of the laws of man in light of the laws of God.

I alert you that if you practice law you must be prepared to answer people who ask how you can be a good member of the Church and a lawyer. This question stems not only from misunderstanding but also from the fact that the law and lawyers are generally controversial, and many of our court and administrative proceedings are adversarial in nature. The Prince of Peace did not advocate controversy, but he was involved in it. The adversary system, imperfect as it is, has evolved as the best means of extracting the truth out of controversy. Is not truth to be sought above other virtues?

Lay people will ask how you reconcile your religious convictions with being an advocate for a "criminal" or a "crook." Many forget the fundamental principle that people are presumed innocent until convicted. I sincerely believe that no committed member of the Church who is trying to keep the laws of God needs to compromise his or her religious and moral convictions in the practice of law. The canons of ethics, with which I hope you will become fully acquainted, support and are in harmony with the moral teachings of the Church. These ethical standards fully encourage many of the moral principles of our Church, specifically those high standards of honesty, integrity, loyalty, truthfulness, and sincerity.

In my opinion there need be no conflict between what the Savior has taught through the Church and what you do as a professional lawyer. Indeed, if you are careful about observing the high moral standards that the Church represents, you will stand out in your profession. Sir Thomas More did. Although he was beheaded, he fitted well the description of Job, "a perfect and an upright man, one that feareth God, and escheweth evil . . . and . . . holdeth fast his integrity" (Job 2:3). The great lawyers I have known have also had great souls.

As an advocate, in a large measure you can establish the moral tone of the case by your own integrity. Because you represent someone who has allegedly done something reprehensible, it does not mean that you approve of that conduct.

You will have more choice in whom you represent than did the lawyers of my era. When I began my practice of law, all members of the bar had the duty to give every person charged with a crime the best defense they could under the law, without charge. There were no public defenders nor public defense funds. We did not enjoy the luxury of patting ourselves on the back for doing *pro bono* work. We were obligated to. We had no choice. In the federal courts the clerk would start down the alphabetical roll of the Utah Bar, assigning common criminals to be defended by the next name to come up, be he the senior member of the bar with the highest Martindale-Hubbell rating in the largest firm, or the most penurious, newly admitted member. It was an aggravating chore but a noble effort.

In one of my early appointments as defense counsel, I appeared before our venerable ninety-year-old federal judge, Tillman D. Johnson. I was appointed to defend a young man charged with taking a stolen motorcycle across state lines. As we approached the bench, Judge Johnson, whose eyes were dimmed with age, said: "Which one of you is the accused?"

The canons of ethics and the rules of court with which you must be familiar are helpful rules of conduct to abide by, but I have always believed that they are the lesser law. An attorney's own careful conscience and his own standards of high integrity ultimately ought to govern his conduct. This is particularly true of the graduates of this law school, most of whom are conversant with and have taught and tried to live in accordance with the laws of God. This is all in harmony with scripture: "He that keepeth the laws of God hath no need to break the laws of the land" (D&C 58:21).

I direct your attention to the first general epistle of John, chapter two, verse 27: "But the anointing which ye have received of him abideth in you, and ye need not that any man teach you: but as the same anointing teacheth you of all things, and is truth, and is no lie, and even as it hath taught you, ye shall abide in him."

I think you can rely on those two verses to help you make moral decisions. I do not think, however, you can rely on them to teach you the rules of law. Do not expect your professor, who may be a high priest, to concentrate his lessons out of the scriptures, although occasionally he may wish to do so. His obligation is to teach you the secular rules of civil and criminal law and matters that relate to them, such as procedures. Your obligation is to learn the rules of law and related matters. The whisperings of the Holy Spirit will no doubt help you, but you must learn the rules of law, using Churchill's phrase, by "blood, sweat, and tears." There is an old Portuguese saying, "*Deus ajude os que trabalhe*" (God helps those who work). Just having a good heart does not get the job done.

May I now be more specific in terms of reconciling the laws of God in terms of having to live under the laws of man. I have always felt that the law could be a truly noble profession. That belief stems in part because the Savior is our advocate with the Father (D&C 110:4). That means everyone at times, in the broad sense, is entitled to or needs an advocate.

I will confess to you that, when I say my personal prayers, I do not ask for justice, I ask for mercy. Since the Savior is our advocate with the Father, then everyone is entitled to justice: to have wrongs righted and, if truly repentant, to have a generous portion of mercy mixed in. That is my answer to the question of how can a lawyer represent "guilty" people. If the guilty are not entitled to an advocate, who then will be entitled to intercession before the judgment bar of God?

Of course, you can limit your practice to commerce and set yourself up as judge and jury, thus staying above the heart-breaking and the heart-rending matters that people bring into law offices. You can justify your conduct by saying to yourself, "This person is not worthy of my help."

I must confess to you that, during the 20 years when I served as bishop or stake president and practiced law in a small office, I did not find much satisfaction in representing the large, soulless corporations with the deep pocket; I found more pleasure helping just common folks whose property and savings may have been at risk. They came into the office distraught and anguished. After they were told, "I think we can get this matter straightened out," they were greatly comforted.

While the time of the sole practitioner may about be gone, I still believe that you can be a good lawyer, have a good life, serve your church, your family, and your community, and not be a member of a large, prestigious law firm. Certainly you will have more independence and a more moderate lifestyle.

An attorney is a counselor. To help a client sort out the risks, exposures, and choices is a great service. Litigation itself is costly, hazardous, and often should be the last resort. Two attorneys of integrity and good faith can often negotiate a solution to difficulties with a better result and with better feelings than a judge who, hearing the matter for the first time, has to decide for or against one or the other.

How do you reconcile your involvement in litigation with the Savior's Sermon on the Mount?

I should like to quote Arthur Nielsen, learned and experienced trial lawyer, currently special counsel to Brigham Young University in Jerusalem:

I do not believe that Jesus was trying to abrogate the principle of justice in our society. He was endeavoring to eliminate injustice. If a person has done another an injustice so that the latter has to sue him at the law to obtain justice, the offender should do more than merely pay that which is due; . . . he should give his cloak also. If a person smite thee on thy right cheek, do not retaliate with an aggressive blow, but show forth compassion rather than hostility. But where efforts of conciliation or reconciliation or compromise are not productive, we should not refuse to champion the cause of justice to institute the proper legal action or to defend against the possible injustices being done.[1]

This philosophy is in harmony with direction given in Section 134 of the Doctrine and Covenants:

We believe that men should appeal to the civil law for redress of all wrongs and grievances, where personal abuse is inflicted or the right of property or character infringed, where such laws exist as will protect the same; but we believe that all men are justified in defending themselves, their friends, and property, and the government, from the unlawful assaults and encroachments of all persons in times of exigency, where immediate appeal cannot be made to the laws, and relief afforded (D&C 134:11).

And I now move to another important subject.

Members of this Church, professional and otherwise, have a balancing act to perform. How much time and effort should be devoted and dedicated to one's temporal calling as against the responsibility to one's family and the Church? This depends in part on what make of car we wish to drive, how large a home we wish to live in, and how big of a bank account we wish to enjoy. In my life my family and my Church callings came first. We lived carefully, and I tried not to become obsessed with financial gain. These conflicting interests were accommodated and, as I told President Jeffrey R. Holland recently, if I had to do it over, I would do it the same way. Large overhead, new technology, I suppose, require shockingly high billings for legal services. This means that some deserving people will not be able to afford your services. One of your challenges will be to make the economic rewards your last consideration rather than the first.

President Henry D. Moyle of the First Presidency, who had been one of the more successful attorneys of this state, gave me some advice as I started to practice the law. He said, "Don't worry too much about the money. If you take care of your office, it will take care of you." More than once I had clients pay me more than I asked and billed. I like to think that I was more interested in them and in solving their problems than I was in their money. I really could not do otherwise in many cases because their little businesses they had struggled with, their homes, their futures, and their good names, were in my hands.

Young attorneys often feel that they must win all of their cases. I am afraid I once wished that I could have won them all, but it does not work out that way. Trying to win at all costs can be fatal in the long run. It will certainly ruin your career and irreparably damage your reputation. As you become more experienced as a counselor, you will learn that you do not have to win all your cases. Because of the law and facts, some cases just cannot be won, but a good defense in such cases can result in more justice. All you have to do is your best. If you are at ease with this philosophy, you will be more successful than if you operate under the theory that every case must be won.

Settling cases is a noble art. This is also an area where integrity can be lost through deception. Again I quote my friend Arthur Nielsen:

> The attorney should at all times be honest, truthful, and not attempt to deceive the court on either the law or the facts or conceal that which should be disclosed. An attorney should also avoid deception when dealing with another attorney. Frequently, when negotiating with another attorney, one may be tempted to lie or conceal the truth. Although an attorney may be under no obligation to disclose facts to his opponent, he should not knowingly allow the other party to deal with him under the mistaken knowledge of what the facts are. Some attorneys have said that this is too much of an altruistic condition, but I feel that you can always state your position and leave it up to the other party to identify his [or hers]—without "educating" him [or her] as to what it ought to be. An attorney should avoid making any statement or refuse to make an answer unless he is prepared to state the truth.[2]

There is a great risk in justifying what we do individually and professionally on the basis of what is "legal" rather than what is "right." In so doing, we put our very souls at risk. The philosophy that what is "legal" is also "right" will rob us of what is highest and best in our nature. What conduct is actually "legal" is, in many instances, way below the standards of a civilized society and light years below the teachings of the Christ. If you accept what is "legal" as your standard of personal or professional conduct, you will rob yourself of that which is truly noble in your personal dignity and worth. You can be just as tough as you want as an advocate, but you must never, never lower your own integrity. To do that, you have to keep in control of yourself, your emotions, and your feelings at all times, particularly in the heat of battle.

Judge David K. Winder of the United States District Court for Utah recently told some admittees to the bar:

> The expedient or short-sighted lawyer who fails to fulfill verbal understandings with other lawyers, who presents dubious evidence, who deals loosely with the record, or who misleads judges, is quickly "pegged." In our bar and every bar there are certain lawyers who achieve the enviable and priceless status of a good name. That status is developed gradually by word of mouth, from judges in the privacy of their gatherings and from lawyers in theirs. And, unlike the litigation you will be handling, be aware that once the verdict of your professional peers is in there is no formal "due process," no rebuttal and no appeal from that verdict.[3]

How do you study or practice the laws of men in the light of the laws of God? You must keep your own soul; you must not give it away. You must not compromise; by all means you should not sell it. I wish to testify that the sponsoring institution of this law school is the Church of Jesus Christ. This is my testimony. I pray that the Lord will bless you in your studies and activities so that you may do good upon the earth and render service to your fellowmen. In the name of Jesus Christ, amen.

This fireside address was given at the BYU Law School on November 22, 1987. Reprinted from the Clark Memorandum, *Fall 1988, 16–20.*

James E. Faust received his J.D. from the University of Utah in 1948 and was President of the Utah Bar Association 1962–63. He received the Distinguished Lawyer Emeritus Award from the Utah Bar Association in 1995 and the Marion G. Romney Law and Public Service Award from the BYU Law School in 2002. President Faust has served as a General Authority since 1972. He is currently Second Counselor in the First Presidency of The Church of Jesus Christ of Latter-day Saints.

Notes

1. Private letter.
2. *Id.*
3. David K. Winder, Utah State Bar Speech to Admittees, 6 October 1987.

First Things First

Michael W. Mosman

The question that brings us together tonight has bedeviled LDS graduate students for many years: how to balance the rigorous demands of graduate school, family, and church responsibilities. Looking as far back as the biography of J. Reuben Clark's public years, it has been a perennial struggle. Your presence here is a testament to your determination to meet it faithfully.

I vividly remember my own fears and the heartfelt conversations with my law school classmates as we talked in the hallways or pondered this challenge in the library at night. That was some time ago—as you can see just from looking at me—and we have met with varying degrees of success or failure in the ensuing years. Looking back, I can see that the way each of us chose to handle the demands of graduate school greatly foreshadowed the way we would respond to the demands of professional life. In other words, far more hung in the balance than I realized as we made decisions about how to live our lives during law school.

For most of us, graduate school presents dramatically increased demands on our time and abilities compared to our undergraduate experience. This was certainly true for me. After one week of law school, I felt a little like Dorothy in *The Wizard of Oz* after the tornado set her down. I wasn't sure what had just happened, but I knew I was "not in Kansas anymore." It is also not uncommon, at least early on, to believe that you have been mistakenly placed in some highly advanced class in which almost everyone else has had the prerequisites, which you somehow missed. I remember feeling that it was a little unfair to put me in law school with people who obviously had practiced law somewhere for several years.

The temptation in such a setting is to decide that graduate school will require an all-out effort with nothing held back. With that in mind, I have set up my remarks as a series of three questions or concerns. These are posed by a hypothetical student I will call James (see Doctrine and Covenants 39; 40), who has tentatively decided to devote all of his time and talents to success in graduate school, while putting church and family obligations "temporarily" on the back burner. My own responses follow. As my children can attest, my answers typically go on a lot longer than the initial question.

James: Don't make such a big deal out of this. It's not like I'm going to leave the Church or something. I know it's true. I just need to focus on my schooling for a limited period of time, and if I do, it will set my family up for the rest of our lives. What's wrong with that?

Response: Implicit in your question is the idea that there is something unique or unusual about the demands of graduate school that justifies relaxing our covenants with the Lord during that time. The assumption is that you are not seeking permanent retirement from service in the kingdom, but a brief sabbatical. The fundamental premise of this question is that you are facing a once-in-a-lifetime challenge that you will never face in quite the same way again.

That premise is false.

The temptation to put the Church on the back burner to study in graduate school is no different in quality or intensity than the temptation to do so in order to start a small business, gain a promotion, prepare for a jury trial, or maintain a tenuous hold on a job during a recession.

I use the word "temptation" deliberately. It is important not to delude ourselves that this desire to put school temporarily ahead of church and even family is some deep philosophical quandary or Abrahamic test. At bottom, it is nothing more glamorous than a temptation. Your professors have subtly planted in you the twin seeds of ambition and fear. Some of you have listened and have begun to feel the unappeasable hunger of a desire for worldly success and its dark side, the fear of failure—that is, the fear of being little in the world's eyes. As you must know, if you give in to these temptations this time, it will only be more difficult to resist the next time around. There will be many occasions where the temptation to put your pride and fear ahead of your family and church will be as acute as anything you feel in graduate school.

Let me use a personal example. As a young associate in a large law firm, I was pulling the laboring oar in a lawsuit that threatened to unravel a large corporate merger and do great harm to one of the firm's major clients. In addition, the basis of the suit involved allegations that our firm had made serious mistakes in a securities offering. Two of the principal partners of the firm, the men who signed my paychecks and decided if I got to come to work the next week, were overseeing the case. We worked endless, tense hours. I recall coming home one night quite late and being so irritated that I had not been able to mow my lawn that I turned on the porch light and mowed it while still in my suit.

The two partners and I met one Saturday. The court hearing that would effectively decide the case was early the next week. I was fully prepared, but more out of panic than necessity, the partners set another lengthy strategy session for Sunday. I had not worked on Sunday through law school and federal court clerkships, and I did not want to start then. At the same time, I was not blind to the fact that the men calling the meeting held my career in their hands, and they were not likely to be impressed that I had a Sunbeam class to teach. I could not be sure of the outcome when I told them I was ready for the hearing, that I had other obligations on Sunday, and that I could not make the meeting.

I tell this story not to talk about the Sabbath but to show that in your careers there will be instances where the pressure to make exceptions to your gospel commitments can be very great. Those who establish their response to such pressure while still in school will find themselves better able to withstand the pressure later.

In sum, the premise of this first question is false. You think this is a one-shot deal. In reality, it is simply the first of many tests of your commitment.

The concept of taking a sabbatical from full commitment to the demands of discipleship is invalid for another reason. It misapprehends our relationship with the Lord and his Church. A vacation or sabbatical is for employees. But our connection to the Lord is described in scripture as a marriage. We would not say to our spouse: "I will always be faithful to you, except while I am in law school. I know you'll understand." Similarly, the Lord searches for those who will serve him no matter what the hazard.

There is yet another danger. We are responsible not only for what we do, but for what we fail to do. Who knows what divine purposes brought you here to this university at this time? Who can say what great service you could render while you are here? Many of you come with gifts, talents, and energy that could be put to extraordinary use in this part of the kingdom. Single-minded pursuit of success in graduate school may cause you to miss many chances to bless the lives of those around you.

I have felt, and still feel, the great weight of things I have failed to do. It was mentioned that I was a law clerk at the Supreme Court. This was an extraordinarily busy year of my life. During that same time, I lived in a ward in Alexandria, Virginia, that experienced numerous convert baptisms of people who had just come to this country from Liberia. I was assigned to home teach a fairly new convert who had been brought into the Church by a great member missionary named Emmanuel Dufur Donka. During a particularly busy time, I missed home teaching this new brother one month. I hasten to add that I was taught better by my father, and this was the first time this had ever happened to me. The next month, I tried to arrange a visit. During that time, he had quit coming to church, and had moved, and I could not find him. That experience, deeply painful to me to this day, brought home to me what President Taylor taught: that we must answer for those who were within our sphere of influence whom we failed to help.[1]

There is another, even more fundamental reason to avoid spiritual sabbaticals. They can result in an undetected yet dangerous weakening of our testimonies. Most of us have an emotional attachment to having a testimony. Once we gain a testimony, we do not like to think of ourselves as having lost it. For this reason, many people do not face the fact that their testimony is dying until it is almost too late. Recently I have learned a little about concrete. One of the things I learned is that a crack in the concrete is often not the first sign of a small problem but nearly that last sign of a very big problem. Testimonies can be the same way. President Lee once said that a testimony "is as hard to hold as a moonbeam."[2] For some of us, that light is very nearly extinguished before we acknowledge there is a problem.

What to do about the loss of testimony is the subject of another day. But if it is happening to you, do not deceive yourself. You are not losing your testimony because your newly honed powers of reasoning have cast the gospel in a harsher light. If I have learned anything in the practice of law, it is that the so-called "powers of reason" serve the purposes of liars and self-deceivers at least as well as they serve the purposes of honest men. If your testimony is dying, it is because you have neglected it.

It is my firm belief that the very things we hold back from God eventually become the source of some of our greatest sorrow. Do not hold back your school years. The law has been called a jealous mistress. As with any mistress, you will, if you give in to her, eventually despise her. I predict that if you hold back your graduate school years from God, you will eventually come to loathe your career. Its shrill demands will become odious to you. Put them on the altar instead, and let God sanctify them for you.

Finally, unless you are aware, you will permanently lose precious family moments. They go, and they do not come back. Each child, at each stage, is like a beautiful mirage, melting into the next phase and never to be captured again. Do not squander any stage; the memory of them will one day be more precious to you than diamonds, and your absence from any of them will weigh heavily on your heart.

I know of a man who turned down lucrative job offers in major eastern cities in order to come to a smaller western city where he could spend more time with his family. The difference between the highest offer he turned down and the one he took was about $52,000. Knowing that he would probably have most of his weekends free, he referred to it as "a thousand dollars a Saturday." This man chose wisely. I have had many Saturdays that I would not trade for a thousand dollars. Over the course of your careers, you will learn that you can exchange your time for money. Try to learn the corollary expressed by Chief Justice Rehnquist that you can also exchange your money for time.

James: I would like to live my religion fully, but I am afraid. Graduate school is hard. What if I don't graduate high in my class? What if I don't finish at all? How will I get a job? If I don't give it everything I've got, what will become of me?

Response: I don't know. But when faced with a significant challenge, you can trust in your own strength, or you can trust in the Lord. I never had so much confidence in my own intelligence and abilities that I felt I could go toe-to-toe with the competition with only my wits to back me up. I knew I needed the Lord's help.

James: But some who do as you say don't do well, and they struggle to find jobs.

Response: True. It is misleading to think that if you put the Lord first during school that you will be a big success and become rich and famous. There are, in fact, great numbers of righteous Saints in all walks of life who have accomplished less than they might have in their public lives because of their commitment to the Church and their families. It is true, as has been said, that religious devotion is no excuse for professional mediocrity. But while it does not excuse mediocrity, it can keep us from the pinnacle. Faithful Saints, including some of you, experience struggles and setbacks and even failure. But their overwhelming testimony is that God has helped them and blessed them in priceless ways that they would not have known otherwise. And when trials come—the wayward child, the bout with cancer, the financial reversal—they know where to turn and in whom they have put their trust. They know where to find him, because they have steadfastly been true to him.

I challenge you to compare their lives to the empty existence of so many of the senior partners I have known, who have given up everything for their careers. In the end, it has left them with nothing that lasts, and it shows in their eyes.

John Lund, who once served here as a bishop, taught that we should never abandon what we know because of what we don't know. You don't know what will happen in your careers if you keep God first, and you have no promise that you will be either rich or famous. But you do know that this is God's church and kingdom, that your time on this earth is precious, and that you are here to prove that you will freely choose God over the honors of this world.

Ultimately the choice, as Elder Packer has said, is not between fame and obscurity, or between wealth and poverty, but between good and evil.[3]

Don't get me wrong. I love my work; I consider it a great privilege to have the job I do. But at a very fundamental level, I do not care if my commitment to the Savior costs me success in my profession. As Paul said, I would suffer "the loss of all things, and do count them but dung, that I may win Christ" (Philippians 3:8). But let me say also to you that my witness, and the witness of many others who could stand before you, is that in trying to put God and family first, God has sanctified my career for me—given me greater opportunities for service, enhanced my abilities, and protected me from harm. In short, I have been utilized by him, even in my career, to help build the kingdom of God on the earth. May he do so for you, and may you allow him to do so, is my prayer.

This stake fireside address was given to University of Idaho and Washington State University graduate students in October 1992. Reprinted from the Clark Memorandum, *Fall 1999, 41–43.*

Michael W. Mosman received his J.D. from Brigham Young University in 1984 and clerked for Justice Lewis F. Powell, Jr. of the U.S. Supreme Court 1985–86. He is currently United States Attorney for the District of Oregon.

Notes

1. "If you do not magnify your callings, God will hold you responsible for those whom you might have saved had you done your duty." *Journal of Discourses,* 20:23.

2. J. M. Heslop, "President Harold B. Lee Directs Church; Led By The Spirit," *Church News,* 15 July 1972, 4.

3. Boyd K. Packer, "The Choice," *Ensign,* Nov. 1980, 21.

Fundamentals and Initiatives

Russell M. Nelson

I am deeply grateful for the privilege of meeting with each of you on this special occasion. I bring greetings from President Benson, President Hinckley, President Monson, and members of the Quorum of the Twelve. We sincerely appreciate this law school, its faculty and student body. And we especially admire those faithful partners who sustain the efforts of their student-spouses. As a doctor, I have had the opportunity of lecturing to many medical groups, but the privilege of speaking with a congregation of lawyers is a rare one for me.

But my study of law is not rare. It is a continuing commitment, which has provided the under-girding strength for all I have tried to do. Of course, my study of law has pertained largely to those divine or natural laws—put in place by our Creator—that govern the structure, function, and healing powers of the human body. These would be classified in contrast to precedents of common law or statutes enacted by legislatures. I know very little about Marbury versus Madison, or the case of Brown against the Board of Education of Topeka, Kansas.

But I will identify law as an important facet of my message tonight that I have entitled, "Fundamentals and Initiatives." I see the proper balancing of these two considerations—fundamentals and initiatives—as one of the great challenges of life.

Let us first turn our attention to the fundamentals, which include my feelings of reverence for the law.

I have learned that the wise physician asks himself at least two basic questions when confronted with any patient who is ill. Question number one: Will this illness subside with the passage of time, or will it become steadily more severe? Let me illustrate with a couple of examples. If a patient has a broken rib, it will get better with the passage of time. On the other hand, if a patient has a broken mitral valve in the heart, the patient will steadily deteriorate and die.

Question number two is considered if the answer to question number one is an ominous prognosis. If the illness is steadily progressive, can that deteriorating course be changed by medical or surgical intervention? In a fractured mitral valve, the downhill progression can be reversed with surgical repair or replacement of that broken valve.

The conscientious physician devotes much of his study to learn the natural laws that govern the area of his concern. We could say the same for the aerospace engineer or the jet pilot whose understanding of the physical laws of "foil" and "lift" is vitally important.

Let us mentally portray this first fundamental principle as a circle of *DIVINE LAW*. Divine law is incontrovertible. It includes not only the laws of physics and physiology, but divine commandments as well. It pertains to things of eternal and everlasting worth, such as family, father, mother, children, ordinance, covenant, and doctrine. Divine law is the most basic of the fundamentals, obedience to which may begin the building of a life of greatness. Reference is made in the scriptures to this first fundamental:

> All kingdoms have a law given;
>
> And there are many kingdoms; for there is . . . no kingdom in which there is no space, either a greater or a lesser kingdom.
>
> And unto every kingdom is given a law; and unto every law there are certain bounds also and conditions (D&C 88:36–38).

The second fundamental principle is also basic to success. It is the circle of *RULES*. This ring includes the laws of man that can be made and also changed by human endeavor. In the Church, we are subject to rules written in the *General Handbook of Instructions*. Not only do we obey our own church rules, but we heed those of the society in which we live. We charge our members to be "subject to kings, presidents, rulers, and magistrates," and to obey, honor, and sustain the law (Article of Faith 12).

Government by law—both in word and practice—is the strength and bulwark of any democracy. No individual is to be above or below the law. This circle of rules must be added to the fundamentals upon which we build our lives. Of course, this will be the circle of your special interest as you shape, honor, and defend such laws of society for the benefit of all.

The next fundamental principle is that of *POLICIES*. Policies are established, for example, by governing boards and presidential bodies who may also change those policies. In the Church, we believe in continuing revelation to presiding leaders who have been given authority and responsibility. The men you sustain as prophets, seers, and revelators respond to inspiration from Him who said, "whether by mine own voice or by the voice of my servants, it is the same" (D&C 1:38).

Next, consider the importance of *GUIDELINES*. Guidelines can be written to help those at work, at school, at home, or at church. I know a man who really understands guidelines. He assists the General Authorities by studying all proposals to purchase or improve real property for the Church. I asked him once how he was able to formulate so many important recommendations he must make to the Brethren. He simply replied, "I work within my guidelines."

If we examine these rings from another perspective, perhaps we can see what he meant. He establishes guidelines well within the circle of policies set by the Brethren. They, in turn, function within rules of the Church and civil government. And those rules are well within bounds set by divine law.

Now let us discuss the final fundamental—that of *STYLE*. This circle includes personality, determination, and spirit. A scripture uniquely applies to personal style:

> ... he that is compelled in all things, the same is a slothful and not a wise servant;
>
> ... men should be anxiously engaged in a good cause, and do many things of their own free will, and bring to pass much righteousness;
>
> For the power is in them, wherein they are agents unto themselves (D&C 58:26–28).

(See Figure 1.)

Figure 1

As we crown this stack with the ring of *STYLE*, note the importance of the central rod that is firmly attached to the basic ring of *DIVINE LAW*. This tie-rod may be likened to the scriptural term, "the rod of iron."

Variations in personal style should range within established guidelines, implemented policies, official rules, and divine law.

When properly stacked, these rings resemble a pyramid in shape. If our behavior is centered in Christ, and the iron rod attaches us firmly at any level of our activity to the fundamentals of God's commandments and things of eternal worth, then we won't so likely be tipped over by winds of adversity.

The heaviest weight in the pyramid is on the bottom. That gives great stability. In a way, it is similar to the heavy ballast in the bottom of an ocean liner, placed there so the ship won't be blown over in a storm.

Periodically we learn of individuals who are either not well anchored or obsessed with a particular idea that extends beyond the limits imposed by guidelines, policies, rules, or even divine law. Such a style may be portrayed as eccentric. This is an unstable situation that leads to wobbly imbalance.

Having considered the fundamentals, let us turn our attention now to the ideas alluded to in the second half of my title—individual initiative. This topic relates to one's freedom to act as a citizen in society or as a responsible member of the Church. The image of the cone of individual initiative takes the inverted shape of the pyramidal cone of fundamentals, which we have just discussed. It is shaped more like a top.

(See Figure 2.)

Let me explain. As individuals, we have no latitude to break the commandments of God. They are absolutes for our conduct. "Thou shalt not commit adultery," for example, is an irrevocable commandment and part of *DIVINE LAW*.

There is a little more room for initiative under the *RULES* by which we live. Handbooks can be edited, new statutes can be passed, even a constitution can be amended.

New *POLICIES* can be even more easily established—but only by those who formulated them in the first place.

GUIDELINES give even greater freedom for adaptation to particular circumstances.

The zone of greatest individual initiative is in the ring of *STYLE*. We previously referred to the word of the Lord that "he that is compelled in all things, the same is a slothful and not a wise servant" (D&C 58:26). So we are expected to exercise much individual initiative.

With this cone of individual initiative put in motion, imagine our rapidly rotating this cone to resemble a spinning top or a whirling gyroscope.

A top spins well on a sturdy pivot-point. It also spins well only if there is no lopsided projection to deform its shape.

In our model, the laws of physics dictate that the forces generated by the spin provide lift in both outward and upward directions.

To me, this teaches a lesson. If individual initiatives are free from abrasive burrs and well based on a firm foundation, there is great potential for personal spiritual growth.

The Lord said, "what manner of men ought ye to be? . . . even as I am" (3 Nephi 27:27). How can one's personal progress approach that of the Lord's hopes for us? It is by exercising individual initiative upwards and outwards, while remaining within the limits of the fundamental bounds and conditions we have discussed.

INDIVIDUAL INITIATIVE

Figure 2

So much for the theory. This strategy can be applied to the lives of real people.

Let me illustrate with a specific example. In the March 3, 1990, issue of the *Church News*, there was a report of the official recognition of the Church by the government of Czechoslovakia. A photograph showed Elder Hans B. Ringger and me meeting with Dr. Josef Hromadka, Deputy Prime

Minister of that country. The fourth person in that picture was Jiri Snederfler, district president of the Church in Czechoslovakia. The accompanying account was truly historic! But another unpublished story preceded that story reported by the media.

As general authorities of the Church, we have been petitioning for official recognition in Czechoslovakia for several years. When Elder Ringger and I met with the minister of Religious Affairs of the country for the first time, we asked him what must be done to gain official recognition that would allow members of the Church in Czechoslovakia to meet in dignity and in full compliance with the law. He replied, "First, you will have to submit statutes indicating your religious beliefs. And they must be submitted not by you 'foreigners,' but by members of your Church here in Czechoslovakia. One of those members must be willing to meet with us and submit those statutes in person. Following that, we will consider your request."

Bear in mind that at this time, some citizens of Czechoslovakia were incarcerated in jail for expression of religious belief or dissident thought. You all know that the new president of the Czechoslovakian Republic, Vaclav Havel, shortly before he became president, was among those prisoners. Not only that, but for nearly four decades, our faithful Latter-day Saints had met quietly only in their homes.

After our meeting with the Minister of Religious Affairs, Elder Ringger and I conferred privately with our district president and his wife, Olga. We explained what was required. Then we asked him, "Are you willing to expose yourself as a member of The Church of Jesus Christ of Latter-day Saints? Are you willing to take the risk, knowing that it might mean jail or death if you were to identify yourself as the leader of the Church in this country?" We assured him that as his ecclesiastical authorities, we could not and would not make that request of him. We could only ask him to determine what his conscience would allow him to do.

Bravely he replied, "Of course I will do it! I will reveal myself. I will meet with the magistrate. I will take the statutes to him personally. I will submit myself to his mercy." Then he concluded, "I will take whatever risk is necessary and even pay with my life, if needed, for the cause of the Lord and his Church because I know the gospel is true!" His wife gave her approval as tears of love moistened her eyes.

God bless Brother and Sister Snederfler for their courage. They are the unsung heroes in the drama that made this significant announcement possible. Because of them, the Church will enter a new era of growth in Czechoslovakia. A mission will be reestablished there in July 1990 after an absence of forty years.

Brother and Sister Snederfler are noble examples of individual initiative balanced on fundamentals. They have been magnified and made great in the eyes of God and their fellowmen.

Valiant action occasionally entails risk. One's reputation, one's very life may be put on the line. Modern scripture suggests that this may be required of each of us. In speaking of our day when the Lord would come to make up his jewels, He spoke of the trials to which his Saints may be subjected:

> Therefore, they must needs be chastened and tried, even as Abraham, who was commanded to offer up his only son.
>
> For all those who will not endure chastening, but deny me, cannot be sanctified (D&C 101:4–5).

In a way, every leader in the Church has to endure trials. Every stake president, bishop, elders quorum president, and teacher has similar and challenging opportunities for individual initiative. When balanced in motion and upon sound fundamental principles, deeds of greatness can result.

Your legal training will require your becoming experts in the letter of the law. You will become craftsmen with words of the English language. But even more challenging will be your ability to master the spirit of the law.

The spirit is all important. President Benson often tells us that the most important thing about our work in the Church is the spirit.

A similar expression was uniquely voiced last month by Dr. Hromadka, Deputy Prime Minister of the Republic of Czechoslovakia. We conversed with him about the challenges faced by a new government in a land where so much is needed. We asked if we, as members of The Church of Jesus Christ of Latter-day Saints, could be of any help to his people. He knew that our Church is well recognized for its efforts in providing humanitarian relief throughout the world. We shall never forget his reply. He said, "We don't need material goods or technology. We need a new spirit. We need moral values. We need the Judeo-Christian ethic back in our curriculum. Please help us to make this a time of spiritual renewal for our nation!"

The new president of Czechoslovakia, Vaclav Havel, won the admiration of his audience when he addressed a joint session of the United States Congress. He did not hold an empty hat in hand. He asked only for spiritual assistance, not just for himself, but also for his neighbor.

This man, who had been unjustly imprisoned for so long and could have felt unkindly toward his captors, said, "I cannot hate; I will not hate." As he spoke to the combined assembly of the United States Congress, he made this impassioned plea for spiritual help:

> The worst thing is that we are living in a decayed moral environment. We have become morally ill, because we have become accustomed to saying one thing and thinking another. We have learned not to believe in anything, not to have consideration for one another, and only to look after ourselves. Notions such as love, friendship, compassion, humility, and forgiveness have lost their depth and dimension, and for many of us they represent merely a psychological idiosyncrasy, or appear to be some kind of stray relic, something rather comical in the era of computers and space rockets.

What a marvelous message! President Havel's hopes for love, friendship, compassion, humility, and forgiveness harken right back to counsel given through the ages by living prophets of God. They have stressed the importance of practicing those principles broadly and, especially, within the walls of our own homes.

I am informed that about 50 percent of you students here tonight are married. And I suspect others may take that important step if your prospective mates are successful in catching you.

May I offer a little advice that may be helpful in your domestic relationships? Be mindful that there is no guarantee of a long life here in mortality.

The sporting world was shocked earlier this month. A 23-year-old basketball star, Hank Gathers, had just completed an "alley-oop" play with a spectacular slam dunk. He then headed up court with a big smile. Seconds later he collapsed and, in spite of prolonged efforts at resuscitation, he died.

While I don't presume to know any more about his particular clinical history than has been published in the papers, I do know this. So-called "skipped" heart beats are common. We all experience them from time to time. Some of those are recorded on the electrocardiogram (ECG) as premature ventricular contractions, or PVCs. If one of those PVCs occurs precisely at the onset of the T wave of the ECG, the heart is especially prone to a fatal shift of its rhythm. A normal rhythm can suddenly switch to ventricular fibrillation—a random motion of muscle fibers—which is incompatible with life because the heart can no longer propel blood. It is my assumption that this is what happened to Hank Gathers. The same can happen, regardless of physical conditioning, to any of us at any time.

Every day of life is a precious gift from God. I sincerely believe these words of King Benjamin:

> If you should render all the thanks and praise which your whole soul has power to possess, to that God who has created you, and has kept and preserved you . . .
>
> If ye should serve him who has created you from the beginning, and is preserving you from day to day, by lending you breath, that ye may live and move and do according to your own will, and even supporting you from one moment to another—I say, if ye should serve him with all your whole souls yet ye would be unprofitable servants.
>
> And behold, all that he requires of you is to keep his commandments; and he has promised you that if ye would keep his commandments ye should prosper in the land (Mosiah 2:20–22).

That scripture teaches the importance of humility, gratitude, obedience, and faith in promised blessings.

It reminds us how fortunate we are to be touched by the majestic spirit of Rex E. Lee, president of Brigham Young University. His example of courage and candor, fidelity and love, constitutes a model worthy of our emulation. He teaches us to keep our vision on the eternities ahead, yet to live and enjoy each day as if it were our last.

We can learn much from such courageous men and women of greatness. Though our eyes are fixed on distant goals, we do today's work today. We can pay our bills on the day we receive them. Today, we can really treat our neighbors as we would like to be treated. We can tell our partners of our love daily.

Occasionally I awaken in the night and tenderly run my fingers through the curly hair of the companion lying beside me. I'm so grateful for her. I suppose some of that gratitude stems from long periods of separation imposed upon us from time to time. How I missed her when I served in the Army on duty overseas! How I missed her when spending arduous nights rendering emergency surgical care at the hospital! And now those long and lonely nights must be endured again when I have assignments overseas for the Church.

Your spiritual self-evaluation is of great importance. Most of you will practice law on a fee-for-service basis. Collect that fee to enable you to serve others. Don't collect the fee as the reason for your service. And, occasionally, you will wish to render service without a fee. That is a great privilege—one of the refreshing distinctions between a profession and a trade.

Your professional work is to support your family. Your family does not exist to support your work.

Your profession will necessarily bring you into contact with the corrupted, which can be corrupting in itself. Your own spiritual strength must be your safeguard.

A society with no other scale than a legal one is not worthy of sons and daughters of God. Any morality based solely on the letter of the law falls short of the great potential of the human soul.

So I plead for a proper balance between fundamentals and initiatives. Actions based on eternal principles enlarge the soul. Through such actions we literally can become more like the Lord. We need not be boastful, but we can literally achieve the goal Jesus Christ expressed for us. "What manner of men ought ye to be?" he asked. Then he answered his own question: "Even as I am" (3 Nephi 27:27). As we so build we will be exhilarated, enlarged, ennobled, and magnified beyond our fondest dreams.

Please know of our deep love for you and of our great confidence in you. Our prayers are with you and your loved ones for your success now and always. I invoke the blessings of the Lord upon you as I testify that God lives, that Jesus is the Christ, that his restored church provides the pathway by which we can achieve balanced growth in this life and eternal glory in the life to come. In the name of Jesus Christ, Amen.

This fireside address was given at the BYU Law School on March 18, 1990. Reprinted from the Clark Memorandum, *Fall 1990, 12–17.*

Russell M. Nelson received his M.D. from the University of Utah in 1947 and his Ph.D. in surgery from the University of Minnesota in 1954. He is currently a member of the Quorum of Twelve Apostles.

WHAT IS PROPERTY UNTO ME?

Let them repent of all their sins, and of all their
covetous desires, before me, saith the Lord;
for what is property unto me? saith the Lord.
(D&C 117:4)

Satisfaction in the Law

David G. Campbell

Tonight I would like to discuss two disturbing developments in the legal profession—developments I believe to be related. They have been much discussed during recent years, but few people seem to see any connection between them.

The first development is the ever-increasing emphasis on the commercial and economic side of law practice and a corresponding decrease in lawyer public service. One need only pick up a copy of any modern legal magazine to see the commercial emphasis. It is trumpeted in articles and surveys that measure professional success almost exclusively in terms of income and status.

The decrease in public service is more difficult to detect, but nonetheless real. It was highlighted in February when the ABA House of Delegates found it necessary to pass an amendment to the Model Rules of Professional Responsibility. The amendment states that lawyers should render at least 50 hours of pro bono legal services each year.[1] Forty hours should be spent providing legal services to the poor, with another ten devoted to improving the law, the legal system, or the legal profession. The remarkable aspect of this amendment is not that it occurred, but that it was deemed necessary by the leaders of our profession. Delegates from around the nation concluded that modern lawyers need an ethical imperative if they are to spend the equivalent of one hour per week providing legal assistance to the poor. Equally concerning is the fact that significant lawyers and groups of lawyers opposed the new rule. They apparently thought it improper or ill-advised to require lawyers to provide pro bono services to the poor.

The second development—one that probably should not be mentioned during an awards ceremony for third-year law students—is the widely

61

documented dissatisfaction modern lawyers feel with their profession. A 1990 survey by the *National Law Journal*, for example, found that only 31 percent of all lawyers were "very satisfied" with their professional lives.[2] Nearly two-thirds complained that law has become less of a profession and more of a business. More than half view other lawyers as obnoxious. Seventy percent dislike the long hours and tension of practicing law.

I believe there is a relationship between the increasing unhappiness of lawyers on one hand and our profession's modern emphasis on economics, with its corresponding de-emphasis on public service, on the other hand. I see this connection largely because of several experiences our firm has had in pro bono practice and the effect those experiences have had on my own happiness as a lawyer.

Twelve years ago our firm agreed to undertake the pro bono representation of John Henry Knapp, a well-known inmate on Arizona's death row. Knapp had been convicted seven years earlier of deliberately setting a fire that had killed his two daughters in the bedroom of their home. As you can imagine, a crime so repulsive had received widespread publicity in Arizona. By the time our firm was approached about the case, Knapp had exhausted his appeals and lost several petitions for post-conviction relief. Several times the Arizona Supreme Court had issued warrants for his execution, only to have them stayed by yet another judicial challenge. Worst of all, Knapp had confessed to committing the crime, making his plight all the less sympathetic.

Knapp had been charged and convicted largely because of a state arson investigator's conclusion that the Knapp fire was not accidental—that it had been started with a combustible liquid. Suspicions that initially arose from the rapid growth, intense heat, and unusual burn patterns of the fire were confirmed, at least in the investigator's mind, when he found an empty can of Coleman fuel in the front hall closet of the Knapp home.

Having concluded the fire was caused by arson, Arizona officials turned their suspicions to the only two adults in the house at the time of the fire—John Knapp and his wife, Linda. Several nights after the fire, under close and vigorous interrogation at the police station, John Knapp confessed that he had started the fire deliberately. John recanted the confession almost immediately, but the confession was enough to convict him of first-degree murder and secure for him the sentence of death—a result applauded by outraged citizens of Arizona.

When our firm entered the case seven years later, there was little hope for John Knapp, and few people who cared to help him. Initially we agreed to look at the case simply as a favor to an overworked and thoroughly frustrated criminal defense lawyer who believed John Knapp to be an innocent man but who had exhausted all of his time and energy for the case. Lawyers in our firm who looked closely into the facts and met John Knapp soon also concluded that he was an innocent man. Time does not permit me to recount all of the efforts undertaken during the next eleven years, but let me mention a few of the high points.

At John Knapp's murder trial, the defense had argued that the Knapp girls set the fire themselves. John was unemployed at the time of the fire, the heat in the house had been turned off by the electric company, and John and his wife had resorted to Coleman lanterns and stoves for lighting, heating, and cooking. The girls had been seen playing with matches more than once. The defense theorized that the girls awoke on the cold morning of the fire and started playing with matches in their cluttered bedroom, inadvertently setting the fire that caused their deaths.

The prosecution debunked this theory, arguing that an accidental fire would have burned slowly, leaving the girls and their parents ample time to detect the fire and either extinguish it or escape from the house. Prosecution experts testified that the rapid and intense heat of the fire simply was inconsistent with the progression of a slow-burning accidental fire. It had to have been aided by some form of combustible liquid such as Coleman fuel.

By the time we became involved in the case seven years later, fire science had made great strides, particularly with respect to a phenomenon known as flashover. Flashover occurs when a fire in a confined area causes heated gases to collect at the ceiling level. The gases quickly become superheated, reflecting intense heat back down on objects in the room. This reflected heat causes the room literally to burst into flames, and the confined space quickly becomes a raging inferno. Tests at Harvard University had shown that even a small fire, through flashover, can quickly cause an entire room to burst into flames. The flashover phenomenon was not generally understood when John Knapp was tried for the murder of his daughters in 1974.

Our firm ultimately hired several fire experts from around the country to examine the evidence from the Knapp fire. These experts concluded that all of the indicators relied on by the Arizona arson expert were consistent with an accidental flashover fire. Our defense team even built a replica of the small bedroom, down to the placement of furniture and other objects in the room, and ignited a small amount of paper to show how quickly a flashover fire could spread. Within minutes the small room became the raging inferno that the arson experts had testified could only have been caused by a combustible liquid.

In 1987, after six years of attempting to obtain a hearing on post-conviction relief, we were permitted to place this flashover evidence before an Arizona superior court judge. After reviewing the evidence, the judge found that it "would probably change the [guilty] verdict," and granted John Knapp a new trial.

At Knapp's original trial prosecutors had placed in evidence the Coleman fuel can found in the closet of the Knapp's home after the fire. They referred to it as "the death can." The prosecutors told defense counsel and the court that they had tested the can for fingerprints but that all prints on the can were smudged. While preparing for the new trial years later, we insisted upon the disclosure of all information in the state's files. To our surprise, we learned that the fingerprints on the Coleman fuel can were not smudged as the prosecutors had asserted during the first trial. Eleven clearly identifiable prints had been found on the can before the first trial, and none of them belonged to John Knapp. All of them belonged to Linda Knapp—John's wife. This evidence suggested that John Knapp had not used the can to start the fire and then returned it to the hall closet, as the prosecution claimed. Linda Knapp apparently had been the last person to touch the can, and she told investigators she had placed the empty can in the closet several days before the fire occurred.

But we still were faced with the very troubling fact that John Knapp had confessed to committing the crime. We learned several significant facts about the confession.

On the night of the confession John Knapp was suffering from a severe migraine headache—a recurring condition for which he had been receiving medical care. The detectives who questioned Knapp later testified that his pain was so severe during the interrogation that he literally was pulling hair from his head. The confession, given in a nine-foot-by-nine-foot room under close questioning by two investigators, and while John Knapp was suffering a migraine headache, was at least suspect.

John Knapp recanted his confession almost immediately, saying that he had confessed to protect his wife. Knapp later claimed that he told his wife, in a phone conversation from jail the day after the confession, that he had confessed to protect her because the police had told him the fire was set deliberately and he did not want her to be charged with the crime. At trial the prosecution rebutted this explanation by noting that Knapp had spoken with his father-in-law shortly after the confession but had not stated to him that the confession was false.

Seventeen years later, as we were approaching Knapp's newly won retrial, the prosecutors finally revealed that the telephone conversation Knapp claimed to have with his wife in 1974 had in fact been tape-recorded by the State and never disclosed to defense counsel. We obtained a copy of the tape. As lawyers from our firm listened to the recording for the first time, they heard the voice of a tearful John Knapp, 17 years younger, telling his wife that he did not set the fire that took the lives of his children and that he had confessed because he feared she would be charged with the crime if he did not take responsibility for the fire. The tape, of course, strongly corroborated Knapp's explanation of the confession.

There is much more I could tell you about this case. John Knapp is now a free man, living in Pennsylvania and working at a full-time job. In more than two years of freedom, as in the years before the fire, John Knapp has had no difficulty with the law. After spending 13 years on death row—at one point coming within 36 hours of execution—John Knapp has become a contributing and responsible member of society.

There is a remarkable corollary to this story. Shortly after John Knapp was released from prison, our firm received a letter from a young man named Ray Girdler, who was serving two consecutive life sentences for the arson deaths of his wife and child in a mobile home fire near Prescott, Arizona. Girdler wrote, "I too am innocent," and asked our firm to help him. We chuckled about the new specialty we apparently were developing and responded with a polite letter declining to become involved.

In short, Ray Girdler persisted, and we eventually agreed to look at his case. What we found was astonishing. Ray Girdler had been convicted of the arson deaths of his wife and daughter on the testimony of the same investigator who testified at John Knapp's murder trial. Lawyers from our firm quickly determined that the arson conclusions in the Girdler fire were even more doubtful than those in the Knapp fire. And in the Girdler case there was no confession, no motive, no Coleman fuel can—only the testimony of an arson investigator who concluded that the fire had not been accidental.

After an extended evidentiary hearing, the Yavapai County judge who had sentenced Ray Girdler to two consecutive life sentences ordered that a new trial be held. We then convinced the court to hire an outside expert to examine the evidence of arson. The expert quickly concluded that the Girdler fire had been entirely accidental. He found the Arizona investigator's conclusions of arson to be professionally negligent and morally unforgivable, and recommended in the strongest terms that the charges against Ray Girdler be dropped. The prosecutor agreed.

Ray Girdler, like John Knapp, is now a free man. After spending eight years in prison under consecutive life sentences, Ray now lives in Phoenix where he is resuming his college studies and recently was promoted to manager of a retail store.

I suspect you would not be surprised if I told you that our firm's defense of John Knapp and Ray Girdler have been among the most satisfying aspects of my law practice. And I did not work on either case. They were handled by other lawyers in our firm. As a partner in the firm I helped to finance the effort, and even that meager contribution has been very rewarding.

I am not here tonight to urge you to take up the cause of death-row inmates. I recount the Knapp and Girdler cases as examples. I have found similar satisfaction from other, less dramatic pro bono projects, such as helping a poor mother of three to fend off an unscrupulous debt collector, assisting another woman in retaining her trailer home, and helping the Arizona state bar in closing down some lawyers who were engaging in patently misleading advertising. What little pro bono work I have done has been enormously rewarding—more so than any other aspect of my litigation practice.

That is why I believe there is a connection between the two developments I described at the beginning of my remarks. It is not a coincidence that dissatisfaction with the profession is reaching its peak at a time when lawyers must, by ethical requirement, be forced to spend even one hour per week helping those in need. Lawyers who lament to the *National Law Journal* that law is becoming more a business than a profession ought to remember these words of Roscoe Pound:

> Historically, there are three ideas involved in a profession, organization, learning, and a spirit of public service. These are essential. The remaining idea, that of earning a livelihood, is incidental.[3]

These words seem out of place, even antiquated, to our modern legal profession—a profession that focuses more attention on earning money than on public service. But remember, that is the same modern profession that lawyers now find quite unsatisfying.

You law students might not recognize it, but as a lawyer you will have marvelous powers. You can open locked doors, break down walls, find solutions to impossible problems. The plight of John Knapp and Ray Girdler illustrate that there are people in our society who find themselves helpless before the law. Without the assistance of a lawyer, these people often are incapable of helping themselves. In today's world of legal complexities, even a simple landlord-tenant problem can become an insurmountable barrier to one untrained in the law. Honest people of modest means often find themselves at tremendous disadvantage in their personal, family, and business dealings when they lack legal counsel. Those of us who have a monopoly on legal services must provide the assistance if it is to be provided at all.

Thus, whether you're heading for private practice, government service, or an in-house position in business, I believe you will find your greatest professional fulfillment in doing for others what they cannot do for themselves. Charles Dickens once wrote that "any Christian spirit working kindly in its little sphere . . . will find its mortal life too short for its vast means of usefulness."[4] That truth applies as fully to the practice of law as it did to Scrooge's counting house.

It is my hope that you will undertake your life in the law as Woodrow Wilson counseled, "with a view to the amelioration of every undesirable condition that the law can reach, the removal of every obstacle to progress and fair dealing that the law can remove, the lightening of every burden the law can lift and the righting of every wrong the law can rectify."[5] If that is too tall an order, then I challenge you to accept the ABA's goal of devoting 50 hours per year to helping others with your legal skills. Such devotion will find for you much happiness in the law.

This address was given at the BYU Law School awards ceremony on March 25, 1993. Reprinted from the Clark Memorandum, *Fall 1993, 24–29.*

David G. Campbell received his J.D. from the University of Utah in 1979 and clerked for Justice William H. Rehnquist of the U.S. Supreme Court 1981–82. He is currently a partner at Osborn Maledon in Phoenix, Arizona.

Notes

1. Don J. DeBenedictis, "Fifty Hours for Pro Bono," *ABA Journal* (April 1993), 32.

2. Margaret Cronin Fisk, "Lawyers Give Thumbs Up," *National Law Journal* (28 May 1990), S2.

3. Roscoe Pound, "What Is a Profession?" 19 *Notre Dame Lawyer* 203, 204 (1944).

4. Charles Dickens, *A Christmas Carol* (New York: Washington Square Press, 1963), 51.

5. Woodrow Wilson, "The Lawyer and the Community," 35 *Reports of the American Bar Association* 419, 435 (1910).

Confirm Thy Soul in Self-Control

D. Todd Christofferson

It is an honor to address you, members of the J. Reuben Clark Law Society and guests. Thank you for the generosity of your invitation to speak on this occasion. As a theme for my remarks, I have borrowed a line from the well-known anthem "America the Beautiful." It is both a plea and a noble aspiration: "Confirm thy soul in self-control." While I hope that the thoughts I will offer are not inconsistent with my calling in the Church, I hasten to state that they are my own observations, opinions, and conclusions and should not be construed as a statement by or the position of The Church of Jesus Christ of Latter-day Saints.

My first job out of law school was as law clerk to the Honorable John J. Sirica, then chief judge of the U. S. District Court for the District of Columbia. It was August 1972, and within days the U. S. attorney's office presented a grand jury indictment against Howard Hunt, Gordon Liddy, James McCord, and four Cuban-Americans for their role in the break-in at the Democratic National Committee headquarters located at the Watergate office complex in Washington. Thus began a two-year saga of legal proceedings under the rubric of "Watergate."

It was, as you can imagine, an incredible experience for one fresh out of law school, and not only for me. On one occasion in the midst of trials and hearings and White House tapes, Judge Sirica said to me, "I hope you appreciate this. Not many law clerks get an experience like this." Then after a momentary reflection, he added, "I guess not many judges do either."

I remember the feeling of pride I had in the legal profession during the argument over the grand jury subpoena to the president to produce his tape recordings of several meetings in the White House and Executive Office Building. It was an historic moment. Not since the time of Thomas Jefferson had a president of the United States been requested to produce evidence in a criminal proceeding. In Jefferson's case the matter had been resolved short of enforcement measures. There was really no precedent with respect to a contested subpoena. In the large ceremonial courtroom of the U. S. courthouse in Washington, with the statues of Solon and Moses looking on, special prosecutor Archibald Cox, representing the grand jury, and Professor Charles Alan Wright, representing President Nixon, stood before Judge Sirica to present the case for and against the subpoena. I felt I was watching a battle of the Titans. Both were great men of the law, and in such moments I knew I had entered a noble profession. Indeed to a large extent, it was lawyers who successfully brought the nation through the Watergate crisis.

On the other hand, to some extent it was lawyers who made Watergate what it was in the first place. As I sat through the break-in trial, subsequent cover-up case, and other proceedings observing some of the defendants and witnesses who were lawyers with not so clean hands, I had moments of doubt. I began to ask myself what accounted for the difference between an Archibald Cox and a John Mitchell, both apparently decent men, both skilled in the profession, and yet one, Mr. Mitchell, apparently willing to approve a scheme of illegal electronic eavesdropping and wiretaps for a possible political advantage. I began to wonder what would protect me from succumbing to the pressures that might, in the future, come from clients or others to step over the moral and ethical line to secure a crucial advantage. I saw that, in one case, a junior White House officer about my age, in complying with his superior's orders to destroy certain files, had committed a criminal act without fully realizing it. Could I recognize in every instance, I asked myself, where the line is?

I found an answer to these concerns in the course of listening to the White House tapes. When President Nixon finally did produce the sub-poenaed tape recordings of White House meetings and telephone calls, Judge Sirica screened them to identify those portions relevant to Watergate, which were, in turn, to be passed on to the special prosecutor and grand jury. With headphones, and using a tape recorder graciously provided by the White House (one of the recorders that had been used to record the tapes initially), the judge and I listened to hour after hour of meetings between Nixon, his aides John Erlichman and Bob Haldeman, legal counsel John Dean, and others.

In the course of listening in on these discussions, I became convinced that Richard Nixon had not had prior knowledge of Gordon Liddy's scheming nor John Mitchell's acquiescence in those schemes. Not long after the arrests of James McCord and the Cuban-Americans at the Watergate office building, however, Nixon was informed of the relationship between the burglars and his reelection committee, learning that it had funded their activities. I deduced from the conversations that Nixon also had some information about the role of his good friend John Mitchell. It was at this point, I think, feeling the expediency of helping a friend and of avoiding embarrassment to his reelection campaign, if not to himself, that the president of the United States committed a criminal act: obstruction of justice. He approved his aides' recommendation that they get the CIA to intervene with the FBI in such a way as to throw the FBI off the money trail—the $100 bills found in James McCord's pockets that would lead them to the Committee to Reelect the President. And so, in succumbing to the pressures of the moment, he stepped off the rock of principle.

The supposedly simple solution did not suffice for long, nor did a continuing series of expedient measures that followed. The bandages, so to speak, were always inadequate. So what began as a small cut grew and festered until it until it became a mortal wound. President Nixon on many occasions could have said, "No, we will not do this. We must be truthful and, if a storm comes, ride it out." It would have required courage, but, had he done so, there would have been no Watergate as it came to be and no resignation under threat of impeachment.

Some do "get away with" dishonest or unethical, even immoral conduct in this imperfect world, but there is no real security except in the consistent adherence to principle. If one ever makes an exception, as did the president with Watergate, his safety evaporates. Contrary to the opinion of some, I do not think President Nixon was a bad man nor that an evil nature accounts for his mistakes. I believe he was essentially a good man who allowed himself exceptions to the moral standard he generally lived by. Watergate taught me that any exception to moral principle, no matter how well reasoned or rationalized, poses a real danger to individuals, to the rule of law, and to society. In the words of Pope John Paul II:

> When it is a matter of the moral norms prohibiting intrinsic evil, there are no privileges or exceptions for anyone. It makes no difference whether one is the master of the world or the "poorest of the poor" on the face of the earth. Before the demands of morality we are all absolutely equal.[1]

In one sense, the ABA's Model Rules and Code of Professional Responsibility work against us as we seek to adopt and guide by high moral norms without exceptions. They do this, at times, by focusing on very fine points and close distinctions, encouraging in some a tendency to rationalize and a propensity to walk as closely to the line as possible, though they hope not to cross it. In a 1996 article in the *Wisconsin Law Review*, Professor Marianne M. Jennings, a 1977 graduate of the BYU Law School, took a good-humored swipe at what sometimes comes across in the Code and the Rules as a search for loopholes and exceptions. She titled her article "The Model Rules and the Code of Professional Responsibility Have Absolutely Nothing to Do with Ethics: The Wally Cleaver Proposition as an Alternative."[2]

Reviewing a series of headlines reporting the actions of certain lawyers that clearly violated basic moral standards of honesty and fairness, Professor Jennings observed:

> Somehow I envisioned the practice of law as something a bit more noble than seeing how much I could get away with. And here we reach the central thesis of this piece: Can we move to a higher standard than how much we can get away with?

> [Footnote 19: I call this thesis the Cleaver proposition, named after the infamous Wally who said, "You know, Beaver, there's only so much junk you can get away with before you get creamed." Getting creamed at Mayfield Elementary meant something different than getting creamed as a lawyer. But the underlying principle is the same: sooner or later we get in trouble when we engage in junky behavior. The public perception is that lawyers have the emotional maturity and behavior of Beaver Cleaver. We're getting closer to being creamed every day. James H. Cossitt proposed a less star-studded approach to lawyer ethics. He wrote that conduct by lawyers should survive the "smell" test. (See James H. Cossitt, "The Smell Test," Bus. L. Today, July–Aug. 1996, at 8.) Wally would put it this way: "Gee, that really stinks."][3]

I am not suggesting that we abandon the Model Rules and Code of Professional Responsibility. These and the opinions of the ABA Standing Committee on Ethics and Professional Responsibility can be of significant practical help in supporting and reinforcing our commitments to speak truthfully, honor obligations, and respect confidences. They define a line that once crossed mandates disciplinary action. But we should not expect rules to perform a task that, by their nature, they cannot achieve. They simply cannot fill the role of ultimate compass or guide.

Codes and rules can serve to strengthen praiseworthy commitments on the one hand or to encourage "what-can-I-get-away-with" lawyering on the other. The outcome depends on whether or not we remain loyal to the fundamental values or principles that underlie the rules. Cut loose from the core principles that have supported our civilization for centuries, ethical norms lose their vitality, just as a branch cut from a tree or a plant severed from its roots.

President J. Reuben Clark, Jr., had this concept in mind when he addressed religious educators of The Church of Jesus Christ of Latter-day Saints nearly 60 years ago. To these instructors of teenagers and young adults he said:

> The teaching of a system of ethics to the students is not a sufficient reason for running our seminaries and institutes. . . . The students of seminaries and institutes should of course be taught the ordinary canons of good and righteous living, for these are part, and an essential part, of the Gospel. But there are the great principles . . . that go way beyond these canons of good living. These great fundamental principles also must be taught to the youth; they are the things the youth wish first to know about. . . .

... [W]e shall not feel justified in appropriating one further tithing dollar to the upkeep of our seminaries and institutes unless they can be used to teach the Gospel in the manner prescribed. The tithing represents too much toil, too much self-denial, too much sacrifice, too much faith, to be used for the color-less instruction of the youth of the Church in elementary ethics.[4]

President Clark correctly perceived that ethics do indeed become "colorless" without the foundation of moral principles that endow those ethics with life and vigor. These principles are often rooted in venerable religious doctrines like those embodied in the commands, "Thou shalt love thy neighbor as thyself" (Leviticus 19:18; Mark 12:31), "Thou shalt not bear false witness" (Exodus 20:16), and "Honor thy father and thy mother" (Exodus 20:12). Emanating from such teachings are the principles of service, compassion, honesty, fairness, loyalty, responsibility, and justice. These give essential vitality to codes and canons, which then can reinforce and help clarify the application of these guiding principles.

The great benefit of a life founded on principle is that it permits self-direction and self-government. The law that governs one's conduct is within; external rules are secondary or supplementary. This affords maximum liberty in professional life and in life generally—not maximum license, but maximum liberty. When principles guide choices, few rules are needed. Principles can move from one situation to another providing a paradigm that focuses the facts and points a proper course. Rules alone are not up to that task. We can never conceive and draft enough rules to cover all events and circumstances, and, even if we could, who could ever read and remember them all? Model rules and a code were not what Richard Nixon needed. He needed an unwavering commitment to honesty. In Nixon's case, lodestar principles could have guided him successfully through the Watergate minefield, or rather would have enabled him to stop Watergate in its tracks at an early stage.

So it is with the brotherhood and sisterhood of the bar. Ethical rules cannot replace moral principles. If a commitment to principles is lacking, we can never produce an adequate volume of rules as a substitute or a sufficiently large army of monitors and bureaucrats to enforce them. John Adams, our second president, is reported to have said, "Our Constitution was made only for a moral and religious people. It is wholly inadequate to the government of any other."[5] Similarly, if lawyers cannot largely govern themselves by principle, no written constitution or code will suffice to force us onto an ethical path.

The proliferation of rules of conduct in the profession and of rules and regulations in society is simply testament to the fact that our commitment to principles is diminishing. Self-control, and the sense of responsibility that engenders it, are not much emphasized. The tendency is rather to focus on rights and encourage individuals to see the rest of the world as responsible to affirm their rights. Responsibility is shifted to others.[6]

Not long ago I was a guest of the Museum of Tolerance at the Simon Wiesenthal Center in Los Angeles. One interactive exhibit focusing on personal responsibility is called the "Point of View Diner." It is designed as a traditional 1950s diner complete with a counter and booths, red vinyl seats, and individual jukeboxes that are actually computer monitors. At one end of the diner is a large television screen showing a simulated nightly news program. The news program I saw was the report of a fictional accident in which a drunk teenage driver, returning from the prom with his date, ran into another vehicle and was killed. The screen shows the aftermath—a close-up of the death car where police and firemen are working to free the injured girlfriend. Looking on in anguish is the dead teenager's mother.

On the jukebox screen one can see the players of this drama and hear them answer questions that the visitor selects from a list on the screen. For example, in one response, the injured girlfriend, who used a fake ID to buy liquor for Charlie, the deceased driver, says, "I loved Charlie; it's not my fault! Everyone drinks. Give me a break! He asked me to get it; I didn't make him drink it." The liquor store owner asserts it is unrealistic to expect him to determine the validity of every ID. "The problem isn't me. Don't you think the responsibility lies with the kid who got drunk?" Charlie's mother acknowledges that she knew about his drinking but is defiant in reaction to a question implying that her own lax parenting had something to do with the tragedy.

After having seen the news report and the answers to these interview questions, visitors use buttons on the jukeboxes to vote on the comparative responsibility of the players: Charlie, his date, his mother, and the liquor store owner. The levels of responsibility are ranked one through five, five being the highest.

My guide made a surprising comment about the reaction of high school students. The vast majority assign a very low level of responsibility to Charlie for what happened. They see the mother, the liquor store owner, and Charlie's date as more at fault than Charlie himself, who chose to drink and who caused the accident in which he was killed. After reflecting about this attitude, it seems to me to reflect a philosophy that is gaining acceptance among all age groups in our society. It is a philosophy in which each person sees himself or herself more and more the victim of circumstance and other people's choices, and therefore, less and less responsible for his or her own choices and their consequences.

If you can shift responsibility for your life to parents, friends, teachers, society, or even God, you can excuse in yourself any failing and will expect others to make right any trouble that comes your way or that you cause for others. This desire to evade responsibility is not a new phenomenon;

throughout history people have been tempted to take this easy way out. When Moses returned from his 40 days on Mt. Sinai and called Aaron to account for making the golden calf, Aaron responded:

> Let not the anger of my lord wax hot: thou knowest the people, that they are set on mischief.
>
> For they said unto me, Make us gods, which shall go before us: for as for this Moses, the man that brought us up out of the land of Egypt, we wot not what is become of him.
>
> And I said unto them, Whosoever hath any gold, let them break it off. So they gave it me: then I cast it into the fire, and there came out this calf (Exodus 32:22–24).

No, seeking to avoid or deny the unpleasant demands of responsibility is not new in this world. What is new in our time is how widely the philosophy of irresponsibility is being accepted and even institutionalized. For example, current trends in tort law are modifying the traditional rules of negligence to require that every victim of an accident be compensated by people who have money, whether or not the people with money play any material role in causation. We seem to be heading toward the creation of some general right to be compensated by someone, somewhere, for every misfortune or disappointment that occurs in life. One wonders, when we have all become victims, who will be left to compensate us?

The doctrine found in the scriptures is something quite different. God requires those of us who are accountable, who have the capacity of choice, to assume responsibility for ourselves. He gives us our moral agency and expects us to guide our lives according to true principles. Among other things, this means that we are obligated to repent when we make mistakes. If we were not obligated to confess and change and make restitution, if our behavior was glossed over and God was responsible to handle the consequences, we would be nothing more than his puppets. Anything that happened in our lives and what became of us in the end would depend entirely on His interventions. That, you will recall, was Lucifer's idea about how things should operate. He, in fact, would have been more than happy to take care of everything and control our lives. He volunteered to do it. But if we jettison responsibility, we also forfeit self-control and the liberty it makes possible.

My plea is that we do what we can to inspire principled conduct and acceptance of responsibility, first in ourselves, next at home, and then wherever our influence extends. This is not simply for the great decisions and moments in life, but most important, in the minutiae of daily life. In a commencement address delivered in April 1994 at Brigham Young University, John Q. Wilson, a political science professor at UCLA, noted that simple acts of personal responsibility are both the hardest and the most important work we have to do. He said:

Commencement speakers are supposed to urge you to rise to the highest challenge, pursue the impossible dream, excel at the loftiest ambitions. I will not do that. It is too easy, and too empty. The easiest thing to do is to support great causes, sign stirring petitions, endorse grand philosophies. The hardest thing to do—and it is getting harder all the time—is to be a good husband or wife, a strong father or mother, an honorable friend and neighbor.

Professor Wilson continued:

> The truly good deeds are the small, everyday actions of ordinary life: the employee who gives an honest day's work; the employer who rewards loyalty and service; the stranger who stops to help someone in need; the craftsman who builds each house as if he himself were going to live in it; the man who unhesitatingly accepts responsibility for the children he has fathered; the father who wants the respect of his children more than admission to the executive suite; the mother who knows that to care for an infant is not an admission of professional failure; the parents who turn the television off even when their children want to watch just one more hour of some bit of Hollywood drivel; the neighbors who join together to patrol a neighborhood threatened by drug dealers; the hiker who carries his own trash out of the park; the landlord who paints out the graffiti without waiting for the city authorities; the juror who judges another on the basis of the principle of personal responsibility before the law. These are the heroes of daily life. May you join their ranks.[7]

There can be no substitute for self-control based on internalized true principles. By personal experience I know that, after all we can do, we may rely on One whose love we little comprehend to do what we cannot. I honor the Savior and bear witness of His grace. I pray His rich blessings upon you.

This address was given to the Orange County and Los Angeles County Chapters of the J. Reuben Clark Law Society on September 29 and 30, 2000. Reprinted from the Clark Memorandum, Spring 2001, 2–7.

D. Todd Christofferson received his J.D. from Duke University in 1972. He is currently a member of the Presidency of the Seventy.

Notes

1. John Paul II, *The Splendor of Truth: Veritatis Splendor,* para. 96 (1993); cited in Robert J. Muise, "Professional Responsibility for Catholic Lawyers: The Judgment of Conscience," 71 *Notre Dame Law Review* 771 at 781–82 (1996).

2. Marianne M. Jennings, "The Model Rules and the Code of Professional Responsibility Have Absolutely Nothing to Do with Ethics: The Wally Cleaver Proposition as an Alternative," 1996 *Wisconsin Law Review* 1223 (1996).

3. *Id.* at 1227.

4. J. Reuben Clark, Jr., "The Charted Course of the Church in Education" in *J. Reuben Clark: Selected Papers on Religion, Education, and Youth,* ed. David H. Yarn, Jr. (Provo, Utah: BYU Press, 1984), 249, 254.

5. Cited in Ezra Taft Benson, *Teachings of Ezra Taft Benson* (Salt Lake City: Bookcraft, 1988), 597.

6. The thoughtful Russian dissident and historian Aleksandr Solzhenitsyn, in an interview with *Time* magazine several years ago, responded to this question: "You have said the moral life of the West has declined during the past 300 years. What do you mean by that?" Solzhenitsyn responded:

> There is technical progress, but this is not the same thing as the progress of humanity as such. In every civilization this process is very complex. In Western civilizations—which used to be called Western-Christian but now might better be called Western-Pagan—along with the development of intellectual life and science, there has been a loss of the serious moral basis of society. During these 300 years of Western Civilization, there has been a sweeping away of duties and an expansion of rights. But we have two lungs. You can't breathe with just one lung and not the other. We must avail ourselves of rights and duties in equal measure. And if this is not established by the law, if the law does not oblige us to do that, then we have to control ourselves. When Western society was established, it was based on the idea that each individual limited his own behavior. Everyone understood what he could do and what he could not do. The law itself did not restrain people. Since then, the only thing we have been developing is rights, rights, rights, at the expense of duty.

"Russia's Prophet in Exile," *Time,* 24 July 1989, 60.

7. John Q. Wilson, "The Moral Life," Brigham Young University commencement address, 21 April 1994.

Integrity: The Evidence Within

Neal A. Maxwell

It's been about 21 years since I first learned as Church Commissioner of Education, in a conversation with Elder Marion G. Romney, that it was his strong desire, on which he soon made good, to have a law school. Since then, I think what has been amassed in the way of accomplishments is greater than even he would have ever imagined could occur in such a short time. The illustrative measurements I'll use here just by way of introductory comments leave out, in my opinion, the more significant accomplishments that have to do with being good fathers, mothers, husbands, wives, neighbors, and citizens. But we have: 20 sitting judges (17 state, 2 federal, and 1 tribal), 1 congressman, 2 congressional candidates, a major industrialist, numerous state legislators and law professors, 3 mission presidents, 20 stake presidents, numerous Relief Society presidents, Primary presidents, bishops, high councilors, etc., graduates practicing in 17 foreign countries, and 7 who have clerked for U.S. Supreme Court Justices.

It's very impressive, and I think the box score, so to speak, is greater than any of us who have watched with interest would have ever expected.

Of course, the on-rolling success of the Law School will be reflected as it now is in the lives of its graduates. And its real accreditation will be a spiritual accreditation.

I repeat quickly two thoughts from a speech given a decade ago to the Utah State Bar:

> Please don't let professional intensity cause you to falter in your own families. A good day in court cannot compensate for a bad day at home. Winning points at the office round table is not as vital as that which happens at your supper table. Go on being a true friend to your family and neighbors as well as a good friend of the court.

One piece of current counsel before I speak to my major theme. Please pace yourselves! Those of you whom I know are highly conscientious and have need of this counsel. On my office wall is a quote from Anne Morrow Lindbergh, which says: "My life cannot implement in action the demands of all the people to whom my heart responds." It's a needed reminder for me, and I rather expect for you as well.

Paralleling that counsel is this episode involving a report by a colleague to President Brigham Young. The colleague made his report and was anxious to leave so as not to impose on President Young. But President Young said, "Oh, please sit a spell with me. I am weary of men and things." How often do we "sit a spell" with spouse, children, colleagues, or friends?

I should like to address the topic of integrity, which for tonight's purpose will be defined as an undivided, uncorrupted, and unimpaired spiritual wholeness. We are not therefore speaking of mere reciprocity as in "honor among thieves," but of wholeness in relation to God's principles. Hence integrity is an important remedy for the almost consuming tendency of compartmentalization in our society and in some of our lives. Compartmentalization is destructive of identity and productive of hypocrisy. It retards putting off the natural man because there are so many places he can hide!

As I begin, I acknowledge that whether or not my remarks are at all helpful to you, this opportunity to reflect on what I yet lack with regard to integrity has been appreciated. Integrity is crucial to happiness; it is also portable. It will, brothers and sisters, to the degree developed, go through the veil of death with us, and it will rise with us in the Resurrection. How marvelous, isn't it, that God's long suffering, when you and I fall short with regard to integrity, gives us fresh chances to do better!

Of President Marion G. Romney, the initiator and early nurturer of the Law School, recipient of the Order of the Coif, his biographer, Elder F. Burton Howard, wrote:

> As [Elder Romney] opened his first law office, he resolved to arrive thirty minutes earlier than any of his associates. . . . He continued this practice for twelve years, during which he read the Book of Mormon nine times. . . .
>
> He learned that the solution to problems was generally to be found through reason and precedent. Thus, he saw no conflict between his approach and the scriptural admonition to "prove all things; [and] hold fast that which is good" (1 Thessalonians 5:21). [Marion G. Romney did not] see any reason to compartmentalize his life into religious and secular segments.[1]

As the founder of the Law School that example should be powerful for all of us.

The virtue of integrity is that it can respond to so many situations. Integrity is never imitated by rivalry! General Robert E. Lee, for instance, was asked for his opinion of a colleague. Lee replied candidly but generously. Lee's questioner then said, in effect, "Well, he doesn't speak so highly of you," to which General Lee replied, "Sir, you have asked me for my opinion of him, not his opinion of me!" Clearly—to borrow a phrase from Walter Bagehot—Robert E. Lee "had furnished his mind . . . with fixed principles," which in my opinion, is the best form of interior decoration!

John the Baptist had quite a following, but commented meekly and with integrity on Jesus' growing influence that "[Jesus] must increase, but I must decrease" (John 3:30). How one wishes for that kind of meekness and candor in public life today. A similar response occurred in the few brief moments in Church history when President Harold B. Lee lay near death. President Romney, his counselor, had come quickly to the hospital. Soon Spencer Woolley Kimball arrived, president of the Council of the Twelve. He meekly asked, "President Romney, what can I do to help you?" A few minutes later President Lee was dead, and President Romney said, "President Kimball, what can I do to help you?"

Our tongues are usually quick to reflect any lack of integrity. Brigham Young said,

> When a person opens his mouth, no matter what he talks about, to a person of quick discernment, he will disclose more or less of his true sentiments. You cannot hide the heart, when the mouth is open.[2]

Since verbosity does disclose the heart, it has been observed that sometimes it is "in silence [that] man can most readily preserve his integrity."[3]

Competency and integrity were both present in the person of General George C. Marshall. In an early effort to preserve his integrity as chief of staff, Marshall refused to be palsy-walsy with his commander in chief. Early on, President Franklin D. Roosevelt addressed Marshall as "George." General Marshall quickly responded, "It's General Marshall, Mr. President."[4] Loyalty was blended with integrity!

Later, loyal General Marshall wanted very much to lead the Allied invasion force which was his deservedly to claim. But Roosevelt wanted him to stay on as chief of staff, and Marshall did. Thus Eisenhower got to lead the Allied crusade, and the rest is history. Marshall was more concerned about rendering service than with what his résumé would show! Meekness was blended with integrity!

Perhaps in its own way, genuine meekness is a special reflection of integrity's proximate reaction to ultimate reality, such as, where we really stand in relation to the God who created us and gave us his Only Begotten Son.

When integrity is missing, betrayal may take its place. In Kirtland, when Wilford Woodruff encountered Joseph, the Prophet held his hand and looked longingly and scrutinizingly into Wilford's eyes. Discerningly, Joseph said how glad he was to know Woodruff was his friend, for "I hardly know when I meet those who have been my brethren . . . who of them are my friends. They have become so scarce."[5] How blessed we are that Joseph persisted and completed his mission—even amid those who lacked meekness and integrity!

The episode just recited may explain this quote from President Woodruff from which the title of my remarks is taken. He said:

> To me the principle of *integrity* is one of the greatest blessings we can possibly possess. He who proves true to himself or his brethren, to his friends and to his God, will have *the evidence within* him that he is accepted; he will have the confidence of his God and of his friends.[6]

True "integrity" does provide "the evidence within" of one's acceptance in a Higher Court! As professionals you deal with evidence. But you also understand (and this is part of what is different about this law school) that "faith is the . . . evidence of things not seen" and, likewise, how certain knowledge as Paul said is spiritually discerned (Hebrews 11:1; see 1 Corinthians 2:10).

Just as when one's conscience calls, it is with a voice which only he can hear. So, too, some assurances that come are highly personalized.

Perhaps it is the general paucity of integrity in public life that results in its being so noticed by all of us. There is something special about the authority of example. This episode from the American Revolutionary War involves sacrificing and unpaid officers:

> Washington called together the grumbling officers on March 15, 1783. . . . He began to speak—carefully and from a written text, referring to the proposal of "either deserting our Country in the extremest hour of her distress, or turning our Arms against it. . . ." Washington appealed simply and honestly for reason, restraint, patience, and duty—all the good and unexciting virtues.
>
> And then Washington stumbled as he read. He squinted, paused, and out of his pocket he drew some new spectacles. "Gentlemen, you must pardon me," he said in apology. "It appears that I have grown gray in your service and now I find myself also growing blind."
>
> Most of his men had never seen the general wear glasses. Yes, the men said to themselves, eight hard years. They recalled the ruddy, full-blooded planter of 1775; now they saw . . . a big, good, fatherly man grown old. They wept, many of these warriors. And the Newburgh plot was dissolved.[7]

No wonder Flexner, Washington's biographer, wrote of our first president, "In all history few men who possessed unassailable power have used that power so gently and self-effacingly for what their best instincts told them was the welfare of their neighbors and all mankind."[8]

Yes, "almost all men" abuse authority and power, but Washington was not among them (see D&C 121:39).

But Washington did not come to the American presidency fully formed. Instead, as a younger officer Washington learned from the reproof inherent in his earlier mistakes. Of his capacity for introspection, Flexner said:

As his character and his world view expanded, more meanings became clear to him. He accurately defined his failures and worked out the reasons why he had failed. The results of this protracted self-education were to prove of the greatest importance to the creation of the United States.[9]

However, brothers and sisters, self-improvement requires integrity in order for one to benefit from introspection.

Inherent in integrity is the blessing of being more settled, which makes integrity conductive to generosity. Generosity in politics, for instance, is so rare, and we are bound to notice it.

As you know, Churchill had steadily and vigorously attacked Neville Chamberlain's failed policies of appeasement. He once said Chamberlain looked at foreign affairs "through the wrong end of a municipal drain pipe."[10] Nevertheless at the time of Chamberlain's death, Churchill and Parliament generously observed:

> History with its flickering lamps stumbles along the trail of the past, trying to reconstruct its scenes, to revive its echoes, and kindle with pale gleams the passion of former days. . . . The only guide to a man is his conscience; the only shield to his memory is the rectitude and sincerity of his actions. It is very imprudent to walk through life without this shield, because we are so often mocked by the failure of our hopes and the upsetting of our calculations; but with this shield, however the fates may play, we march always in the ranks of honor.[11]

Life gives us so many clinical experiences to help us, but it takes introspection and integrity working together to break down the compartmentalization.

Integrity also insists that we draw upon our instructive memories, including past mistakes. Churchill chose these words as the motto for his last volume of his World War II history: "How the Great Democracies Triumphed, and so Were able to Resume the Follies Which Had so Nearly Cost Them Their [Lives]."[12]

Without integrity, memory is diminished!

Integrity can help us as it combines with meekness to keep us from the excesses of ego. You and I can so easily be victimized by role suction, that powerful, almost silent process by means of which we can become so entrapped in a particular role that we reflect its accompanying viewpoints automatically, not reflectively. Hence the saying you and I all know, "Where we stand depends on where we sit." Granted, where we sit can bring wider perspectives, but it can also induce a refusal to reflect or to face the results of reflection.

In World War I, General Douglas Haig (along with other generals and their political leaders) got "locked" in the awful and inconclusive trench warfare. One historian described Haig as, "inflexible, intolerant . . . the perfect commander for an enterprise committed to endless abortive assaulting."[13]

Just how disastrous was the "abortive assaulting"? One morning, waves of British soldiers climbed out of their trenches and began to walk forward. "Out of 110,000 who attacked, 60,000 were killed or wounded on this one day. . . . Over 20,000 lay between the lines, and it was days before the wounded in No Man's Land stopped crying out."[14]

Unlike Washington, who learned from his errors, Haig's "diary contains no admission of his errors, no recognition of his fallibility."

Without integrity, it is so easy to "gratify our pride," or "our vain ambition" and even to "cover our sins" (D&C 121:37). In fact, this pattern is a *leitmotif,* recurring again and again in human affairs!

For instance, Prime Minister Stanley Baldwin flinched from the facts just preceding World War II because of worry over being re-elected. He later confessed as prime minister, a "confession" which stunned many in Parliament:

> Supposing I had gone to the country and said that Germany was rearming and that we must rearm, does anyone think that this pacific democracy would have rallied to that cry at that moment? I can think of nothing that would have made the loss of the [general] election from my point of view more certain.[15]

A very damaging, startling admission.

President John F. Kennedy fretted over the growing U.S. buildup in Vietnam, but as in this reported episode, he shared Baldwin's reluctance:

> The President said . . . he knew . . . what the influential Senator wanted to hear, that he [Kennedy] was beginning to agree about a compete military withdrawal. "But I can't do it until 1965—until after I'm re-elected." To do it before could cause "a wild outcry" against him.[16]

With those episodes from history as a backdrop, what of you and me? What of our individual samples of humanity—those lying within our circles of influence—whom God has given to us to love and to serve with integrity?

Our circles of influence vary in size, but size is less important than the quality and integrity of what we do within those circles. J. R. R. Tolkien wrote wisely,

> It is not our part to master all the tides of the world, but to do what is in us for the succor of those years wherein we are set, uprooting the evil in the fields that we know, so that those who live after may have clean earth to till. What weather they shall have is not ours to rule.[17]

Without integrity, brothers and sisters, there are so many ways in which you and I can fail to "succor" and to uproot the evil in the years and the situations wherein we are set.

You and I have been asked to put off the natural man and the natural woman. In your profession, as in every other, there are so many inducements to keep the natural man and woman comfortably intact—if only to do battle with other natural men and natural women! No wonder becoming the men and women of Christ is the great and persistent challenge (see Mosiah 3:19)!

If we are spiritually improving, whenever another individual encounters us—"at all times and in all things, and in all places"—he or she will experience a spiritual wholeness and a constancy—not perfection, but serious discipleship (Mosiah 18:9).

Occasionally, by worldly standards spiritual wholeness will prove costly. Disciples' rewards are often not only deferred, they are often quite different. Our retainers will come in the coin of a different realm. At times, therefore, we really do give up certain things of the world in order to maintain integrity.

"Do what is right; let the consequence follow" contains homely but splendid advice. Happily, faithful members of the Church have been promised the gift of the Holy Ghost, who will show us "what is right"[18] in all things and in all situations (see 2 Nephi 32:3–5).

Living in such a way that we can be shown what to do is a demanding challenge, and it takes integrity.

Erastus Snow warned of the barriers that we interpose to God's spirit when we seek to gratify our own wills instead of his. What are these barriers, brothers and sisters, except more compartmentalization?

Two verses of scripture give an immensely significant insight into Jesus' integrity. They tell us that he suffered "temptations of every kind" (Alma 7:11) but "gave no heed unto them" (D&C 20:22). With his keen intellect and unusual sensitivity, he would surely have noticed each and all of the temptations. Yet he "gave no heed" unto them. It is giving heed unto temptations that gets us in trouble! My mission president used to say we may not be able to stop all evil thoughts from coming into our minds, but we don't have to offer them chairs and tell them to sit down.

Many of us may not have any major problems with integrity, but we have lots of small gaps in our integrity. One may not lie, but a nuance of an expression, otherwise accurate, nevertheless inflects to convey advantage. We may not personally engage in bashing others, but we do engage sometimes in conversational cloak-holding by failing to speak up.

If integrity were more operative, its emancipating effects on the human scene would be enormous. It would free us to focus our energy, time, and talents on the real issues rather than on game playing or maneuvering. Moreover, with higher levels of shared trust, there would be greater shared perceptivity as to problems and solutions.

As in all things, the ultimate example is Jesus. I never tire of bearing witness of him—not alone that he lived and lives, but also how he lived! Even in what might be described as small episodes, he gives us such large lessons. He was a fully integrated, righteous individual, fully congruent in character.

Some small episodes as I close: Previous to the events immediately preceding the crucifixion, Pilate and Herod had been "at enmity." Yet, at a point of crisis, they "made friends together" (Luke 23:12). Opportunities existed for Jesus to take advantage of this temporary alliance had he been willing to "shrink" from going through with the Atonement (see D&C 19:18, 19). Pilate found no fault with Jesus; Pilate was reachable. So was Herod, who had been desirous "to see [Jesus] of a long season" and "hoped to have seen some miracle done by him" (Luke 23:8). Though standing before Herod and fully aware of the ruler's expectations and the opportunity to please him, Jesus, nevertheless, "answered him nothing" (Luke 23:9, see also Mosiah 14:7).

Jesus' integrity was not for sale. There would be no demonstration to purchase amelioration. Jesus maintained his integrity even in the midst of an opportunity a lesser individual would have gladly seized.

Earlier, when his enemies came for Jesus—the Light of the World—in Gethsemane, they ironically came with lanterns and torches (see John 18:3). Amid that and so many other ironies, Jesus kept his poise. He endured so much irony, and irony is the crust on the bread of adversity. Irony, in my opinion, tests integrity more than almost anything else, and Jesus endured it.

Drenched in deep suffering at the time of his arrest, Jesus might have let himself become so swollen with understandable self-concern—he's working out the Atonement for the human family—that there would have been no capacity to think of others at all. Instead, empathic Jesus restored the severed ear of a hostile guard (see Luke 22:50–51). His way was not the way of the sword (see Matthew 26:52).

On the cross Jesus spoke only several recorded sentences. One was to assure that his mother, Mary, would be cared for by the Apostle John. Another reassured a pleading thief by Jesus' side. While Jesus was literally saving the world, he still nurtured proximate individuals. He was and is the Perfect Shepherd, full of integrity and full of empathy! When you and I suffer, sometimes we pass it along, don't we?

Jesus always individualized remarkably. The Nephite Twelve, for instance, were interviewed by him "one by one" (3 Nephi 28:1). Clearly, he knew beforehand what their individual desires were, yet he still gave each individual an audience. Contrast how able-and-idealistic Woodrow Wilson tried to get his league of nations approved. As his biographer said:

[Wilson] did not consult with the Senators and Representatives. When he wanted to tell them something, he sent for them. There was little give and take when they appeared. He explained what was desired, and dismissed the callers. When men offered information he already possessed, he cut them off by saying, "I know that."[19]

Universal Jesus is so personal! Jesus honored the integrity of each moment instead of worrying about audience size. He was especially disclosing to a believing and solitary woman of Samaria:

> The woman saith unto him, I know that Messias cometh, which is called Christ: when he is come, he will tell us all things.
>
> Jesus saith unto her, I that speak unto thee am he (John 4:25–26).

It was the same audience size with an imprisoned Paul: "And the night following the Lord stood by him, and said, Be of good cheer, Paul: for as thou hast testified of me in Jerusalem, so must thou bear witness also at Rome" (Acts 23:11).

Jesus' sensitivity and integrity combined so beautifully. To the mother of James and John, who wrongly craved status for her sons in the world to come, Jesus gave mild reproof, "Ye know not what you ask," further indicating the Father had already made that determination (Matthew 20:22). Jesus never shrank from giving counsel, but he always took into account the receiving capacity of the hearers. It takes caring to customize and perceptivity to know how. One could care but not know how. Or one could see what needs doing but not care sufficiently to do it. Integrity mobilizes all the other virtues!

Jailed John the Baptist sent followers, doubtless concerned with John's situation, to inquire of Jesus about his Messiahship. "Do we look for another?" they said (Matthew 11:3). Jesus praised, not scolded John, indicating that no greater prophet had been born of woman (see Matthew 11:11). To the inquiring delegation, he said go and tell John that the blind see, the lame walk (see Matthew 11:4, 5). What is your phrase? *Res ipsa loquitur?*

Of the once confident Peter who had faltered briefly, Jesus later pointedly and reprovingly asked him three times, "Lovest thou me?" (John 21:15–17)—evoking, as you know, Peter's heart-wrenching responses. This was apparently a necessary spiritual cleansing. It seems to me, brothers and sisters, that post-doctoral disciples often have the toughest curriculum.

Jesus was so perfect in his integrity that he never sought to prosper or to conquer, in the words of the Book of Mormon, "according to his genius" (Alma 30:17). Yet he was the brightest intellect ever to grace this planet!

How many mortals have done precisely opposite while wanting recognition for their dominance! Contrast meek Jesus and his integrity with the poet Shelley's lines about one mortal ruler celebrated by a statue:

> Two vast and trunkless legs of stone
>
> Stand in the desert. . . . Near them, on the sand,
>
> Half sunk, a shattered visage lies,
>
> . . .
>
> And on the pedestal these words appear:

"My name is Ozymandias, king of kings;

Look on my works, ye Mighty, and despair!"

Nothing beside remains. Round the decay

Of that colossal wreck, boundless and bare

The lone and level sands stretch far away.[20]

The key may be seen in what concerned Jesus in the depths of his agony in the Atonement. What concerned him? "That [he] might not . . . shrink" (D&C 19:18)! Mercifully for all of us, he did not pull back. He did not shrink but, instead, completed, with full integrity, his "preparations unto the children of men" (D&C 19:19).

No wonder Paul declared, "in [Christ] all things hold together" (Colossians 1:17, RSV). He certainly held together during that awful Atonement! He not only had the integrity to do the Father's will, but, just as he had premortally promised, he gave all the glory to the Father!

As I conclude, the words of Jacob come to mind: "O be wise; what can I say more?" (Jacob 6:12).

May you and I develop sufficient additional integrity so that we can receive the blessing Wilford Woodruff promised and obtain "the evidence within," so that, though imperfect, we can be "accepted" and "have the confidence of God." And then, on one later day, shall our "confidence wax strong in the presence of God" (D&C 121:45).

God bless you and yours, in the name of Jesus Christ. Amen.

This address was given at the BYU Law School Alumni Dinner on October 23, 1992. Reprinted from the Clark Memorandum, *Fall 1993, 10–17.*

Neal A. Maxwell received his M.A. in political science in 1961 and an honorary Doctor of Laws degree in 1969 from the University of Utah. He received the Liberty Bell award for public service from the Utah State Bar in 1967. Elder Maxwell has served as a General Authority since 1974. He is currently a member of the Quorum of Twelve Apostles.

Notes

1. F. Burton Howard, *Marion G. Romney, His Life and Faith* (Salt Lake City: Bookcraft, 1988), 89.

2. *Journal of Discourses*, 6:74.

3. Meister Eckhart, *Directions for the Contemplative Life*.

4. David McCullough, *Truman* (New York: Simon & Schuster, 1992), 534.

5. Matthias F. Cowley, *Wilford Woodruff* (Salt Lake City: The Deseret News, 1909), 68.

6. *Journal of Discourses*, 8:266 (emphasis added).

7. Bart McDowell, *The Revolutionary War: America's Fight for Freedom* (Washington, D.C.: National Geographic Society, 1967), 190–91.

8. James Thomas Flexner, *Washington: The Indispensable Man* (Boston: Little, Brown and Company, 1974), xvi.

9. *Id.* at 38.

10. William Raymond Manchester, *The Last Lion, Winston Spencer Churchill: Visions of Glory, 1874–1932*, 1st ed. (Boston: Little, Brown, 1983), 786.

11. Robert Rhodes James, ed., *Churchill Speaks: Winston S. Churchill in Peace and War: Collected Speeches, 1897–1963* (New York: Chelsea House, 1980), 734.

12. Winston S. Churchill, "Triumph and Tragedy," in *The Second World War*, vol. 6 (Boston: Houghton Mifflin Company, 1953), ix.

13. Paul Fussell, *The Great War and Modern Memory* (London: Oxford Press, 1975), 12.

14. *Id.* at 13.

15. Roy Jenkins, *Baldwin* (London: Collins, 1987), 27.

16. Barbara W. Tuchman, *The March of Folly: From Troy to Vietnam*, 1st ed. (New York: Alfred A. Knopf, 1984), 303.

17. Gandolf in *The Return of the King* (New York: Ballantine Books, 1965), 190.

18. "Do What Is Right," *Hymns* (1985), no. 237.

19. Gene Smith, *When the Cheering Stopped* (New York: William Morrow and Company, 1964), 30.

20. Percy Bysshe Shelley, "Ozymandias," 1817.

The Challenge:
Basing Your Career on Principles

Alexander B. Morrison

In their best-selling book of a few years ago, entitled *In Search of Excellence,* Peters and Waterman point out that the greatest fear people have is not that they will die—it is not the fear of separation from loved ones, or even of extinction—but the fear that life will not have mattered, that its struggles and triumphs, tears, and laughter will all have been in vain.[1]

In the cynical world in which we live, confronted each day as we are by "man's inhumanity to man," by the cruelty and indifference of much of human existence, it seems to many that life does indeed have little meaning.

We live in a society saturated with self-absorption, which promotes and rewards excessive materialism, mocks and derides moral principles, and worships secularism. Increasingly, Western society is bereft of the enduring virtue of honor, of which Pericles, the great Athenian statesman, said two and a half millennia ago: "For it is love of honor that never grows old; and honor it is, not gain, as some would have it, that rejoices the heart of age and helplessness."

Faced with the wintry reality of life, with all its contradictions and imperfections, cruelty and injustice, one can feel some sympathy for those who, in their despair, proclaim that life is but a hollow charade, an obscene joke, or, in the words of Shakespeare's Macbeth, "a walking shadow, a poor player that struts and frets his hour upon the stage, and then is heard no more . . . a tale told by an idiot, full of sound and fury, signifying nothing."[2]

But I must tell you in the strongest possible terms that those who feel like that are wrong, tragically and terribly so. "Men are, that they might have joy," the scriptures tell us (2 Nephi 2:25). Our task is to fulfill the measure of that destiny by tasting the sweetness of the joy the Lord wishes for us. As we do so, the scales of cynicism, pride, indifference, and disregard for others will fall away from our eyes, and we will begin to see who we are and what God expects us to do with our lives.

My only wish today is to help contribute to your search for understanding. I have no quick-fix "do-it-yourself" recipe book to offer—only a few principles that are well worn but proven. As we apply basic principles, we gain a perspective of things as they really are. We see in life's challenges opportunities to serve.

The darkness of night portends the dawning of a new and better day. The greatest Englishman of this century, Winston Churchill, knew of the opportunities to serve during difficult days when he spoke at Harrow School in October of 1941. He said:

> Do not let us speak of darker days; let us speak rather of sterner days. These are not dark days: these are great days—the greatest days our country has ever lived; and we must all thank God that we have been allowed, each of us according to our stations, to play a part in making these days memorable in the history of our race.

I group my advice under several headings: prepare yourselves temporally and spiritually, and see that preparation as one grand eternal round; set your priorities straight; learn the spirit of service and the joy of work; and let devotion to duty and honor be the hallmarks of your life.

Prepare Yourself Temporally and Spiritually

If you are to serve yourself, your family, community, country, and church properly; if you are to be your brother's keeper in the sense that you accept your measure of responsibility for others, you must be prepared. You cannot contribute if you don't have the skills and knowledge to do so. Sincerity will not suffice and goodwill will not win. Consider Winston Churchill's words as he described the day he became prime minister on May 10, 1940. If ever there was a time for action and not for preparation, that was it. The French army was collapsing piecemeal before the ferocious fury of the German blitzkrieg. Britain stood alone, nearly defenseless. There was serious doubt the British Expeditionary Force could be saved. Churchill said of that day:

> As I went to bed at about 3:00 a.m., I was conscious of a profound feeling of relief. At last I had authority to give direction over the whole scene, and I felt as though I were walking with destiny, that my past life had been a preparation for this honor, for this trial. I could not be reproached, either for having made the war or for lack of preparation for it, and yet I felt I knew a good deal about it and I was sure I would not fail.

He was prepared! No preparation can occur in the absence of work. What the world mistakes for genius is, as Edison pointed out, 90 percent perspiration and 10 percent inspiration. If you wish to serve, prepare yourself through study, work, and faith.

As you struggle to learn and relearn in the intellectually demanding field of the law, I urge you to cultivate a flexibility of attitude, a willingness to venture into fields not yet cultivated by you, a catholicity of interest that sees all learning as interrelated. You must make learning an eternal quest. If I may be permitted a personal comment, the chance to learn is to me one of the greatest privileges of life and one of the great attractions and fascinations of the restored gospel. Indeed, two doctrines of the Church attracted me as a young university student in Edmonton nearly half a century ago: eternal marriage and eternal progression. I remain grateful for them and perhaps more knowledgeable about their importance now than I was as a callow youth.

President Spencer W. Kimball encouraged us to lengthen our stride. That advice applies in the temporal realm as much as in the spiritual. Learn to stretch your mind, to reach a little further each day in testing the limits of your intellectual capacity. We are told that most of us use less than 25 percent of our intellectual abilities. We can all do much more than we now do. That stretching may be painful. It will certainly be exhausting. But it is ever so exhilarating. Indeed, it is intoxicating! Make it a lifelong habit to flex and stretch your intellectual muscles.

There is a Chinese proverb that states:

To live and not to learn is not living;

To learn and not to understand is not learning;

To understand and not to do is not understanding.

Seek to understand. Develop and retain an eternal curiosity. Some of you may remember Merlin's advice to King Arthur:

The best thing for being sad . . . is to learn something. That is the only thing that never fails. You may grow old and trembling in your anatomies, you may lie awake at night listening to the disorder of your veins, you may miss your only love, you may see the world about you devastated by evil lunatics, or know your honor trampled in the sewers of baser minds. There is only one thing for it then: to learn. Learn why the world wags and what wags it. That is the only thing which the mind can never exhaust, never alienate, never be tortured by, never fear or distrust, and never dream of regretting. Learning is the thing for you.[3]

In a few words: Seek always to learn!

Get Your Priorities Straight

Several years ago President David O. McKay in speaking to a group of Church employees put into perspective what we should concentrate on in our lives. He said:

> Let me assure you, Brethren, that someday you will have a personal priesthood interview with the Savior himself. If you are interested, I will tell you the order in which he will ask you to account for your earthly responsibilities.
>
> First, he will request an accountability report about your relationship with your wife. Have you actively been engaged in making her happy and ensuring that her needs have been met as an individual?
>
> Second, he will want an accountability report about each of your children individually. He will not attempt to have this for simply a family stewardship but will request information about your relationship to each and every child.
>
> Third, he will want to know what you personally have done with the talents you were given in the preexistence.
>
> Fourth, he will want a summary of your activity in your Church assignments. He will not be necessarily interested in what assignments you have had, for in his eyes the home teacher and a mission president are probably equals, but he will request a summary of how you have been of service to your fellow man in your Church assignments.
>
> Fifth, he will have no interest in how you earned your living but if you were honest in all your dealings.
>
> Sixth, he will ask for an accountability on what you have done to contribute in a positive manner to your community, state, country, and the world.[4]

You will note that the Lord puts first emphasis on family—your relationships with spouse and children. He is certainly less interested in how you earn your living, though He is most concerned whether you are honest in your dealings. Whatever else you do, provide time for your family. If you are as busy and active as you should be, it will not always be easy to do so. Sometimes you will not get it right (at least I certainly haven't), but keep on trying. Call down the powers of heaven to help you in your struggle. I promise you the needed assistance will be yours.

"It takes more nobility of character," Steven Covey has said, "to do whatever is necessary to build that one relationship [the family] than to labor diligently and faithfully for the many others outside it."

One of the great tragedies of life is to observe men—and increasingly women—who struggle up the ladder of their careers, perhaps, though certainly not necessarily, over the backs of colleagues, and in the process, through carelessness, neglect, or selfishness, lose their families. They divorce their spouse, from whom, in the euphemism of the day, they claim to have "grown apart" in their search for "personal fulfillment," whatever that is. Their children drift away, finding no warmth, no giving, no help, no understanding, and then, perhaps in the twilight of their lives, these gray husks of men find that all they've done has turned to ashes. The ladder up which they climbed was leaning against the wrong wall. It led not to light and joy but to darkness of mind and spirit.

It need not be so. Many there are whose lives are tributes to the happiness that comes from commitments made and renewed daily. President Gordon B. Hinckley tells a sweet and loving story that illustrates, far better than I could, the strength and joy that come from having proper priorities in life. He relates the following:

> I think of two friends from my high school and university years. He was a boy from a country town, plain in appearance, without money or apparent promise. He had grown up on a farm, and if he had any quality that was attractive it was the capacity to work. He carried bologna sandwiches in a brown paper bag for his lunch and swept the school floors to pay his tuition. But with all of his rustic appearance, he had a smile and a personality that seemed to sing of goodness. She was a city girl who had come out of a comfortable home. She would not have won a beauty contest, but she was wholesome in her decency and integrity and attractive in her decorum and dress.
>
> Something wonderful took place between them. They fell in love. Some whispered that there were far more promising boys for her, and a gossip or two noted that perhaps other girls might have interested him. But these two laughed and danced and studied together through their school years. They married when people wondered how they could ever earn enough to stay alive. He struggled through his professional school and came out well in his class. She scrimped and saved and worked and prayed. She encouraged and sustained, and when things were really tough, she said quietly, "Somehow we can make it." Buoyed by her faith in him, he kept going through these difficult years. Children came, and together they loved them and nourished them and gave them the security that came of their own love for and loyalty to one another. Now many years have passed. Their children are grown, a lasting credit to them, to the Church, and to the communities in which they live. . . .
>
> . . . Forty-five years earlier people without understanding had asked what they saw in each other. . . . Their friends of those days saw only a farm boy from the country and a smiling girl with freckles on her nose. But these two found in each other love and loyalty, peace and faith in the future.
>
> There was a flowering in them of something divine, planted there by that Father who is our God. In their school days they had lived worthy of that flowering of love. They had lived with virtue and faith, with appreciation and respect for self and one another. In the years of difficult professional and economic struggles, they had found their greatest earthly strength in their companionship. Now in mature age, they were finding peace and quiet satisfaction together. Beyond all this, they were assured of an eternity of joyful association through priesthood covenants long since made and promises long since given in the House of the Lord.[5]

Having prepared yourself, or, more accurately, having begun the eternal task of preparing yourself, go forth to serve, expressing always the joy of work, seeing it as a spiritual necessity as well as a temporal imperative. As you do so, I admonish you to keep ever in your mind these inspired words of King Benjamin: "I would that ye should impart of your substance to the poor, every man according to that which he hath" (Mosiah 4:26).

We lighten Christ's yoke as we accept some of the burdens of others, as we help them to have hope rather than dark despair, as we apply a healing balm of Gilead to their scarified, suffering souls.

A few years ago the *Wall Street Journal* recounted a heartwarming tale of suffering, compassion, and Christlike service.[6] Some 20 years ago, Dr. Ian Jackson, a world-famous craniofacial surgeon, was on a charity mission from his native Scotland to Peru. There he met David Lopez, a tiny Indian boy, just two years old, who had virtually no face at all. A gaping hole covered the areas where his mouth and nose should have been. There were no upper teeth or upper jaw. To drink, David simply tilted back his head and poured the liquid straight down. His lower teeth could actually touch his forehead. Most of David's face had literally been eaten away by a terrible parasitic disease called leishmaniasis.

Relief workers begged Dr. Jackson to help. He was leaving for Scotland the next day, but he agreed to try to rebuild David's face if the boy could come to Scotland. Eventually a way was found, and the Jacksons went to Glasgow Airport to pick up David. As he walked down the ramp, they saw a tiny boy wearing scuffed white boots and a hand-knit poncho. A woolen cap was pulled so low on his head that only his big brown eyes and the round hole beneath them were visible. The Jacksons took David into their home and into their hearts. There followed long years of surgery—more than 80 operations in all—as Dr. Jackson attempted to give David a new face. All of the doctor's services were donated. Each summer, as other children played, David would be in the hospital, his head swathed in bandages.

The painstaking, pioneer surgical efforts to rebuild David's face went on for 15 years. Today David looks like a young man who has been in a serious automobile accident, but he is well adjusted and fully functional. He used to be teased and tormented about his looks, but over the years, that has died away.

The Jacksons now live in the United States, where Dr. Jackson continues to be one of the leading craniofacial surgeons in the world. In 1982 Mrs. Jackson flew to Peru to try to find David's parents. After a long journey downriver from a remote Catholic mission, David's father was found. He explained that the boy had been born healthy, but when he developed leishmaniasis after having been bitten by an infected sandfly, he was taken to the mission to seek treatment. The father gave permission to the

Jacksons—who had developed a deep love for David—to adopt him as their own. Since 1984 David Lopez has been David Jackson.

I don't know whether Dr. Jackson is a Christian or not. But I do know he is doing God's work. "When ye are in the service of your fellow beings ye are only in the service of your God" (Mosiah 2:17).

As we lose our lives in compassionate service to others, we develop a deeper understanding of our dependence on God. I return again to the wisdom of King Benjamin: "And now, if God, who has created you, on whom you are dependent for your lives and for all that ye have and are, doth grant unto you whatsoever ye ask that is right, in faith, believing that ye shall receive, O then, how ye ought to impart of the substance that ye have one to another" (Mosiah 4:21). Said faithful Nephi, "I know in whom I have trusted. My God hath been my support; he hath led me through mine afflictions in the wilderness; and he hath preserved me upon the waters of the great deep. He hath filled me with his love, even unto the consuming of my flesh. . . . Behold, he hath heard my cry by day, and he hath given me knowledge by visions in the nighttime. . . . And upon the wings of his Spirit hath my body been carried away. . . . I will trust in thee forever" (2 Nephi 4:19–21, 23, 25, 34).

Now of course you can't do all that needs to be done to help change this world, but you can do your best and hope that others will follow.

As you strive to serve others, I urge you to look beyond those who are your clients. They deserve your very best, of course, but your concern must not stop with them. You must look to the broader community in which you live and work. Voluntary service to others will be an increasingly significant characteristic of caring communities in the new millennium. It takes many forms, including work in your church, neighborhood schools, and professional and service organizations and assistance to the disadvantaged—the poor, children, immigrants, etc. In Utah, lawyers are being encouraged by Legal Services, the Disability Law Center, and the Legal Aid Society to donate each year the monetary equivalent of two billable hours to provide free legal services to those in need. The Church has announced that if the drive to do so raises $300,000, it will donate an additional $100,000.[7] I commend that sort of initiative to you, tailored, of course, to fit the needs of your own community.

It will take both courage and commitment if you are to help change the world as it must be changed. Do not lose your idealism. Do not slip into the sophisticated cynicism of those who sell their moral integrity for this world's goods. Do not become so tied to your mortgage payments, career ambitions, company loyalties, or professional associations that you become afraid or unwilling to search for the truth and to speak out in its defense. Corporate greed, bureaucratic empire-building, and political venality all flourish because otherwise good men and women are unwilling to say no to what they recognize in their hearts is wrong. "I was only obeying orders," they say. "You can't fight City Hall." Of such is born the moral outrage of our time. In less spectacular fashion, but of equal importance, such a decline in commitment to moral integrity leads to an indifferent, almost passive acceptance of the myriad of minor corruptions of our society.

The demands of the future relate not only to man's physical needs but to all of the dimensions of human existence. It is ironic that the rise of materialism has resulted in a decline in the quality of man's spiritual life. This potentially fatal imbalance can only be redressed if we begin to pay proper attention not only to the things that are Caesar's but also to those that are God's (see Matthew 22:21). Man obviously needs food, shelter, clothing, clean water, education, and health care. But he also needs love and hope and those other attributes of the spirit that collectively contribute to the quality of life. In Teilhard de Chardin's words, we must seek for a future "consisting not merely of successive years but of higher states."[8] The current witless pursuit of materialism bears within it the seeds of death for industrial societies and perhaps for the world as we know it. We must move beyond a unidimensional view of man to consider all that is needed to give meaning and value to life, all that contributes to the formation of the whole man.

Let Devotion to Duty and Honor Be Your Hallmarks

There will be opportunities—some blatant, some seductive—for you to lose your integrity every day. The adversary will see to that. It may be the lure of compromising your principles of honesty: the chance to make a somewhat soiled dollar in a somewhat shady deal. Or it may be the temptation to break one of the other moral laws: to lie a little, cheat a little, or be a little dishonest, to have just one drink, or to be unfaithful to your spouse just once. Almost always the temptation will come wrapped in glitter and gloss, dressed up to look like what it is not, the devil's counterfeit. And to the extent you succumb you will be weakened and deprived of your manhood or womanhood. The work of the Lord will be impeded, and the Devil will laugh. Conversely, as you rise above temptation, you will grow in spiritual stature and enjoy the approbation of good men and women everywhere. "Duty," said the great Confederate military commander Robert E. Lee, "is the most sublime word in any language. Do your duty in all things. You cannot do more. You should not expect to do less."[9]

Duty achieves its highest expression when carried out within the framework of and adherence to a firm set of moral standards. Many observers have commented on the slackening of moral fiber in the Western democracies over the past several decades. In his celebrated commencement address at Harvard a few years ago, Alexander Solzhenitsyn drew attention to the most outstanding weakness of the Western democracies: their growing lack of courage. In Solzhenitsyn's view, this decline in courage is particularly striking among the ruling and intellectual elites. In part it may arise from having too many of this world's possessions, too easily come by. Those who remain courageous (and there are many) have little impact on public life.

"Political and intellectual functionaries," Solzhenitsyn continues, "exhibit depression, passivity, and perplexity in their actions and in their statements, and even more so in their self-seeking rationales as to how realistic, reasonable, and intellectually and even morally justified it is to base state policies on weakness and cowardice."[10] Although Solzhenitsyn was referring primarily to political courage of the kind needed by national leaders, the courage of nations begins with the courage of individuals.

Courage is the great need of our time, courage to accept the ineluctable truth that greatness can never be achieved without adversity, that struggle is the prerequisite for growth. Edmund Burke taught this well when he said:

> Adversity is a severe instructor, set over us by one who knows us better than we do ourselves, as He loves us better, too. He that wrestles with us strengthens our nerves and sharpens our skill. Our antagonist is our helper. This conflict with difficulty makes us acquainted with our object and compels us to consider it in all its relations. It will not suffer us to be superficial.[11]

Yes, adversity is the refiner's fire that bends iron but tempers steel. It is in the fire of struggle and stress that greatness is forged. A measure of your greatness as men and women will be your response to adversity, the courage you have as you wrestle with problems that can strengthen your nerves and sharpen your skill, as Burke said.

Hastiness and superficiality have been termed the psychic disease of the 20th century. The pace of modern life, which seems to grow more frantic each year, penalizes thoroughness and promotes haste. Society demands speed—speed at all costs, speed regardless of the consequences to the health and happiness of individuals, speed at the expense of diminishing supplies of irreplaceable resources. We demand instant communication, ever more rapid means of transport, faster decisions. Business deals are conceived in Toronto, planned in Edmonton, and consummated in Vancouver or New York or Tokyo, all in a few hours time—but not without a price being paid. Often the price is tragically high: anxieties that must be calmed with tranquilizers or alcohol, children who grow up not knowing their father (or, increasingly, their mother), and lives spent in acquiring rather than giving.

It will take courage for you to step far enough away from the glamour and excitement of the speedway of life to see it for what much of it really is: a poor, tawdry counterfeit of what life can be. I for one am delighted to note that increasing numbers of people are doing just that, deciding that the game isn't worth the candle, and that there are more important things to do in this world than to act like a speeded-up version of the Roadrunner. I can't tell any of you, nor would I wish to, what speed to run your life at. All I ask is that you be honest enough to take a hard look at what you really want and courageous enough to act on your decision, even if it means fewer material possessions and less worldly acclaim.

Finally, I remind you that the final stage in the development of an exceptional professional is that of teacher and mentor of the next generation—the young men and women just entering the profession and in need of the example and guidance of those who have already scaled the heights and who are the skilled practitioners of their craft. Law school provides the intellectual framework for the practice of law, but does little to actually teach students how to be lawyers. That is done as the new graduate learns the realities of practice at the knee of one who is more experienced.

Each generation has a solemn obligation to give a helping hand to those coming behind, who will in their turn be the carriers of the torch. A profession that loses that vision has at best an uncertain future.

The choice is clear: If you want to do more than exist, if you want to soar as on eagle's wings to the outermost limits of your potential as a human being, you must pay the price. That price is an amalgam of discipline and desire, lightened by hope and love, bound together by the steel hoops of work and service, tempered in adversity, undergirded by faith, and overlaid with courage. This is your challenge, and I send you forth to accept it.

This address was given to the Edmonton, Alberta Chapter of the J. Reuben Clark Law Society on February 26, 1999. Reprinted from the Clark Memorandum, *Spring 1999, 32–39.*

Alexander B. Morrison received his Ph.D. from Cornell University in 1956. He served as a member of the First and Second Quorums of the Seventy 1987–2000 and was named an emeritus General Authority in 2000.

Notes

1. See Thomas J. Peters and Robert H. Waterman, Jr., *In Search of Excellence: Lessons from America's Best-Run Companies* (New York: Warner Books, 1984), xxi, quoting Ernest Becker, *Escape from Evil* (New York: Free Press, 1975), 3–6, 51; and Ernest Becker, *The Denial of Death* (New York: Free Press, 1973), 3–4. See also chapter 3 "Man Waiting for Motivation," *In Search of Excellence*, 55–86.

2. *Macbeth*, 5:5.26–28.

3. T. H. White, *The Sword in the Stone*, 183.

4. Reported by Cloyd Hofheins in a talk to the seventies quorum of Provo Utah Oak Hills Stake, 16 May 1982, as quoted in Stephen R. Covey, *The Divine Center* (Salt Lake City, Utah: Bookcraft, 1982), 54–55.

5. Gordon B. Hinckley, "First Presidency Message: And The Greatest of These Is Love," *Ensign* (March 1984): 3–4.

6. Neal Templin, "Look of Love: As His Face is Molded, Boy Finds His Surgeon Becoming His Father," *Wall Street Journal*, 13 November 1992, A1, A16.

7. "Attorneys Dig Deep to Help Poor," *Deseret News*, 27 January 1999, A12 (editorial). [Editors' note: The drive was successful. See "Legal-Aid Campaign Reaches a Goal, Gets Matching Funds," *Deseret News*, 1 September 1999, A11.]

8. Pierre Teilhard de Chardin, *The Future of Man* (New York: Harper & Row, 1969), 192.

9. In John Bartlett, *Familiar Quotations* (Boston: Little, Brown and Co., 1968), 620.

10. Alexander Solzhenitsyn, "A World Split Apart," Commencement Address Delivered at Harvard University, 8 June 1978.

11. "Reflections on the Revolution in France," in *Edmund Burke*, Harvard Classics, 50 vols. (1909), 24:299–300.

Bridges

Dallin H. Oaks

I had a sobering duty as a justice of the Utah Supreme Court. I had to vote to disbar a graduate of the Brigham Young University J. Reuben Clark Law School. With that action I stopped assuming that people who have had the right kind of education automatically have the right kind of moral sense.

Law school is a distorting experience in many ways. No one said it better than my classmate and good friend, Roger C. Cramton, former dean of Cornell Law School, in his article "The Ordinary Religion of the Law School Classroom."[1] He talked about a number of value assumptions in the law school classroom and their impact on the thinking of law students. I want to comment on three of those value assumptions.

One of Dean Cramton's value assumptions is what he calls the "instrumental approach to law and lawyering." Under this approach, law is nothing more than an instrument for achieving social goals. The goals are, of course, those of the client. The lawyer need not be concerned with selecting goals or with the value questions associated with them because the lawyer is simply the skilled craftsman who works out the *means* by which predetermined goals are achieved.

The result of this assumption reminds me of the doctor who told an educator that medical science would soon perfect the means to sever the human mind from the rest of the body and with appropriate support systems keep the brain alive indefinitely with no connection with the heart. "That's really not new," the educator replied. "We've been doing that in our college for years." I am sure you can see what the instrumental approach, which is inherent in much that is done in the law school classroom, does to the value sensitivities and the value orientations of the budding lawyer. There are reasons for this instrumental approach, even sound pedagogical reasons.

But anyone exposed to it needs to be alert to its evil consequences on our moral and value sensitivities in order to be inoculated against them.

The second point of Cramton's he states as follows:

> A skeptical attitude toward generalizations, principles and rules is doubtless a desirable attribute of the lawyer. But skepticism that deepens into a belief in the meaninglessness of principles, the relativism of values or the non-existence of an ultimate reality is dangerous and crippling.[2]

Put another way, the skeptical attitude toward generalizations, principles, and received wisdom—a desirable attribute for some purposes—inclines the student toward concluding that principles are meaningless and values are relative.

A third assumption of Dean Cramton is that the law school classroom serves up a steady diet of borderline cases with scarcely any mention of routine legal problems of easy solution.

> Legal problems that have a routine and easy solution are not considered in law school. The student is faced with a steady diet of hard cases—borderline situations that might reasonably have been decided either way. Since there is a good argument both ways, and the case could reasonably have been decided either way, the student is led to believe that life is that way, that law is that way—there are no *right* answers, just *winning* arguments. This diet of border-line cases thus contributes to value skepticism.[3]

Those observations from Dean Cramton provide an introduction to the principal message I want to give you this evening.

Some of you may remember that when I was called to the Council of the Twelve I was serving on the Utah Supreme Court. I had authored a dozen opinions that were pending in other chambers or were just about ready to circulate. I had participated in oral arguments and preliminary votes on a hundred or more other cases that were pending in the chambers of the other four justices on the Utah Supreme Court. Consequently, if I had responded immediately to the call by showing up in general conference, I would have been disabled as a practical matter from continuing to work on those cases. Having stepped across the wall between church and state, I would have had no way to get back on the other side to complete my judicial duties without being tainted in some way, especially in a litigious environment.

I discussed this with the First Presidency, and they made the decision to present my name, have me sustained, and then tell me to stay away until I was ready to be ordained and take up my responsibilities. That is what I did. It was about three or four weeks after I was sustained in April Conference, 1984, when I resigned as a judge, went to the Church Office Building to meet for the first time with the leadership of the Church, was ordained, and began my duties.

During this period when I was winding up my cases, I had time to think about the calling in which I would spend the rest of my life. I asked myself what kind of apostle I would be. I took an inventory of my credentials, experience, and qualifications and compared them with the kinds of things which, in my imperfect understanding, I imagined I would be called upon to do. I asked myself, "Throughout the remainder of your life will you be a judge and lawyer who has been called to be an apostle, or will you be an apostle who used to be a lawyer and a judge?"

There is a very large difference between those two. I knew how to do some of the things that I would be called upon to do. I thought that my legal experience might be called upon in some way. I knew about committees; I knew about personnel; I knew about public affairs. I also knew a little bit about human nature in general and myself in particular. I was sure that we all have a tendency to focus our efforts on those things that are familiar and easy—where we feel at home. We are repelled by those things that are unfamiliar and difficult.

The most important parts of my calling—the only parts that are really unique in the service of the Lord—were those parts that I knew nothing about—those parts where I would have to start all over at the beginning. I knew that if I concentrated my time on the things that came naturally and the things that I felt qualified to do, I would never be an apostle. I would always be a former lawyer and judge. I made up my mind that was not for me. I decided that I would focus my efforts on what I had been called to do, not on what I was qualified to do. I determined that instead of trying to shape my calling to my credentials, I would try to shape myself to my calling.

Each of us brings a set of qualifications to whatever we are called to do. We can shape our callings to our qualifications or we can try to shape ourselves to our callings. I mention this because it is not only a challenge to each of us in church service, but it also has something to do with the professional performance of lawyers.

Does training in the law dull one's sense of justice, or one's moral and ethical sensibilities? Does it matter what clients and causes we serve with the skills that we have developed?

You are in training for a noble profession, which our society could not do without. It has served humanity ably, responsibly, and effectively throughout my lifetime and for many lifetimes before me. But the whole system of law and the legal profession can be corrupting if we do not understand all of it. When you are busy learning the ins and outs of it, it is probably timely to remind you of the potential corruption of it. It can be corrupted.

When I considered prayerfully what I could say to you about this subject and about my deep concerns for the fundamental integrity of those who study and practice law, I had an inspiration to recall the story of *The Bridge over the River Kwai.*[4] I saw the movie many years ago, but I had never read the book. I found a copy in a used-book store. As I studied it, I found the example I sought to illustrate my point. The principle is a very simple one.

The story told in the book is not a true one, but it is based on a true setting: World War II in Southeast Asia where the Japanese took about 60,000 prisoners from the British, Australian, Dutch, and American forces that were guarding the various bastions of their nations. Five hundred of these prisoners, according to the tale, wound up in a camp on the River Kwai in the jungles on the border between Burma and Siam (now Thailand). The Japanese desired to build a railway linking their great seaport at Singapore with the Bay of Bengal. There was great military significance in having a railway that could take the ship traffic that came through sheltered sea lanes to Singapore and move it overland to a point where it could be put to military use against the Allied forces in India.

So it was that the Japanese in the story began to build a railroad hundreds of miles in length between Singapore and the Bay of Bengal. A major obstacle was the River Kwai—a large stream in a chasm over which a great bridge had to be built. The Japanese constructed a prisoner-of-war camp at this site that held 500 prisoners. By luck, Colonel Nicholson, the British colonel and senior military officer in that camp, was an experienced engineer.

Colonel Nicholson's bridge building came to the attention of Allied intelligence in India. For very understandable military reasons, they assembled a commando force to go and blow up that bridge. As the story goes forward, we see the commandos planning the raid and the prisoners, under Colonel Nicholson, building the bridge.

Nicholson was a disciplinarian who got them to build it right. He had the engineering skills to design and build a bridge that was unbeatable for its purpose, and he did so.

The small commando team arrived at the jungle site and prepared to blow up the bridge. They monitored the construction from their observation post in the hills above and from their frequent infiltration into or near the camp.

Colonel Nicholson and his prisoner workers completed the bridge. The ceremonial first train was approaching. The charges had been planted to blow it up, which the commandos planned to do just as the initial train crossed the bridge. A wire had been strung from the explosives to a detonator some distance away so that a visual observation could determine the exact time to bring the bridge down. The train was puffing up with a whole load of enemy troops, generals, dignitaries, ammunition, and all the stores—the initial cargo over the bridge on the River Kwai. Shears, one of the commandos, whispers, "Nothing can stop us now. Fate has no more tricks to play. The train will surely be here in twenty minutes."[5] He scrambles down from the observation post to get a little closer to the action.

Colonel Nicholson inspects the bridge and is satisfied that it's technically excellent. The author gives a long, loving description of this military engineer's pride in his professional craftsmanship. Then Nicholson sees the wires. The level of the river has dropped over night, and wires to the detonator, that should have been under water, are exposed. He runs down the bank calling for the Japanese colonel who commands the prisoner-of-war camp to come and see. They stand at the water's edge near the unbelieving commando, Shears, who is hiding in the weeds. Shears runs out with his knife and kills the Japanese Colonel. He has been trained to do that work quickly, and he does it. Colonel Nicholson stares at him, unbelieving, as the train chugs forward to the bridge.

Shears throws off the lifeless body of his enemy, climbs up the bank to Colonel Nicholson, and introduces himself: "British officer, sir! Force 316 from Calcutta. Commandos. Orders to blow up the bridge."

"Blow up the bridge?" Colonel Nicholson asks, still not understanding. It takes a little while for him to realize what is happening. When he finally understands, he shouts, "Help!" at the top of his lungs. The Japanese guards come running.[6] The *film* has a happy ending. Colonel Nicholson falls across the detonator, the bridge goes up, and the train crashes in the gorge. The *book* is not that way at all. The train gets across the bridge. There is a small charge on the other side of the bridge, and it blows the train off the track. Two cars fall in the river, but the bridge is left standing. All the commando raid really accomplished was to create a very large diversion and to kill a few of the enemy. All of the commandos lost their lives, except one man who made his way back to report. In a conversation with his superior officer in India, he complains that Colonel Nicholson did not understand what was going on. And Shears, the commando with the knife at the water's edge, did not understand what was happening either. The surviving commando laments:

> He should have been more perceptive, more discerning. Then he would have understood that in our job it's no good cutting any old throat. You've got to cut the right throat. Isn't that so sir?
>
> More insight, that's what he needed; then he would have known who his enemy really was, realized it was that old blockhead [Nicholson] who couldn't stand the idea of his fine work being destroyed. A really perceptive mind would have deduced that from the way he strode along the platform. I had my glasses trained on him, sir; if only it had been a rifle! He had the sanctimonious smile of a conqueror on his lips, I remember. A splendid example of the man of action, sir, as we say in Force 316. He never let misfortune get him down; always made a last effort. It was he who shouted to the Japs for help! . . .

He had a highly developed sense of duty and admired a job well done. He was also fond of action—just as you are sir, just as we all are. This idiotic worship of action, to which our little typists subscribe as much as our greatest generals! I'm not sure where it all leads to, when I stop to think about it. I've been thinking about it for the last month, sir. Perhaps that silly old fool was really quite a decent fellow at heart? Perhaps he really had a genuine ideal? An ideal as sacred as our own? . . . Perhaps . . . the same source that provides the impetus which lies behind our own activities? That mysterious atmosphere in which our natural impulses stir us to the point of action. Looking at it like that, perhaps the "result" may have no meaning at all—it's only the intrinsic quality of the effort that counts.[7]

I do not know of a better example of the glories of a technical job well done—craftsmanship in the face of enormous adversity—and the hazards of ignoring whose cause you are serving by your blind craftsmanship, than this homely little adventure play.

I am not here to argue against the fact that everybody needs representation. I am not here to argue with the adversary system. But I am here to say that the same kind of reasoning (or lack of it) that totally obscured the vision of Colonel Nicholson can have and has had its morally deadening effect on lawyers. I could even name names. They are people I knew many years ago when I was serving as a foot soldier in some large litigation wars and saw the seamy underside of legal conflict that is rarely visible to those who sit on the appellate bench or work in a law school classroom. If you are not aware, you will be sometime. All of this has a lot to do with legal ethics. It has a lot to do with morality. It has a lot to do with what I hope is a suitable antidote for the worthy but distorting concentration on craftsmanship that is part of what Dean Cramton called the "ordinary religion of the law school classroom."

Some words of Alexander Solzhenitsyn provide a takeoff on the final subject I wish to mention before I conclude.

Western society has given itself the organization best suited to its purposes, based, I would say, on the letter of the law. The limits of human rights and righteousness are determined by a system of laws; such limits are very broad. People in the West have acquired considerable skill in using, interpreting, and manipulating law, even though laws tend to be too complicated for an average person to understand without the help of an expert. Any conflict is solved according to the letter of the law and this is considered to be the ultimate solution. If one is right from a legal point of view, nothing more is required, nobody may mention that one could still not be entirely right, and urge self-restraint, a willingness to renounce such legal rights, sacrifice and selfless risk: it would sound simply absurd. One almost never sees voluntary self-restraint. Everybody operates at the extreme limit of those legal frames. . . . I have spent my life under a communist regime and I will tell you that a society without any objective legal scale is a terrible one indeed. But a society with no other scale but the legal one is not quite worthy of man either. A society which is based on the letter of the law and never reaches any higher is taking very scarce advantage of the high level of human possibilities. The letter of the law is too cold and formal to have a beneficial influence on society. Whenever the tissue of life is woven of legalistic relations, there is an atmosphere of moral mediocrity, paralyzing man's noblest impulses.[8]

From those words I will skip over to others written recently in *Chronicles,* a publication of The Rockford Institute, by the director of Corporate Communications for Walgreen's.

Businesses of every kind are much enamored these days with the demanding ideal they call the "pursuit of excellence." Devotion to this pursuit is so widespread as to qualify as a form of "natural religion" to which everyone can pay homage without the snickers that accompany talk of things divine.[9]

The pursuit of excellence about which we hear so much is very closely related to the worship of self and the worship of technique illustrated in *The Bridge over the River Kwai.* I continue the quote:

The professional person is powerfully motivated today by the search for excellence. Let us hope that search can transcend the desire to just have more and extend to "being more." . . . The *true* pursuit of happiness involves a *personal*—a moral—as well as a professional effort. And if that man or woman is receptive to the Judeo-Christian tradition he or she realizes that the rewards of this effort [that is the effort to be more not just to make more] are imperishable.[10]

It may seem a strange thing for me to make such a plea to students, my brothers and sisters who are essentially poverty stricken. But if you don't think seriously now about *being* more, not just *making* more, husbands and wives are likely to make so many promises to one another that the fulfillment of those promises is going to bend the lawyer out of shape in the formative years of his or her practice of law. And once you are bent out of shape in the legal profession, it is very difficult to get straightened out again.

There are a lot of hard choices ahead of you in determining what bridges you will build. I suggest that the books you use to tell you how to build a bridge are not going to tell you who to build it for, or in whose cause you will spend your professional qualifications.

I surely do not want to be understood as saying that you shouldn't represent a criminal defendant. I need to tell you that the client who gave me the greatest personal satisfaction was a young Polish boy whom the Supreme Court of Illinois appointed me to represent in his appeal to that court. I lost the appeal seven to nothing and acknowledged the result as just. But I had a great deal more satisfaction in helping that young man have due process of law than I had representing some prestigious but sometimes quite underhanded corporate clients.

I'm not trying to make this advice easy by telling you who your clients should be. But I am suggesting that there is a large world of causes out there and that while one little piece of representation doesn't make one of those causes, a succession of representations of a particular character can add significantly to a mosaic and amount to a pattern. I am asking you to think about that, and I'm also asking you to think about what kind of rewards you want from the practice of law. Ask yourself whether those rewards amount to the reward of getting or the rewards of serving and becoming.

The Apostle Paul said, "Set your affection on things above, not on things on the earth" (Colossians 3:2). He wrote to his young companion Timothy to withdraw from men of corrupt minds, "destitute of the truth, supposing that gain is godliness" (1 Timothy 6:5). What a sermon there is in those words "supposing that gain is godliness." That is a lesson not learned by many, not understood or accepted by many in this church today, including a few in the profession for which you are in training.

In the parable of the sower, in the 13th chapter of Matthew, the Savior taught that certain seeds, representing the word of God, fell among the thorns. In explaining this parable later to his apostles, he said that this represented the word that went to people who were caught up in the cares of the world and the deceitfulness of riches, which choke the word and render it unfruitful.

My brothers and sisters, this is an exciting time of your life. Poor though you may be, rich you are and will be. The kind of riches you will gain depends on what you put into your head now in the way of priorities, more than what you learn in the way of techniques and professional craftsmanship. What you have in the way of priorities to guide your skills is of eternal significance. What you have in terms of technical skills is going to be outdated when you draw your last breath.

I know that the gospel is true. I know that this Law School is pleasing to our Heavenly Father. I was close enough to the current of inspiration in the founding of this Law School to have my heart tingle. I know that it serves a purpose. And I am positive that the purpose is not pecuniary. Though I do not understand what it is, I know well what it is not. It is not to augment the tithing revenues of the Church. It is to serve that end the Savior described when he said, "Lay not up for yourselves treasures upon earth, where moth and rust doth corrupt, and where thieves break through and steal: But lay up for yourselves treasures in heaven, where neither moth nor rust doth corrupt, and where thieves do not break through nor steal" (Matthew 6:19–20).

May God bless you to remember that admonition throughout your professional preparation and practice, is my prayer, which I offer as I bear my testimony to you of Jesus Christ, the light and life of the world. In the name of Jesus Christ, amen.

This fireside address was given at the BYU Law School on February 8, 1987. Reprinted from the Clark Memorandum, *Fall 1988, 10–15.*

Dallin H. Oaks received his J.D. from the University of Chicago in 1957, clerked for Chief Justice Earl Warren of the U.S. Supreme Court 1957–58, and served as Utah Supreme Court justice 1981–84. He is currently a member of the Quorum of the Twelve Apostles.

Notes

1. Roger C. Cramton, "The Ordinary Religion of the Law School Classroom," 29 *Journal of Legal Education* 247 (1978).

2. *Id.* at 253.

3. *Id.* at 254–255 (emphasis in original).

4. Pierre Boulle, *The Bridge over the River Kwai,* trans. Xan Fielding (New York: Grosset & Dunlap Publishers, 1954).

5. *Id.* at 203.

6. *Id.* at 215.

7. *Id.* at 145–146.

8. Alexander Solzhenitsyn, "A World Split Apart," Commencement Address Delivered at Harvard University, 8 June 1978.

9. Mammoser, "Letter from Corporate Headquarters," *Chronicles,* Jan. 1987, 38.

10. *Id.* at 39 (emphasis added).

Weightier Matters

Dallin H. Oaks

The book of Matthew contains the Savior's denunciation of the scribes and Pharisees: "Ye pay tithe of mint and anise and cummin, and have omitted the *weightier matters* of the law, judgment, mercy, and faith: these ought ye to have done, and not to leave the other undone" (Matt. 23:23; emphasis added).

I wish to address some "weightier matters" we might overlook if we allow ourselves to focus exclusively on lesser matters. The weightier matters to which I refer are the qualities like faith and the love of God and his work that will move us strongly toward our eternal goals.

In speaking of weightier matters, I seek to contrast our ultimate goals in eternity with the mortal methods or short-term objectives we use to pursue them. The Apostle Paul described the difference between earthly perspectives and eternal ones in these words: "We look not at the things which are seen, but at the things which are not seen: for the things which are seen are temporal; but the things which are not seen are eternal" (2 Cor. 4:18).

If we concentrate too intently on our obvious earthly methods or objectives, we can lose sight of our eternal goals, which the Apostle called "things . . . not seen." If we do this, we can forget where we should be headed and in eternal terms go nowhere. We do not improve our position in eternity just by flying farther and faster in mortality, but only by moving knowledgeably in the right direction. As the Lord told us in modern revelation, "That which the Spirit testifies unto you . . . ye should do in all holiness of heart, walking uprightly before me, *considering the end of your salvation*" (D&C 46:7; emphasis added).

We must not confuse means and ends. The vehicle is not the destination. If we lose sight of our eternal goals, we might think the most important thing is how fast we are moving and that any road will get us to our destination.

The Apostle Paul described this attitude as "hav[ing] a zeal of God, but not according to knowledge" (Rom. 10:2). Zeal is a method, not a goal. Zeal—even a zeal toward God—needs to be "according to knowledge" of God's commandments and His plan for His children. In other words, the weightier matter of the eternal goal must not be displaced by the mortal method, however excellent in itself.

Thus far I have spoken in generalities. Now I will give three examples.

Family

All Latter-day Saints understand that having an eternal family is an eternal goal. Exaltation is a family matter, not possible outside the everlasting covenant of marriage, which makes possible the perpetuation of glorious family relationships. But this does not mean that everything related to mortal families is an eternal goal. There are many short-term objectives associated with families—such as family togetherness or family solidarity or love—that are methods, not the eternal goals we pursue in priority above all others. For example, family solidarity to conduct an evil enterprise is obviously no virtue. Neither is family solidarity to conceal and perpetuate some evil practice like abuse.

The purpose of mortal families is to bring children into the world, to teach them what is right, and to prepare all family members for exaltation in eternal family relationships. The gospel plan contemplates the kind of family government, discipline, solidarity, and love that serve those ultimate goals. But even the love of family members is subject to the overriding first commandment, which is love of God (see Matt. 22:37–38), and the Savior's directive, "If ye love me, keep my commandments" (John 14:15). As Jesus taught, "He that loveth father or mother more than me is not worthy of me: and he that loveth son or daughter more than me is not worthy of me" (Matt. 10:37).

Choice, or Agency

My next example in this message on weightier matters is the role of choice, or agency.

Few concepts have more potential to mislead us than the idea that choice, or agency, is an ultimate goal. For Latter-day Saints, this potential confusion is partly a product of the fact that moral agency—the right to choose—is a fundamental condition of mortal life. Without this precious gift of God, the purpose of mortal life could not be realized. To secure our agency in mortality we fought a mighty contest the book of Revelation calls a "war in heaven." This premortal contest ended with the devil and his angels being cast out of heaven and being denied the opportunity of having a body in mortal life (see Rev. 12:7–9).

But our war to secure agency was won. The test in this postwar mortal estate is not to secure choice but to use it—to choose good instead of evil so that we can achieve our eternal goals. In mortality, choice is a method, not a goal.

Of course, mortals must still resolve many questions concerning what restrictions or consequences should be placed upon choices. But those questions come under the heading of freedom, not agency. Many do not understand that important fact. We are responsible to use our agency in a world of choices. It will not do to pretend that our agency has been taken away when we are not free to exercise it without unwelcome consequences.

Because choice is a method, choices can be exercised either way on any matter, and our choices can serve any goal. Therefore, those who consider freedom of choice as a goal can easily slip into the position of trying to justify any choice that is made. "Choice" can even become a slogan to justify one particular choice. For example, today one who says "I am pro-choice" is clearly understood as opposing any legal restrictions upon a woman's choice to abort a fetus.

More than 30 years ago, as a young law professor, I published one of the earliest articles on the legal consequences of abortion. Since that time I have been a knowledgeable observer of the national debate and the unfortunate Supreme Court decisions on the so-called "right to abortion." I have been fascinated with how cleverly those who sought and now defend legalized abortion on demand have moved the issue away from a debate on the moral, ethical, and medical pros and cons of legal restrictions on abortion and focused the debate on the slogan or issue of choice. The slogan or sound bite "pro-choice" has had an almost magical effect in justifying abortion and in neutralizing opposition to it.

Pro-choice slogans have been particularly seductive to Latter-day Saints because we know that moral agency, which can be described as the power of choice, is a fundamental necessity in the gospel plan. All Latter-day Saints are pro-choice according to that theological definition. But being pro-choice on the need for moral agency does not end the matter for us. Choice is a method, not the ultimate goal. We are accountable for our choices, and only righteous choices will move us toward our eternal goals.

In this effort, Latter-day Saints follow the teachings of the prophets. On this subject our prophetic guidance is clear. The Lord commanded, "Thou shalt not . . . kill, nor do anything like unto it" (D&C 59:6). The Church opposes elective abortion for personal or social convenience. Our members are taught that, subject only to some very rare exceptions, they must not submit to, perform, encourage, pay for, or arrange for an abortion. That direction tells us what we need to do on the weightier matters of the law, the choices that will move us toward eternal life.

In today's world we are not true to our teachings if we are merely pro-choice. We must stand up for the *right* choice. Those who persist in refusing to think beyond slogans and sound bites like pro-choice wander from the goals they pretend to espouse and wind up giving their support to results they might not support if those results were presented without disguise.

For example, consider the uses some have made of the possible exceptions to our firm teachings against abortion. Our leaders have taught that the only possible exceptions are when the pregnancy resulted from rape or incest, or when a competent physician has determined that the life or health of the mother is in serious jeopardy or that the fetus has severe defects that will not allow the baby to survive beyond birth. But even these exceptions do not justify abortion automatically. Because abortion is a most serious matter, we are counseled that it should be considered only after the persons responsible have consulted with their bishops and received divine confirmation through prayer.

Some Latter-day Saints say they deplore abortion, but they give these exceptional circumstances as a basis for their pro-choice position that the law should allow abortion on demand in all circumstances. Such persons should face the reality that the circumstances described in these three exceptions are extremely rare. For example, conception by incest or rape—the circumstance most commonly cited by those who use exceptions to argue for abortion on demand—is involved in only a tiny minority of abortions. More than 95 percent of the millions of abortions performed each year extinguish the life of a fetus conceived by consensual relations. Thus the effect in over 95 percent of abortions is not to vindicate choice but to avoid its consequences.[1] Using arguments of "choice" to try to justify altering the consequences of choice is a classic case of omitting what the Savior called "the weightier matters of the law."

A prominent basis for the secular or philosophical arguments for abortion on demand is the argument that a woman should have control over her own body. Not long ago I received a letter from a thoughtful Latter-day Saint outside the United States who analyzed that argument in secular terms. Since his analysis reaches the same conclusion I have urged on religious grounds, I quote it here for the benefit of those most subject to persuasion on this basis:

> Every woman has, within the limits of nature, the right to choose what will or will not happen to her body. Every woman has, at the same time, the responsibility for the way she uses her body. If by her choice she behaves in such a way that a human fetus is conceived, she has not only the right *to* but also the responsibility *for* that fetus. If it is an unwanted pregnancy, she is not justified in ending it with the claim that it interferes with her right to choose. She herself chose what would happen to her body by risking pregnancy. She had her choice. If she has no better reason, her conscience should tell her that abortion would be a highly irresponsible choice.

What constitutes a good reason? Since a human fetus has intrinsic and infinite human value, the only good reason for an abortion would be the violation or deprivation of or the threat to the woman's right to choose what will or will not happen to her body. Social, educational, financial, and personal considerations alone do not outweigh the value of the life that is in the fetus. These considerations by themselves may properly lead to the decision to place the baby for adoption after its birth, but not to end its existence in utero.

The woman's right to choose what will or will not happen to her body is obviously violated by rape or incest. When conception results in such a case, the woman has the moral as well as the legal right to an abortion because the condition of pregnancy is the result of someone else's irresponsibility, not hers. She does not have to take responsibility for it. To force her by law to carry the fetus to term would be a further violation of her right. She also has the right to refuse an abortion. This would give her the right to the fetus and also the responsibility for it. She could later relinquish this right and this responsibility through the process of placing the baby for adoption after it is born. Whichever way is a responsible choice.

The man who wrote those words also applied the same reasoning to the other exceptions allowed by our doctrine—life of the mother and a baby that will not survive birth.

I conclude this discussion of choice with two more short points.

If we say we are anti-abortion in our personal life but pro-choice in public policy, we are saying that we will not use our influence to establish public policies that encourage righteous choices on matters God's servants have defined as serious sins. I urge Latter-day Saints who have taken that position to ask themselves which other grievous sins should be decriminalized or smiled on by the law due to this theory that persons should not be hampered in their choices. Should we decriminalize or lighten the legal consequences of child abuse? of cruelty to animals? of pollution? of fraud? of fathers who choose to abandon their families for greater freedom or convenience?

Similarly, some reach the pro-choice position by saying we should not legislate morality. Those who take this position should realize that the law of crimes legislates nothing but morality. Should we repeal all laws with a moral basis so our government will not punish any choices some persons consider immoral? Such an action would wipe out virtually all of the laws against crimes.

Diversity

My last illustration of the bad effects of confusing means and ends, methods and goals, concerns the word *diversity.* Not many labels have been productive of more confused thinking in our time than this one. A respected federal judge recently commented on current changes in culture and values by observing that "a new credo in celebration of diversity seems to be emerging which proclaims, 'Divided We Stand!'"[2] Even in religious terms, we sometimes hear the words "celebrate diversity" as if diversity were an ultimate goal.

The word *diversity* has legitimate uses to describe a *condition*, such as when one discusses "racial and cultural diversity." Similarly, what we now call "diversity" appears in the scriptures as a condition. This is evident wherever differences among the children of God are described, such as in the numerous scriptural references to nations, kindreds, tongues, and peoples.

Yet in the scriptures, the objectives we are taught to pursue on the way to our eternal goals are ideals like love and obedience. These ideals do not accept us as we are but require each of us to make changes. Jesus did not pray that his followers would be "diverse." He prayed that they would be "one" (John 17:21–22). Modern revelation does not say, "Be diverse; and if ye are not diverse, ye are not mine." It says, "Be one; and if ye are not one ye are not mine" (D&C 38:27).

Since diversity is a condition, a method, or a short-term objective— not an ultimate goal—whenever diversity is urged it is appropriate to ask, "What kind of diversity?" or "Diversity in what circumstance or condition?" or "Diversity in furtherance of what goal?" This is especially important in our policy debates, which should be conducted not in terms of slogans but in terms of the goals we seek and the methods or shorter-term objectives that will achieve them. Diversity for its own sake is meaningless and can clearly be shown to lead to unacceptable results. For example, if diversity is the underlying goal for a neighborhood, does this mean we should seek to assure that the neighborhood includes thieves and pedophiles, slaughter-houses and water hazards? Diversity can be a good method to achieve some long-term goal, but public policy discussions need to get beyond the slogan to identify the goal, to specify the proposed diversity, and to explain how this kind of diversity will help to achieve the agreed-upon goal.

Our Church has an approach to the obvious cultural and ethnic diversities among our members. We teach that what unites us is far more important than what differentiates us. Consequently, our members are asked to concentrate their efforts to strengthen our unity—not to glorify our diversity. For example, our objective is not to organize local wards and branches according to differences in culture or in ethnic or national origins, although that effect is sometimes produced on a temporary basis when required because of language barriers. Instead, we teach that members of majority groupings (whatever their nature) are responsible to accept Church members of other groupings, providing full fellowship and full opportunities in Church participation. We seek to establish a community of Saints—"one body," the Apostle Paul called it (1 Cor. 12:13)—where everyone feels needed and wanted and where all can pursue the eternal goals we share.

Consistent with the Savior's command to "be one," we seek unity. On this subject President Gordon B. Hinckley has taught:

> I remember when President J. Reuben Clark, Jr., as a counselor in the First Presidency, would stand at this pulpit and plead for unity among the priesthood. I think he was not asking that we give up our individual personalities and become as robots cast from a single mold. I am confident he was not asking that we cease to think, to meditate, to ponder as individuals. I think he was telling us that if we are to assist in moving forward the work of God, we must carry in our hearts a united conviction concerning the great basic foundation stones of our faith. . . . If we are to assist in moving forward the work of God, we must carry in our hearts a united conviction that the ordinances and covenants of this work are eternal and everlasting in their consequences.[3]

Anyone who preaches unity risks misunderstanding. The same is true of anyone who questions the goal of diversity. Such a one risks being thought intolerant. But tolerance is not jeopardized by promoting unity or by challenging diversity. Again, I quote President Hinckley: "Each of us is an individual. Each of us is different. There must be respect for those differences."[4]

On another occasion he said:

> We must work harder to build mutual respect, an attitude of forbearance, with tolerance one for another regardless of the doctrines and philosophies which we may espouse. Concerning these you and I may disagree. But we can do so with respect and civility.[5]

President Hinckley continues:

> An article of the faith to which I subscribe states: "We claim the privilege of worshipping Almighty God according to the dictates of our own conscience, and allow all men the same privilege, let them worship how, where, or what they may" (A of F 1:11). I hope to find myself always on the side of those defending this position. Our strength lies in our freedom to choose. There is strength even in our very diversity. But there is greater strength in the God-given mandate to each of us to work for the uplift and blessing of all His sons and daughters, regardless of their ethnic or national origin or other differences.[6]

In short, we preach unity among the community of Saints and tolerance toward the personal differences that are inevitable in the beliefs and conduct of a diverse population. Tolerance obviously requires a non-contentious manner of relating toward one another's differences. But tolerance does not require abandoning one's standards or one's opinions on political or public policy choices. Tolerance is a way of reacting to diversity, not a command to insulate it from examination.

Strong calls for diversity in the public sector sometimes have the effect of pressuring those holding majority opinions to abandon fundamental values to accommodate the diverse positions of those in the minority.

Usually this does not substitute a minority value for a majority one. Rather, it seeks to achieve "diversity" by abandoning the official value position altogether, so that no one's value will be contradicted by an official or semi-official position. The result of this abandonment is not a diversity of values but an official anarchy of values. I believe this is an example of former Brigham Young University visiting professor Louis Pojman's observation that diversity can be used as "a euphemism for moral relativism."[7]

There are hundreds of examples of this, where achieving the goal of diversity results in the anarchy of values we call moral relativism. These examples include such varied proposals as forbidding the public schools to teach the wrongfulness of certain behavior or the rightness of patriotism. Another example is the attempt to banish a representation of the Ten Commandments from any public buildings.

In a day when prominent thinkers have decried the fact that universities have stopped teaching right and wrong, we are grateful for the countercultural position at Brigham Young University. Moral relativism, which is said to be the dominant force in American universities, has no legitimate place at BYU. The faculty teach values—the right and wrong taught in the gospel of Jesus Christ.

In conclusion, diversity and choice are not the weightier matters of the law. The weightier matters that move us toward our goal of eternal life are love of God, obedience to His commandments, and unity in accomplishing the work of His Church. In this belief and practice we move against the powerful modern tides running toward individualism and tolerance rather than toward obedience and cooperative action. Though our belief and practice is unpopular, it is right, and it does not require the blind obedience or the stifling uniformity its critics charge. If we are united on our eternal goal and united on the inspired principles that will get us there, we can be diverse on individual efforts in support of our goals and consistent with those principles.

We know that the work of God cannot be done without unity and cooperative action. We also know that the children of God cannot be exalted as single individuals. Neither a man nor a woman can be exalted in the celestial kingdom unless both unite in the unselfishness of the everlasting covenant of marriage and unless both choose to keep the commandments and honor the covenants of that united state.

I testify of Jesus Christ, our Savior. As the One whose Atonement paid the incomprehensible price for our sins, He is the One who can prescribe the conditions for our salvation. He has commanded us to keep His commandments (see John 14:15) and to "be one" (D&C 38:27). I pray that we will make the wise choices to keep the commandments and to seek the unity that will move us toward our ultimate goal, "eternal life, which gift is the greatest of all the gifts of God" (D&C 14:7).

This devotional address was given to the BYU student body on February 9, 1999. Reprinted with permission from the Ensign, *Jan. 2001, 12–17; also published in* Brigham Young University Speeches 1998–99, *147–153 and in* Clark Memorandum, *Spring 1999, 2–9.*

Dallin H. Oaks received his J.D. from the University of Chicago in 1957, clerked for Chief Justice Earl Warren of the U.S. Supreme Court 1957–58, and served as Utah Supreme Court justice 1981–84. He is currently a member of the Quorum of the Twelve Apostles.

Notes

1. See Russell M. Nelson, "Reverence for Life," *Ensign,* May 1985, 11–14.
2. J. Thomas Greene, "Activist Judicial Philosophies on Trial," *Federal Rules Decisions* 178 (1997): 200.
3. *Teachings of Gordon B. Hinckley* (1997), 672.
4. *Teachings,* 661.
5. *Teachings,* 665.
6. *Teachings,* 664.
7. "Viewpoint," *Daily Universe,* 13 Oct. 1998, 4.

Pure Religion

Stephen A. West

We are brought together tonight by virtue of two shared faiths—faith in the Church and faith in the law. When I was asked to speak to you, I thought it would be relatively easy to talk to Church members about the Church or to lawyers about the law but not as easy to find common threads that tie the two together. To try to fulfill that responsibility, I would like to share with you some gospel-related experiences and then connect them with the law.

These experiences all came as a result of an exceptional opportunity for service that my wife Martha and I completed last November. We were called to work with our brothers and sisters in the Mt. Pleasant Branch of the Church, where I worked as a counselor in the branch presidency and Martha helped with the Relief Society. Martha's and my roles were to be shadow leaders and to help implement the programs of the Church in the branch. For both of us this was a great learning experience. We learned wonderful things about attitudes, approaches, and people during the 18 months of our service. The entire branch membership is 20 to 35 individuals: one Spanish American, four whites (which included the two of us), and the remainder black members of the Church. Approximately half of the black members were born or grew up in the United States and the other half were born or grew up in Africa.

Let me set the scene for you. The branch is located in a rented row house in the District of Columbia at 14th and Newton Street. A Vietnamese branch, a Hispanic branch, and our central city branch all meet in this facility. This is a difficult neighborhood. Recently the members of a gang called the "Newton Street Crew" were arrested. The gang was composed of residents of Newton Street who lived between 14th and 16th Streets who allegedly had been selling drugs and committing other related crimes in that area. Many of you who are from the Washington area may remember the Shotgun Stalker who, within the past year, shot at eleven people in this small Mt. Pleasant neighborhood. Four people were hit, and three others were killed; one of them was murdered in the alley that runs behind the branch, and the other shootings took place within a few blocks of our building. A number of businesses, both large and small, were once located in this neighborhood; but many of them have remained boarded up ever since the 1968 riots that accompanied Martin Luther King Jr.'s assassination.

On the other hand, there are positive things about the neighborhood. It is a place where many of the current residents have always lived. As a result, they know grandmothers, parents, and children of families that also have remained in this area for years. They can easily distinguish between the "good guys" and the "bad guys." There is a small Spanish church on the corner near our building. In front, during the warmer months a vendor sells papayas, mangos, watermelon, and other fruits from a pushcart to the many people who congregate there.

The branch president has been a member of the Church for about five or six years. He is a man of my age, a father and a grandfather. He is a college graduate, has taken a number of post-graduate courses, and works as a teacher and consultant. He was a civil rights activist during the 1960s. His father was a minister. When he joined the Church, he was the only one of his family to do so.

The other counselor in the branch presidency is a younger man about three or four years out of college. He grew up in Africa. One of his grandfathers was a minister, and the other was a radical leader. He was offered admission to several American universities, including the University of Idaho, which he attended. While in college, he met Mormon missionaries, but he did not "connect" with them at that time. Subsequently, he decided to go to law school and attended Howard; but he was expelled from the law school for being "too radical." As he explains, "It is quite an accomplishment to be too radical at Howard Law School." In his bitterness, he decided to file a *pro se* lawsuit against Howard. He was on a bus on his way to the courthouse when he noticed two Mormon missionaries who soon started talking to him. When he reached his destination, the missionaries got off with him. As they sat and talked for a while in the park, he said he felt the hatred and animosity drain out of him. As a result, he continued to talk to the missionaries; they began to teach him some of the discussions. He later joined the Church and abandoned his efforts to fight with Howard Law School. He is now a consultant for an international organization.

As we worked with the good members of the branch, our old thought patterns were continually being challenged and reshaped. From these humble people, we learned lessons of faith and courage. For instance, one day in Sunday School we were discussing when we should pray and when we should act. During the course of that discussion, one of the members told us that soon after he and his wife had come to the United States from Africa his wife came to him and said, "We must kill our baby because there is not enough to feed three of us, and we must stay alive." We subsequently found out that when his wife had said "kill" she meant that she must have an abortion. He told us that his response to her was, "No, we will pray about this and place it in the hands of the Lord." He said they prayed fervently for help with this decision. He continued, "Within three days of our prayers, I received a job. Subsequently I was promoted on that job, and we were able to complete the pregnancy and have the baby." He concluded, "We named her Victoria, because we had prayed and we were victorious." Today she is an outstanding grade school student. Moreover, she is teaching her parents how to live in the United States, giving them knowledge that they never would have known if she had not been born.

In another discussion in Sunday School, we learned about charity. We were talking about when it is appropriate to give to the poor and needy. One brother told us that as he was walking home one evening he was approached by a man who put a pistol to his chest and demanded all his money. The branch member took his money from his pockets and handed it over to the assailant, adding, "If you need the money that badly, I have more." He then proceeded to open his briefcase, remove additional funds and hand them to the robber. As he did so, he said, "You are not taking this from me; I am giving it to you in the spirit of the Lord because you need it." The robber looked at him in amazement, put the pistol in his belt and said, "Where do you live? I'm going to walk you home because you're too good a man to be on the streets—you are not safe here." As they started to walk to his apartment, suddenly they were surrounded by police cars because a woman had seen the stickup from her window and reported it. The police arrested the robber and took him away. This member, who was the victim, was asked to be a witness at the trial. In his testimony, he stated that although the defendant had demanded his money, he had told him that he gave it to him in the spirit of the Lord and that if he needed it that badly he wanted him to have it. As a result, the judge found the robber guilty but put him on probation, and he did not have to serve time.

In another Sunday lesson I observed what living by the spirit can mean as we teach in the Church. We had a man in his mid-thirties attend the class for the first time. At the end of the lesson the Sunday School teacher, who was a woman about 20 years his senior, asked him to say the closing prayer. I probably would never have had the temerity to ask someone who I had never seen before to say a closing prayer. Nevertheless, she encouraged him with a smile, and he replied, "No, I haven't prayed for years and years, and I could not do it." She answered, "Sure you can. Go ahead, and I will hold your hand." She came over and took his hand and then said, "And if you don't do a good job, that's fine. We will ask somebody else to say a prayer after you if your prayer isn't adequate." Given that reassurance, he bowed his head and gave a wonderful prayer. When he had finished, she put her arm around him and said, "See, that was a great prayer. We don't have any need for anyone else to say something after that." What an effective thing to simply take his hand to support him while he prayed and to tell him that someone else could pray if needed to take the pressure out of the situation.

I learned a great deal about sacrifice from a humble sister in the branch. One day this sister came to sacrament meeting, clutching a baggie containing a piece of bread that was hard and stale and partially moldy. She said to me, "If you are going to belong to a church you ought to contribute, and I can't contribute much, but one thing I can do is bring the sacrament bread." There was no way we were not going to use that bread for the sacrament that day. I sensed that her "contribution" was like the widow's mite. In Mark 12:41–44 we read:

> And Jesus sat over against the treasury, and beheld how the people cast money into the treasury: and many that were rich cast in much.
>
> And there came a certain poor widow, and she threw in two mites, which make a farthing.
>
> And he called unto him his disciples, and saith unto them, Verily I say unto you, That this poor widow hath cast more in, than all they which have cast into the treasury:
>
> For all they did cast in of their abundance; but she of her want did cast in all that she had, even all her living.

I continually learned from the courage and commitment of our branch president, the missionaries, and the members. Typically, we would hold the traditional sacrament, Sunday School, priesthood, and Relief Society meetings on Sundays. Then one evening during the week, we would have a scripture study class, which included playing some games and having refreshments, somewhat like a family home evening meeting. At the time the Shotgun Stalker was at large in the neighborhood, I wondered if we should cancel many of our meetings; but our wise branch president stood before the congregation and announced:

> To cut back or curtail our meetings is exactly what the person or persons who are perpetrating these crimes wants to accomplish. They want to take the good people off of the streets and have them hiding and not coming out. Now is the time when it is most important that we as members of the Church be visible, that we be on the streets, and that we be seen. They must know that they can't intimidate us. This is the time that we should hold our meetings and that we should be out in the neighborhood standing up for what we believe.

So we continued with our full calendar of meetings. Our missionaries remained very visible on the street, meeting and talking to people as always.

And these brave missionaries also became my new heroes. I watched young men from small towns in Arizona, Utah, Idaho, and Nevada come into the neighborhood, into a totally new environment. I saw them walk down the street "high-fiving" the people and visiting with them. I watched the neighborhood people respond by slapping the missionaries' hands and saying, "How are you doing, elders?" The missionaries were not alarmed when people would warn them, "You are not safe here." They would respond with a smile, offer the reassurance that they were happy to be there, and go on about their work.

I learned who the branch members' heroes were as I heard their talks in our meetings. For example, when John Wilson, the D.C. city councilman, died it was obviously very important for many people to speak of what a great man he had been. They explained how he had influenced their lives, how he had helped their neighborhood, how he had helped their schools, how he had helped increase their job opportunities, and how he had been an example to them. As they spoke of John Wilson, they remembered him and worked through the grief that they felt at his death.

People were quoted in our meetings who are not normally quoted in other LDS congregations. The members often quoted Martin Luther King Jr. I recall one of those quotes in particular: "Death is not a period which ends this great sentence of life, but a comma that punctuates it to a more lofty significance."[1] What an interesting and comforting description of death!

I also learned new ways of listening. One day a woman who had suffered a stroke that had confined her to her apartment for a long period of time was brought to our fast and testimony meeting. She was being cared for full-time by another branch member. Her caretaker brought the sister to this meeting in a wheelchair and placed her in the front of the room. She listened intently to the proceedings. She was not able to speak because of her stroke, but suddenly, at an appropriate time, she started to make a gurgling sound in her throat. We couldn't understand what she was saying, but as we looked at her face and saw the tears running down her cheeks, we knew that she was bearing a strong testimony. I learned that day that when words are not discernible, the heart can interpret.

I repeatedly learned new ways of seeing people during my time in the branch. The door to our little row house opens right onto the city sidewalk. One Sunday, in the middle of the high councilor's talk, a homeless woman who was wearing dirty, ragged clothes, coughing up phlegm, choking and carrying a filthy handkerchief appeared at the door. She announced, "I want to sing. I want to pray." She then walked on into the room and proceeded to the front row. She selected a seat next to a sister in the branch who was wearing a white blouse and placed her head on the woman's shoulder. The sister immediately put her arms around this new arrival and held her throughout the remainder of the meeting. The high councilor had been relating the parable of the Good Samaritan as the homeless woman joined us. As this woman coughed and used her dirty handkerchief, the speaker continued with the parable. When he came to the end, he quoted part of the relevant scripture and suddenly our visitor completed the verse the high councilor had begun quoting. Later as we sang, the woman sounded off-key every word of the hymn. I found myself wondering how she knew that scriptural passage, how she knew that hymn. After the meeting had ended, I commented to the high councilor, "What better visual aid could you have of the parable of the Good Samaritan than the woman who put her arms around our visitor?" We both reflected upon the fact that it was probably the first time in a long time that someone had put their arms around our visitor in affection.

My "vision" was tested on other occasions. One evening at Christmas time we were going to take all our members up to the Washington Temple Visitors Center to see the lights and to enjoy the various church choirs that performed there. As I walked into the branch chapel, I saw a man that I had never met before sitting in one of our folding chairs. He had on high top boots, a long overcoat, and a leather aviator's hat with flaps sticking out on either side of his ears. As he looked up at me, he said, "Hi, chief—what's up?" I went over to talk with him, and he asked, "What are we doing, chief?" I told him of our plans, and he said, "I dig it; let's go."

When we arrived at the visitors center, we sat down and listened to a Presbyterian bell choir perform. At intermission he said, "Chief, can we go up and talk to the head man?" I replied that I thought that would be fine, so we went up and talked to the conductor. Right away, my companion started discussing the tonic fifths that the bell choir had been playing. I thought, "How in the world does he know what a 'tonic fifth' is?" He proceeded to have a detailed discussion of baroque music theory with the conductor, a music teacher. As we returned to the branch, I asked the young man how he knew about tonic fifths and baroque music. He told me that he was a music major at the University of the District of Columbia. He explained that he had sold most of his belongings to buy more drums and that he hoped to graduate with a degree in music and do some composing. I was struck by how completely I had misjudged this individual based on my first impression of him.

On another occasion, in the middle of our sacrament meeting, the door of our building opened and in came a man wearing black Nikes with the shoes unlaced, long baggy levis and an underwear top. As he sat down, I noticed the very tough, very grim expression on his face. I watched him throughout the meeting, thinking, "here comes trouble." When we finished sacrament meeting and moved directly into Sunday School, he remained in place, still frowning. At about the mid-point of Sunday School, he got up and walked out.

The following week he joined us again in the middle of a meeting. This time I thought, "Well, he has cased us out and now he's back to cause us trouble." After the meeting he came up and said to me, "Isn't today testimony meeting? I have come to bear my testimony." When I inquired, he said, "I'm a member of the Church and belong to the Capitol Hill Branch." Once more, my vision had needed correction.

As I reflect upon what I have learned about people through this experience, my thoughts turn to a 40-year-old Book of Mormon my grandmother gave me when I graduated from high school. It accompanied me on my mission, and I keep it close with me today. The leather cover has come off, it is tattered, it just has the cardboard backing left, and sections of the book are separating from other sections. Many of the people I encountered during my service in the branch are like my Book of Mormon—tattered, worn, damaged on the outside; but they have great and important things on the inside. They may have been classified by some as "low-income types," but I came to know that they all were first class.

After hearing of the lessons I have learned through this church service, you may be asking yourselves, "What does all this have to do with the law?" Let me try and weave my themes together now. Earlier, I told you that our branch president's father had been a minister—he preached in a church in Topeka, Kansas. He also was the head of the local chapter of the NAACP. In this role, he initiated a lawsuit to integrate the junior high schools of Topeka. The resistance came quickly. The sisters of our branch president's father and his attorney, both teachers in the Topeka school system, were asked to persuade their brothers to drop the suit. When their fathers did not give in to the pressure, the two women teachers were fired. However, the suit progressed and succeeded in integrating the junior high schools.

A subsequent action was initiated to broaden the effects of this first suit, to try to integrate the entire school system of Topeka. Unfortunately, the health of our branch president's father was failing, and he was not able to participate actively in the second suit. When he passed away, the suit was picked up by Ollie Brown, the assistant pastor of the congregation presided over by our branch president's father.

That case, which was the result of collaboration by individuals who were trained in religion and individuals who were trained in the law, continued up through the appellate system until it was finally decided in May 1954 by the court you will be admitted to practice before tomorrow, the Supreme Court of the United States. Its name was *Brown v. the Board of Education,* the landmark case that held that separate by equal schools cannot be equal while separate.[2] It was the case that resulted in the nationwide integration of the public schools, the Supreme Court opinion that we mark the 40th anniversary of this week. "And now you know the rest of the story," as Paul Harvey might say.

Early last year at a memorable event, I was reminded of our obligation to the next generation to pass on this combining of faith in religion and faith in the law. I served as vice chair of the Interfaith Conference of Metropolitan Washington that sponsored this citywide service to commemorate the birthday of Martin Luther King Jr. This Conference is made up of representatives of the Catholic, Protestant, Jewish, Mormon, Muslim, and Sikh religions. The service was held in a large Baptist church in a center-city neighborhood. During the course of the program, about 60 sixth-grade students walked across the front of the sanctuary, holding a large butcher paper banner that spanned the entire front section of this big church. Across the top of the banner the legend, "I Have a Dream" was printed. Underneath that the children had dipped their hands in paint and then pressed them onto the banner. Under each palm print, the owner had written his or her own dream. The words read: "I want to be a pharmacist. *I want to be a lawyer.* I want to be a beautician. I want to be a professional basketball player. *I want to be a lawyer.* I want to be a truck driver. *I want to be a lawyer because of the good I can do for my people.* I want to be a teacher. I want to be a dairy owner," et cetera.

As far as I could see across the Church, fully one-third of these young black children had expressed their desire to be a lawyer. No other occupation was mentioned as often. At a time when we as lawyers are part of a profession under siège and when lawyer jokes and lawyer bashing are prevalent, these sixth graders saw something that so many of our contemporaries have missed—the importance of the role of the lawyer, the ability it provides to make a difference, and the vehicle it offers to help all people.

In conclusion let me leave you with two quotations that capture the complementary joining of the religious and the legal. The Reverend Martin Luther King Jr. spoke of religion and service:

> A religion true to its nature must also be concerned about man's social conditions. Religion deals with both earth and heaven, both time and eternity. Religion operates not only on the vertical plane but also on the horizontal. It seeks not only to integrate men with God but to integrate men with men and each man with himself.[3]

John W. Davis, one of the named partners in the New York City law firm of Davis, Polk, spoke about the blending of law and service:

> True, we build no bridges. We raise no towers. We construct no engines. We paint no pictures—unless as amateurs for our own principal amusement. There is little of all that we do which the eye of man can see. But we smooth out difficulties; we relieve stress; we correct mistakes; we take up other men's

burdens and by our efforts we make possible the peaceful life of men in a peaceful state.[4]

As I began, I spoke of our two shared faiths, faith in the Church and faith in the law. In both of these important areas, may our faith continue to be strong; may we magnify our callings as representatives of the Church and as officers of the court is my prayer in the name of Jesus Christ, amen.

This address was given on May 24, 1994 to graduates of the BYU Law School who had come to Washington, D.C. to be admitted to practice before the U.S. Supreme Court on the following day. Reprinted from the Clark Memorandum, Fall 1994, *14–21.*

Stephen A. West received his J.D. from the University of Utah in 1961 and was senior vice president and general counsel for Marriott International. He is currently a member of the Second Quorum of the Seventy.

Notes

1. Martin Luther King, Jr., "Eulogy for the Martyred Children," in *A Testament of Hope: The Essential Writings of Martin Luther King, Jr.,* ed. James Melvin Washington (San Francisco: Harper & Row, 1986), 222. "The Reverend Dr. King delivered this sermon at the funeral of the little girls who were killed on 15 September 1963 by a bomb as they attended the Sunday school of the 16th Street Baptist Church in Birmingham, Alabama." *Id.* at 221.

2. *Brown v. Board of Education,* 337 U.S. 483 (1954).

3. Martin Luther King, Jr., *The Words of Martin Luther King, Jr.: Selections by Coretta Scott King* (New York: Newmarket Press, 1987), 66.

4. John W. Davis, Address, New York, 16 March 1946, in 1 *Record of the Association of the Bar of the City of New York* 101, 102 (1946), as quoted in Fred R. Shapiro, *The Oxford Dictionary of American Legal Quotations* (New York: Oxford University Press, 1993), 273.

Soldiers of the Spirit

Lance B. Wickman

Last Friday, I was talking with a dear friend and professional colleague of mine, a retired judge of the San Diego Superior Court and the California Court of Appeals, who is of counsel to our law firm, a man for whom I have both affection and high regard. I told him that I was going to be speaking to students at the BYU Law School this evening. "What is your subject?" he inquired. "Ethics," I briefly replied. "Oh," he said with a twinkle in his eye, "Do you know anything about it?"

A sobering question! My dear friends, I can tell you this—whatever I may know about this subject, particularly as it relates to the practice of law as a Latter-day Saint, I have learned not so much in classroom or courtroom as in the silent chambers of the soul in coming to grips with a thousand, nay, a thousand thousand, decisions great and small in the daily course of attempting to practice my religion and my profession at the same time—in coming to understand what it means to be a *Latter-day Saint lawyer.* Do I know anything about it? Well, I will let you be the judge of what I know after you have heard what I have to say. My prayer has been, and is, only that if there is anything of intrinsic merit in what I say that it will be evident and thus of lasting value to you.

It was almost a year ago that my life changed dramatically. I was sitting in my law office in San Diego at noon a few days before April conference when the telephone rang. The voice on the other end was President Gordon B. Hinckley inviting my wife, Pat, and me to meet with him the following day. A very unsettling 27 hours followed. Then, as we sat with the president, he extended this special call to serve as a member of the Second Quorum of the Seventy. But, he explained, my service would not be full-time. I would continue to live in San Diego and practice law. I would serve as a member of the presidency of the North America West Area, which encompasses California and Hawaii (a tough assignment, but someone has to do it!).

Thus began a new phase of life—a life of being alternately "law man" and "church man." When I returned from general conference, I encountered one of our regional representatives, who is also a lawyer. Another lawyer in his firm and I had been on opposite sides of a lawsuit. Good-naturedly, he said, "Does this [my new call] mean that we have to give up now?!" Well, I gave him the only answer that any lawyer worthy of his hourly rate could give: "Of course, it does!" The question was intended, and received, in good humor, but it highlights indirectly a question that lingers in the mind of every Latter-day Saint lawyer (indeed in the mind of every lawyer of integrity) who daily witnesses the contentious, often strident, world of law: How do I conform my professional life with my private life? Am I the same man or woman in my workday activity that I am in my ecclesiastical activity? Can I be?

Happily, I can say categorically that the answer to that question is "yes." I have learned that it really is true that "no man can serve two masters." I have also learned that the profession of law does not require him to do so. I have learned that the lawyer's enemy is not his profession but rather the arrogance that all too often infects those who come into it. Hence, I would like to begin by saying something about this occupational hazard and its antidote. From there, I wish to proceed to share a thought or two about what it means to be both a Latter-day Saint and a lawyer.

The scriptures, as always, provide profound insight. With his new-found missionary companion, Amulek, Alma went forth among the people of the wicked city, Ammonihah, to preach the gospel. Evidently, the lawyers and judges of Ammonihah were among those chiefly responsible for the wickedness of the people. Alma and Amulek preached in fervent testimony to touch their hearts, but the Book of Mormon account records:

> Nevertheless, there were some among them who thought to question them, that by their cunning devices they might catch them in their words, that they might find witness against them, that they might deliver them to their judges, that they might be judged according to the law, . . .
>
> Now it was those men who sought to destroy them, who were lawyers, who were hired or appointed by the people to administer the law at their times of trials, or at the trials of the crimes of the people before the judges.
>
> Now these lawyers were learned in all the arts and cunning of the people; and this was to enable them that they might be skilful in their profession.
>
> And it came to pass that they began to question Amulek, that thereby they might make him cross his words, or contradict the words which he should speak (Alma 10:13–16; emphasis added).

The ensuing discussion between Alma and Amulek and these lawyers, including one in particular named Zeezrom, illustrates the two most common manifestations of lawyer arrogance: the arrogance of power, or manipulative behavior, and the arrogance of sophistry, or what I call the arrogance of being clever.

The first of these, the arrogance of power, or manipulative behavior, stems from the enormous influence that a lawyer potentially wields simply because he knows "the system." It is the unprincipled use of a lawyer's knowledge of law and the legal system to manipulate others to his own selfish end that is the arrogance of power. The following exchange between Amulek and some of his listeners illustrates this evil:

> And now behold, I say unto you that the foundation of the destruction of this people is beginning to be laid by the unrighteousness of your lawyers and your judges.
>
> And now it came to pass that when Amulek had spoken these words the people cried out against him, saying: Now we know that this man is a child of the devil, for he hath lied unto us; for he hath spoken against our law. Now he says that he has not spoken against it.
>
> And again, he has reviled against our lawyers, and our judges.
>
> *And it came to pass that the lawyers put it into their hearts that they should remember these things against him* (Alma 10:27–30; emphasis added).

The *lawyers* put it into the people's hearts that Amulek was purportedly undermining their system of laws when the opposite was true. The manipulations of the lawyers themselves were the enemy to the people. Sadly, this phenomenon is all too present in the conduct of some lawyers today. It is manifest not only in some who attain high political office, which they then attempt to bend to their own purposes, but it is also found in the super-aggressive antics of a few practitioners who seek to use their skill to bully and browbeat opponents to obtain an advantage, unfairly, for their clients. This arrogant manipulative behavior is widespread. Occasionally (but not often enough, in my opinion), the courts themselves will step in and pointedly slap the hands of those who engage in such practices. In *Paramount Communications v. QVC Network*,[1] the Supreme Court of Delaware quotes an extended excerpt from a deposition in which one lawyer crossed the line of propriety and collegiality. He was rude, insulting, and obstructing in his conduct, all in an effort to cow his opponent. In stating its intention not to allow this particular lawyer (from another state) to make future appearances in Delaware courts absent a showing of good cause, the court said:

> Staunch advocacy on behalf of a client is proper and fully consistent with the finest effectuation of skill and professionalism. Indeed, it is a mark of professionalism, not weakness, for a lawyer zealously and firmly to protect and pursue a client's legitimate interest by a professional, courteous, and civil attitude toward all persons involved in the litigation process. A lawyer who engages in the type of behavior exemplified by Mr. [X] on the record of the [Y]

deposition is not properly representing his client, and the client's cause is not advanced by a lawyer who engages in unprofessional conduct of this nature.[2]

Such behavior is one of the reasons that many lay people are less than complimentary about lawyers. But there is another reason, and more widespread, and that is the arrogance of sophistry.

The arrogance of lawyer sophistry—of being clever—is also illustrated in the tenth and eleventh chapters of Alma.

> And there was one among them whose name was Zeezrom. Now he was the foremost to accuse Amulek and Alma, he being one of the most expert among them, having much business to do among the people. . . .
>
> And this Zeezrom began to question Amulek, saying: Will ye answer me a few questions which I shall ask you? Now Zeezrom was a man who was expert in the devices of the devil, that he might destroy that which was good; therefore, he said unto Amulek: Will ye answer the questions which shall be put unto you? (Alma 10:31; 11:21)

Throughout chapter 11 Zeezrom attempts, unsuccessfully, to hoodwink Amulek by putting clever questions to him—foolishly elementary questions from one presumably schooled in the teachings of the prophets—such as: "Is there more than one God?" "How knowest thou these things?" "Who is he that shall come?" "Is it the Son of God?" "Shall he save his people in their sins?"

Then, puffed up in his self-congratulatory prowess as a cross-examiner, Zeezrom said unto the people:

> See that you remember these things [referring to Amulek's answers]; for he said there is but one God; yet he saith that the Son of God shall come, but he shall not save his people—as though he had authority to command God (Alma 11:35).

But, as so often happens with arrogant people, Zeezrom's inflated ego obscured his vision. He failed to see that his foolish questions had only provided Amulek an opportunity for teaching some very fundamental doctrine concerning the redemptive power of Christ and the reality of an ultimate resurrection and judgment. In marked contrast to Zeezrom, Amulek was filled with the Spirit and with a fundamental integrity and honesty that forcefully turned back Zeezrom's shallow intellectual questioning, confounding him. Amulek punctured Zeezrom's fragile bubble of self-importance—of cleverness. To his credit, Zeezrom changed his ways.

But Zeezrom is not the only scriptural example of a lawyer inflated by his own cleverness. Once the Savior was approached by a "certain lawyer," as he is described by Luke, who also fancied himself as clever. Seeking to tempt the Savior, he asked, "Master, what shall I do to inherit eternal life?" In the right context, the question is both profound and important. It is a question asked sooner or later by every honest truth seeker. But this lawyer's interest in the answer was pretended; his purpose was not truth but treachery. His question was also foolishly elementary for one schooled in the law. Jesus said: "What is written in the law? How readest thou?" The lawyer responded, "Thou shalt love the Lord thy God with all thy heart, and with all thy soul, and with all thy strength, and with all thy mind; and thy neighbor as thyself." The answer was a good one, but in so readily giving it the lawyer revealed the transparent insincerity—the sophistry, the attempt at cleverness—in his question. Jesus' divine mastery of the encounter is revealed in the simplicity of his response: "Thou hast answered right: this do, and thou shalt live" (See Luke 10:25–28).

And then Luke, to whom we are indebted for the record of this episode, provides this penetrating insight. Referring to the lawyer, he said: "*But he, willing to justify himself . . .*" The lawyer's true motive was exposed; he sought to justify himself. His purpose in asking the question about eternal life was vain self-aggrandizement. Outwitted, his motive of self-justification was even more evident. "But he, willing to justify himself, said unto Jesus, And who is my neighbor?" The Savior then taught the beautiful parable of the Good Samaritan—the story of one who, in marked contrast to this lawyer, was motivated by selfless service, not selfish posturing (Luke 10:29–37).

But lest the judgments of sacred writ be left unbalanced on the matter of lawyers, Mark offers a glimmer of hope for those following the profession of the law.

> And one of the scribes [lawyers] came, and having heard them reasoning together, and perceiving that he [the Savior] had answered them [some Sadducees] well, asked him, Which is the first commandment of all?
>
> And Jesus answered him, The first of all the commandments is, Hear, O Israel; the Lord our God is one Lord.
>
> And thou shalt love the Lord thy God with all thy heart, and with all thy soul, and with all thy mind, and with all thy strength: this is the first commandment.
>
> And the second is like, namely this, Thou shalt love thy neighbor as thyself. There is none other commandment greater than these (Mark 12:28–31).

Note how similar on the face of the written text are the two interviews with lawyers—one recorded by Luke and the other by Mark—similar at least to this point. However, note the difference in the response of this lawyer:

> And the scribe said unto him, Well, Master, thou hast said the truth: for there is one God; and there is none other but he:
>
> And to love him with all the heart, and with all the understanding, and with all the soul, and with all the strength, and to love his neighbor as himself, is more than all whole burnt offerings and sacrifices (Mark 12:32–33).

This man sought no self-justification. He sought not to be clever or self-promoting. His dialogue was honest, sincere. The integrity of his soul is revealed in his earnest response to the Savior's answer. In the words of the Gospel writer, "he answered discreetly."

"And when Jesus saw that he answered discreetly, he said unto him, Thou art not far from the kingdom of God" (Mark 12:34; emphasis added).

The difference between these two lawyers was not so much in their questions as in their attitude. One spoke "discreetly," that is to say sincerely and without sophistry. And of him the Master said, "Thou art not far from the kingdom of God."

Nonetheless, to underscore the Savior's mastery of any and all who sought to embarrass or condemn him through their sophistry and cleverness, Mark concludes his account of the incident with this telling epitaph, "And no man after that durst ask him any question" (Mark 12:34).

What accounted for the Savior's mastery over his interrogators? To answer that he was the Christ merely begs the question. For then one must ask, What are the qualities that made him the Christ? Discovering those, one will unlock the door to success in law and happiness in living. One thing is patently obvious (and worthy of emulation by every would-be lawyer): He knew the law—*"The Law."* He was a master of *The Law.* Faced with lawyers' questions, he turned to *The Law* for the answer. In each case, faced with a question from one who was expected to know the law, Jesus responded by asking him to state the rule, albeit a rule of ecclesiastical law. It was his mastery of the system of rules we call *The Law* that enabled the Master to engage in persuasive conversation. There is a lesson here for each of us. In the profession of law there is no substitute for knowing *The Law.*

But there was something else, something much more important, something divine in Jesus' handling of these situations. And that "something" is the special blend of personal qualities that comprised his character. Luke uses a single word to describe that blend of qualities: *Virtue.*

> And he came down with them, and stood in the plain, and the company of his disciples, and a great multitude of people out of all Judea and Jerusalem, and from the sea coast of Tyre and Sidon, which came to hear him, and to be healed of their diseases;
>
> And they that were vexed with unclean spirits; and they were healed.
>
> And the whole multitude sought to touch him: *for there went virtue out of him,* and healed them all (Luke 6:17–19; emphasis added).
>
> And a woman having an issue of blood twelve years, which had spent all her living upon physicians, neither could be healed of any,
>
> Came behind him, and touched the border of his garment: and immediately her issue of blood stanched.
>
> And Jesus said, Who touched me? When all denied, Peter and they that were with him said, Master, the multitude throng thee and press thee, and sayest thou, Who touched me?

> And Jesus said, Somebody hath touched me: for *I perceive that virtue is gone out of me....*
>
> And he said unto her, Daughter, be of good comfort: thy faith hath made thee whole; go in peace. (Luke 8:43–46, 48; emphasis added)

Christ's virtue was honed and developed to the point that it was palpable. It could literally be felt by him and by others. It was, plain and simple, *power.*

Recently, in a meeting of the Quorums of Seventy, Elder Carlos Asay of the presidency of the Seventy gave a marvelous presentation, which he entitled "Cherish Virtue." Elder Asay said concerning the Savior:

> Not only was he endowed with godly powers inherited from his Heavenly Father, but he also possessed the powers and strength that come from living a sinless life. He was the epitome of morality, manliness, and goodness. Hence, he had the power or virtue to cast out devils, heal the sick, raise people from the grave [and, we might add, contend with sophists] and do other marvelous and miraculous things. And, he could even discern the flow of virtue from his body when people of faith touched his garments as he passed by them.[3]

Elder Asay pointed out "the Greek translation of the word *virtue* is power or strength."[4] Brigham Young defined virtue (or power) as doing the will of our Father in Heaven:

> That is the only virtue I wish to know. I do not recognize any other virtue than to do what the Lord Almighty requires of me from day to day. In this sense virtue embraces all good; it branches out into every avenue of mortal life, passes through the ranks of the sanctified in heaven, and makes its throne in the breast of Deity. When God commands the people, let them obey.[5]

Elder Asay, after quoting Brother Brigham, then made this telling observation:

"Elder Nelson pointed out to me that one of the two words in the Greek New Testament (dunamis), translated as virtue in English, appears *120* times. Of those 120 times, it is translated as *power 77* times."[6]

Virtue is power! Virtue has a power, an influence, that is, quite literally, matchless. The Book of Mormon contains this profound insight:

> And now, as the preaching of the word had a great tendency to lead the people to do that which was just—yea, it had had more powerful effect upon the minds of the people than the sword, or anything else, which had happened unto them—*therefore, Alma thought it was expedient that they should try the virtue of the word of God* (Alma 31:5; emphasis added).

The example and teachings of Christ illustrate that axiom of life. It is manifest in his brief interviews with the two lawyers. It is evident in Amulek's mastery of Zeezrom. And it is evident in the lives of virtuous men and women in the legal profession. The truly great ones are unfailingly people of honesty, integrity, decency and courtesy—and in that virtue they are also men and women of great power and influence.

A few years ago, I was asked to sit on a select committee of the San Diego County Bar Association. The committee was composed of a few practitioners and judges from the state and federal courts, trial and appellate. Our charter was to fashion the Litigation Code of Conduct, a set of guidelines that would go beyond the basic Rules of Professional Conduct and canonize collegiality and fair play fundamentals that ought to characterize the behavior of officers of the court. Here are a few excerpts from the code we drafted (which incidentally has now been adopted by a number of courts):

> Lawyers should honor their commitments.
>
> Lawyers should uphold the integrity of our system of justice.
>
> Lawyers should not compromise their integrity for the sake of a client, case or cause.
>
> Lawyers should conduct themselves in a professional manner.
>
> Lawyers should be guided by a fundamental sense of fair play.
>
> Lawyers should be courteous and respectful to the court. Lawyers must remember that conflicts with opposing counsel are professional and not personal—vigorous advocacy is not inconsistent with professional courtesy.
>
> Lawyers should not be influenced by ill feelings or anger between clients.
>
> Lawyers should discourage and decline to participate in litigation that is without merit or is designed primarily to harass or drain the financial resources of the opposing party.

That last one calls to mind the words of Abraham Lincoln, written in July 1850, and contained in his "Notes for a Law Lecture":

> Discourage litigation. Persuade your neighbors to compromise whenever you can. Point out to them how the nominal winner is often a real loser—in fees, expenses, and waste of time. As a peacemaker the lawyer has a superior opportunity of being a good man. There will still be business enough.
>
> Never stir up litigation. A worse man can scarcely be found than one who does this.[7]

My favorite rule from our Litigation Code of Conduct is the very last one: "Lawyers should conduct themselves so that they may conclude each case with a handshake with the opposing lawyer." To me, that one embodies all of the others and is the quintessence of the virtuous lawyer. Think of the difference in the public perception of lawyers if our entire profession embraced these basic precepts of decency and virtue! You and I cannot change the whole profession, and we probably are not going to make a wholesale difference in public perceptions. But each of us can decide what kind of lawyer he or she is going to be. Again, it was the great Lincoln who put his finger on it:

There is a vague popular belief that lawyers are necessarily dishonest. I say vague, because when we consider to what extent confidence and honors are reposed in and conferred upon lawyers by the people, it appears improbable that their impression of dishonesty is very distinct and vivid. Yet the impression is common, almost universal. Let no young man choosing the law for a calling for a moment yield to the popular belief—resolve to be honest at all events; and if in your judgment you cannot be an honest lawyer, resolve to be honest without being a lawyer. Choose some other occupation, rather than one in the choosing of which you do, in advance, consent to be a knave.[8]

When our bar association committee finished our work, we recommended to the association that an annual award be established honoring the trial lawyer best exemplifying the credo: "His word is his bond"—an award honoring both professional excellence and personal virtue. This recommendation was accepted, and the award was established. One of the first selected to receive the award is a good friend of mine and an outstanding civil trial lawyer. I attended the banquet where this award was presented to him. It was a lovely affair; several wonderful tributes were paid to this good man by his colleagues, both partners and opponents. All were universally complimentary. The moment came for him to receive the award. He came forward, and in receiving it, said in substance:

> When I was a young lawyer, just starting out, I was anxious to know what it takes to be a successful courtroom attorney. So I went to Judge [Louis] Welch [now retired from the San Diego Superior Court] and asked him that question. He answered me with five words that I have tried to live by. He said, "The decided are always gentle."

The decided are always gentle. What a wonderful philosophy! The Savior was "decided." He knew where he stood. He knew The Law. More importantly, he had a firm grip on his moral compass. (As Elder Neal A. Maxwell has said, "His grip upon himself is our grip upon eternity.") His character was perfectly intact. He was a man of *virtue.* As with the Master, so with every person who knows where he stands. Truly, there is a gentility and strength about the "decided." The great ones are consummate professionals—unfailingly gracious and awesome adversaries! The decided *are* always gentle.

But, there is more. We, you and I, have a special charge. As Latter-day Saints, we have a greater charge than merely being true to a moral code. We are the custodians of the Restoration, the gospel of Jesus Christ. We are more than just lawyers; *we are Latter-day Saint lawyers.* By virtue of the priesthood and our Church membership, as well as our professional membership, ours is a dual obligation. We have an affirmative obligation to use our legal training to make a difference. In his presentation to the Seventy, Elder Asay quoted from *The White Company* by A. Conan Doyle. Said he:

In one of my favorite books, there is an interesting conversation between a young man who seemed destined to become a monk and a young lady who had fallen in love with him. The young man, in a moment of despair, exclaimed:

"God help me! I am the weakest of the weak," groaned Alleyne. "I pray that I may have more strength."

"And to what end?" she asked sharply. "If you are, as I understand, to shut yourself forever in your cell within the four walls of the abbey, then of what use would it be were your prayer to be answered?"

"The use of my own salvation."

She turned from him with a pretty shrug and wave. "Is that all?" she said. "Then you are no better than Father Christopher and the rest of them. Your own, your own, even your own! My father is the king's man, and when he rides into the press of the fight he is not thinking ever of the saving of his own poor body; he recks little enough if he leaves it on the field. Why then should you, who are soldiers of the Spirit, be ever moping or hiding in cell or in cave, with minds full of your own concerns, while the world, which you should be mending, is going its way, and neither sees nor hears you? Were ye all as thoughtless of your own souls as the soldier is of his body, ye would be of more avail to the souls of others."

"There is [truth] in what you say, lady," Alleyne answered; "and yet I scarce can see what you would have the clergy and the church to do."

"I would have them live as others and do men's work in the world, preaching by their lives rather than their words. I would have them come forth from their lonely places, mix with [society], feel the pains and the pleasures, the cares and the rewards, the temptings and the stirrings of the common people. Let them toil and [sweat], and labor, and plough the land, and take wives to themselves. . . . I have learned . . . by looking from my own chamber window and marking these poor monks of the priory, their weary life, their profitless round. I have asked myself if the best which can be done with virtue is to shut it within high walls as though it were some savage creature. If the good will lock themselves up, and if the wicked will still wander free, then alas for the world!"[9]

Alas, indeed! We here tonight are bound together by dual bonds. We are students of *The Law*. We are Latter-day Saints. The marriage of these two distinctive characteristics in each of us should raise us to high-minded purpose in our professional pursuits. For us, the law must never be a lever of manipulation or a vehicle for self-promotion through clever sophistry. But neither can we take our law degrees and, like poor monks of the priory, "lock ourselves up," as it were, and content ourselves with using our special training exclusively for our own selfish ends—"profitless rounds." Our lives must be in personal and professional dimension a seamless fabric of virtue and service. *We are soldiers of the Spirit!* May we be men and women of virtue and valor, not locked up in ourselves but using our virtue and our professional skill to contend with evil and benefit others. In our professional and personal pursuits, may it be said of us by the Master of all as he said of the ancient scribe, "Thou art not far from the Kingdom of God."

This fireside address was given at the BYU Law School on March 12, 1995. Reprinted from the Clark Memorandum, Fall 1995, 2–9.

Lance B. Wickman received his J.D. from Stanford University in 1972. He is currently General Counsel for The Church of Jesus Christ of Latter-day Saints and a member of the First Quorum of the Seventy.

Notes

1. 637 A.2d 34 (Del. 1993).
2. *Id.* at 54.
3. Carlos E. Asay, "Cherish Virtue," 2 (unpublished).
4. *Id.*
5. *Journal of Discourses*, 2:123.
6. Asay, 3 (emphasis in original).
7. Abraham Lincoln, "Notes for a Law Lecture," in *The Collected Works of Abraham Lincoln*, ed. Roy P. Basler (New Brunswick, NJ: Rutgers University Press, 1953), 2:81.
8. *Id.* at 82.
9. Asay, 5–6, quoting A. Conan Doyle, "The White Company," in *The Works of A. Conan Doyle* (New York: Black's Readers Service, 1975), 222.

UNTO WHAT WERE YE ORDAINED?

Wherefore, I the Lord ask you this question—
unto what were ye ordained?
(D&C 50:13)

Professionalism

Bruce C. Hafen

The announced subject of my remarks is something about law school activities. The handout you have received tells you most of what you need to know on that subject in an immediate and practical sense. What the handout does not say, however, is that the purpose of everything we do in this law school, formally and informally, is to make of you an attorney and counselor at law, a lawyer, a member of the bar, part of a learned and noble profession. Whether you come to understand the special meaning of those titles is a matter for your own discovery.

You will not learn, merely from reading the cases, that special combination of skill, insight, and selflessness that work together to create a truly professional counselor at law. But I daresay that if you do not make this discovery, really as a by-product of what we do in the classroom, you will leave this campus three years hence not much more than a relatively sophisticated money grubber and may always wonder why all that lofty language about being a professional seems so full of emptiness.

What does it mean, that word "professional"? Oh, it might mean playing football for money instead of for fun. Or maybe it means competently executed, a "professional" job, something done by a "real pro." You may wonder if the word differs in any material sense from "trade" or "occupation." Some will tell you it means joining up with the "establishment," the guardians of the existing power structure.

I must confess that the word did not mean much to me when I graduated from law school, or even when I practiced. But just lately, for some reason, some concepts filled with meaning—intellectual, social, and spiritual—have come to my mind in association with the word "professional."

I think it began when I was giving an oral examination to an Honors Program student who was planning to enter medical school. I wanted to ask some question that would probe the range of his mind in connection with his vocational choice, but I did not know much about medicine. I believe I finally put the question this way: "The law protects as privileged—that is, not admissible as evidence in a court of law—the confidential communications between a lawyer and his client, a priest and a penitent, and a doctor and his patient. What do these three roles, lawyer, priest, and physician, have in common that justifies this important legal privilege?"

His brow furrowed, a few beads of sweat appeared. Finally, he ventured, "Well, they all go to school a long time, and at least the doctors and lawyers make a lot of money." "Not all of them," I replied. That was all he said, but I continued to think about it.

Then I noticed in some reading I was doing for another purpose (though I'm sure I was aware of it before) that these three were the first, and for many years the only, fields of higher education, the oldest, the most traditional of all *learned* endeavors in western civilization. Much later, the scholar—the university teacher and researcher—was added by some to this list. However, in recent years many occupations, from salesmen to hobos, have claimed an interest in the status imputed by that word "profession."

Just lately, I ran across a brilliant little analysis by a sociologist named Goode of whether "the big three" or "big four," depending on a minor distinction or two, will or should ever be displaced as the central professions. You will be relieved to know that Goode doesn't think any of the other fields will make it, but more important than his conclusion is his explanation of what it is that makes the traditional professions unique.

Some of the characteristics that distinguish a true profession are the following. (I will be using Goode as a point of departure, but do not blame him for what follows.)

(1)   Members of the profession have mastered an abstract body of erudite knowledge that can and does solve complex and highly personal problems.

(2)   The knowledge and skills involved are sufficiently difficult that they are not accessible to the ordinary man, by his own efforts or even with help. Thus, only other professionals in the same field can judge the competence of their fellows.

(3)   The practitioner rather than the client determines the client's needs.

(4)   The profession demands real sacrifice from practitioners both ideally and in fact.

(5)   The problems with which the profession deals are so sensitive and so important that incompetence within the profession is highly dangerous, both to the individual client and to society.

(6)   As a result of the kinds of facts just mentioned, the lay society has no alternative but to trust the professional, even to the extent of laying bare to him its most intimate and threatening fears in a complete leap of faith, thereby entrusting the professional not only

with confidential facts but also with enough power and control over their lives that he can truly bless or tragically exploit them.

(7)   If the professional puts his own self-interest or the interests of others who would exploit his position above that of the client, he not only should not, but actually cannot perform the task he is engaged to perform. Thus, the very nature of the needs he is supposed to meet *requires* trust, devotion to selfless ideals, and objectivity. If those elements do not characterize the professional relationship, he is not really a professional at all, and he is not in fact performing the function recognized over the last several centuries as indispensable. The function he *is* performing, on the other hand, is quite dispensable.

In another interesting treatise[1] on the role of the major professions in American history, it is noted that one fundamental question has been the source of society's anxiety about the role of the learned professions. That question is, "Their interest or God's?" In other words, people have traditionally believed that the allegiance of professionals was to God, or in more recent years, at least to higher values and principles than their own self-interest. But because of the absolute necessity, if problems are to be solved, of entrusting professionals with total power to deal as they will with sensitive personal matters as well as with the resources of society, people have always been, to use a modern phrase, a little antsy about what professionals will do with that power. Whenever it appears that a person with power to bless our lives or curse them might really be motivated by something other than our best interests, we panic and instinctively want to take back that grant of trust that has left us so vulnerable. Once the trust is gone, we keep from professionals what they must have to perform their intended task— our secrets.

Let me take you back now, for a moment, to the question I posed to the Honors student. Shortly after that interview, I asked another Honors student informally how he might have answered that question. His response was more provocative. "What do the lawyer, doctor, and priest have in common?" he repeated. "I think they are all *healers*, those to whom we open up our innermost secrets when something seems to threaten our very lives, physically, spiritually, or in some other way that would destroy our liberty or our property, our chance to live. And we go to them to be healed, to be made whole, and to retain control over our lives."

That student and I have since discussed the possibility that in ancient times the healer, the source of justice and life of both body and spirit, was God and those who actually represented him. The complete dependence of men upon God to bring about justice or maintain the quality of life was a true reflection of man's natural relationship to Him. But when God gradually receded from apparent participation in the lives of most men, as they supposed, those roles still had to be filled. The nature of man and his most crucial problems required it. And thus the other healers arose, and men's faith in them continued, sometimes warranted, sometimes unwarranted. My student friend believes it was because of the ancient power of the true priesthood that the lawyers and judges, the scholars, and the other holders of power, political and otherwise, assumed the tradition of wearing robes in an imitation of the priesthood robes that had originally symbolized the authority and power of the great healer. I leave that possibility for your continued reflection.

But my commentary on the learned professions is not complete because in recent times, the citadel of status and power represented by the professionals has been under heavy assault as society increasingly sees that citadel as a symbol of money and self-interest rather than actual service. Let me quote another recent study of professional life in America:

> The professions justify themselves as organized efforts to assure that society's vital needs are met: the need for justice, for health, for knowledge, for spiritual guidance, for communication, for governance, for the creation and maintenance of a physical environment, for the socially responsible provision of goods and services.
>
> But over the past ten years we are forced to recognize that something is amiss. Vital needs are unmet, and the organized professions seem perversely or arrogantly opposed to change. Vast increases in funding for medicine, education, law and welfare have been accompanied by declines in service to those most in need.
>
> The young have learned this lesson almost too well. Five years ago, Paul Goodman taught a course on "Professionalism" at the New School for Social Research in New York City. Goodman brought in professionals to explain "the obstacles that stood in the way of honest practice and their own life experiences in circumventing them." These professionals were rejected by the students, who called them "liars, finks, mystifiers, or deluded." Goodman realized that the students "did not believe in the existence of real professions at all; professions were concepts of repressive society."[2]

Therefore, this study reports, there has been increasing agitation "to replace the unresponsive hierarchies that now exist to serve entrenched interests with new, humane professions that really serve their clients, particularly the poor."[3] The twin goals of those who actively lead such movements are, "first, to transform the institutions of society (rather than merely augment or support their word), and secondly, to liberate, rather than merely to help, the oppressed and the poor."[4] Note that the advocates of this position believe that "the most important insight of recent years [is] that political organization is not enough, that civil society and culture must be reconstructed"[5] in order to achieve the reforms they believe are needed.

I, too, am a professional. I have felt the inner tug and pull of my interests against those of a client. I have seen some of the hypocrisy to which reference has been made. But my view of the solution to such dilemmas differs from those I have mentioned. The reformers may be quite right these days that the healers and others to whom we have entrusted our power have not always proven worthy of that trust, not only in highly visible places but at the grassroots level as well. However, that does not change the facts established by the ages.

The needs of men for the healing power have not vanished. But if the needs go unmet, if the healers do not heal, I say, that is because of the hearts of the healers, not because of the transitory social fabric of our day. Oh, it is true, if the custodians of life and liberty and justice have turned their power to bless into a power to curse, then that social fabric of which we speak may just come all unraveled. But the symbol of the robes remains as the symbol of the healing power. There is no such power in the symbols of destruction and anarchy, and changes in environment simply do not change men's hearts.

The real question for you, for me, and for all who assume the responsibility of the professional tradition is whether we really do prove worthy of the trust. Can our hearts be changed enough that it really is a selfless interest we serve? I happen to believe they *can*. And also by a leap of faith, this law school has committed itself to the proposition that they *will*, not by force or pedantic incantations, but by your private discoveries, borne of righteous desires.

May I close with a homespun little story? I am told that my sister was visiting her grandparents years ago, when she was about three or four. She longed for their attention after supper but found them invariably reading the newspaper for what must have seemed like an awfully long time. Soon she gave up on breaking through the newsprint wall and began trying to read the discarded pages herself, since it seemed to be so interesting. But she couldn't, try as she would. Then she noticed that both her grandfather and her grandmother were wearing glasses. Aha, she thought, that is how they make sense of all those letters and numbers. So she went to Grandma with the sincere request, "Grandma, could I borrow your glasses so I can read the paper, too?"

Ladies and gentlemen, the power is not in the glasses. It is not in the robes or the titles or the credentials. It is in the man or the woman who has somehow attuned his or her life to the sources of the true healing power, thereby himself becoming a *source* of the power, as the branches on a vine. That can be done, and is done, quite independently of religious affiliations or theological frameworks, as demonstrated by the stirring examples of the true professional whose names and writings you will soon begin to encounter in the great books and cases of the law.

May you discover and give yourself to the same secrets that they did, not only because your life will thus become more rich, but more importantly, because you as a counselor at the law may thus make a profound difference in the lives of the people and the society whom you aspire one day to serve.

This address was given to the charter class of the BYU Law School on August 30, 1973 (four days after the first opening of the school). Reprinted from the Clark Memorandum, *Fall 1999, 12–15.*

Bruce C. Hafen received his J.D. from the University of Utah in 1967 and served as Dean of the J. Reuben Clark Law School 1985–89. He is currently a member of the First Quorum of the Seventy.

Notes

1. Daniel H. Calhoun, *Professional Lives in America: Structure and Aspiration, 1750–1850* (Cambridge, MA: Harvard University Press, 1965).

2. Ronald Gross and Paul Osterman, eds., *The New Professionals* (1965), 10, citing "The New Reformation," *New York Times Magazine,* 14 September 1969.

3. *Id.* at 13, quoting Joseph Featherstone, *Schools Where Children Learn* (1971), x.

4. *Id.* at 17.

5. *Id.* at 25–26.

Truth: A Shield to Memory

Marion D. Hanks

The one thing that a lawyer (and any other human being) needs to do is continue to broaden his or her exposure to that which is delightful, good, and uplifting in this world, limiting, to the extent possible, the opposite. Perhaps you are acquainted with the statement, "God will hold us responsible for all the lovely things we did not enjoy in this world."[1] So we need to enjoy lovely things. I learned this from my mother. She was a very special, lovely person.

My father was a lawyer and a judge in Salt Lake City in days long ago. He died early in his 46th year from peritonitis that he suffered while sitting on a murder case. He went home one evening quite sick, but had some relief during the night, so went back and finished the case. When he reached the hospital and they opened him, there was not a thing they could do—no medicine in that day. So my mother had to kneel by his bed and, in response to his plea, ask God to let him escape from pain that he felt he could no longer endure. She did not want to do that. But she finally did, and he was released.

I watched my mother spend a lifetime holding us together, not with entreaty or admonition or tears or great emotion, but through her strong heart, her love for the Church, her faith, and her sense that we could do it. She had the ability to communicate to us that, if we stuck together, worked hard, lived simply, and came to understand that we are not here solely to serve our own purposes—if, in a sense, we followed the life of the Lord— we could make it.

Among the things she gave us was exposure to literature. One of the pieces of literature I read was Tennyson's *Idylls of the King*. Do you remember the story of Gareth and Lynnette? Gareth was the last son of a family of knights and a lesser king and queen. His father had served as a knight and now was just a memory of a man, lying inert by the fireside, unable to function because of his wounds and illness and age. Some of his brothers were knights at Arthur's table and Gareth wanted to be a knight. He had a special agenda of his own. His mother tried to talk Gareth out of becoming a knight. She argued, in summary: Your father has all these estates. You are a prince. Why not just stay home and enjoy the "perks" of your fortunate birth and all this affluence? This was Gareth's response:

> Mother,
>
> How can ye keep me tether'd to you . . . !
>
> Man am I grown, a man's work must I do.
>
> Follow the deer? follow the Christ, the King,
>
> Live pure, speak true, right wrong, follow the King—
>
> Else, wherefore born?[2]

As the adventure continued, Gareth prepared himself for that kind of a quest—a lifelong quest.

As we think of the profession you are preparing to enter, we are thinking about an honorable and elemental need in human society. We are thinking about a broad view of life, a philosophy of life, and a set of values that can carry us into conflicts with a knowledge of who we are and what we believe, values that will permit us to respond to the adversities of life with clarity—not easily, but with clarity. When we think of being people who can be described as living the pure life, of speaking the truth, and righting wrongs, we are describing the expectation that we hold, and society may hold, for those who practice or represent areas of the law.

Living Pure

I was in a Boy Scout meeting years ago in New York City when Thomas Watson, then chief executive officer and major owner of International Business Machines, finished his second term as president of the Boy Scouts of America. Thomas Watson later was ambassador to Russia; during World War II he was a decorated flyer; he had more millions than most of us have hundreds. He was born to it, and he had been married for 38 years to the same beautiful wife, who sat by him at that meeting. He was one who was quietly committed to abstention from those enticements of society that often go with his station. Thomas Watson was a clean, decent, honorable, wonderful man, and I will not forget what his 8- or 10-minute valedictory was based on that night.

He said there were two nights in his life more important than any others. He mentioned only one. At age 12 he went to his first Scout meeting to learn how to become a Tenderfoot. He went, he said, in fear and trembling. He was the heir of great fortunes even then. He did not mention any of that, but just said, "I went to my first Scout meeting and there a Scoutmaster spoke to us about the pure life. It was one of the two most important nights of my life." He did not speak longer or extenuate that idea—he just said it. And everybody there got the message. This is the kind of life that, while his money would buy him most things, had been the stable, strong, steady course for him. I saluted in my heart such a man.

In Doctrine and Covenants 100:16 we read that God will raise up for himself a pure people and, again, that we who represent him in any way should purify ourselves, purify our hearts, as we go into the fray. It is my honest conviction that unless we are willing to live the pure life, speak truth, and right wrongs—or undertake to do so—we are missing the foundation of what can be and is meant to be a wonderful and beautiful life.

There is a statement by Mr. Churchill that I want to share with you. Let me read what he wrote about the way we live. It is, as Socrates said, not just any kind of an argument in which we engage—it is the argument of how a person shall live. And this is what Winston Churchill wrote and spoke in the House of Commons in 1940:

> History with its flickering lamp stumbles along the trail of the past, trying to reconstruct its scenes, to revive its echoes, and kindle with pale gleams the passion of former days. What is the worth of all this? The only guide to man is his conscience; the only shield to his memory is the rectitude and sincerity of his actions. It is very imprudent to walk through life without this shield, because we are so often mocked by the failure of our hopes and the upsetting of our calculations; but with this shield, however the fates may play, we march always in the ranks of honor.[3]

I have on my office wall two framed pictures. One is of Sir Thomas More, the other of Abraham Lincoln—both great lawyers. And of Thomas More I have read considerably his quotations, his life, his response to Henry VIII's invitation to lose either his honor or his head. It was an easy decision for him—though not easy to carry out—for there was no other answer. He would surrender his life, his head to the guillotine, but never his honor. In the play *A Man for All Seasons,* which portrays the life of Sir Thomas More, there is this interesting little exchange:

Sir Thomas speaks of needing respect for his own soul, and Cromwell, furious, replies,

> A miserable thing, whatever you call it, that lives like a bat in a Sunday School! A shrill incessant pedagogue about all its own salvation—but nothing to say of your place in the State! Under the King! In a great native country!

Conscience compared to that? More answers,

> Is it my place to say "good" to the State's sickness? Can I help my King by giving him lies when he asks for truth? Will you help England by populating her with liars?[4]

And to the common man, the commentator says,

> It isn't difficult to keep alive, friends—just don't make trouble—or if you must make trouble, make the sort of trouble that's expected.[5]

There is before anyone who is in the practice of the law the absolute certainty of many difficult questions and the absolute assurance that, if we are committed clearly and early to the idea that there are some things that are wrong and some things that are right, we will make those decisions with correctness and integrity and the shield of memory and conscience that will permit us to live.

Now, at the cost of reading a little, I would like to share with you the testimony of Charles Malik. You know him as a great man and an internationally important statesman, who once served as general secretary of the United Nations. Pay as close attention as you can, because his words are meaningful and significant:

> There is truth, and there is falsehood. There is good, and there is evil. There is happiness, and there is misery. There is expansiveness, and there is self-withdrawal. There is freedom, and there is slavery.

> There is that which ennobles, and there is that which demeans. There is that which conduces to strength and health, and there is that which conspires to weakness and disease. There is a climate of confidence and trust and peace, and there is when the spirit of contradiction and conflict hits you in the face. There is that which puts you in harmony with yourself, with others, with the universe, with God, and there is that which alienates you from yourself, from the world, and from God. There is that which makes you feel certain and confident, and there is that which insinuates doubt and uncertainty in your soul. There is that which makes you decisive, and there is that which causes you to waver and equivocate. There is that which opens every pore of your existence to the whispers of being, and there is that which causes you to shut up like a clam. There is when you see God on the face of every man you come across, and there is when you pass men by without even noticing them.

> There is when you want to dance and sing, and there is when you have no desire to move or look at anything. There is when you love children and old women and flowers and the drifting clouds and the raging waves, and even the rocks and stones; and there is when you hate everybody and everything—above all, yourself. There is real ecstatic mastery over every impulse in your being, and there is awful flabbiness whereby everything sweeps you away with it. There is life and fullness of being, and there is tending subtly, gradually toward nothingness and death.

> These things are different and separate and totally distinguishable from one another. Truth is not the same as falsehood, happiness is not the same as misery. We will not be far wrong if we say the first elements of these 17 pairs all come from the living God, and the second elements all from the devil.

> The greatest error in modern times is the confusion between these orders of being. Nothing is anything firm in itself—this is the great heresy of the modern

world. But, there is no power on earth or in heaven that can make falsehood truth, evil good, misery happiness, slavery freedom.

Then he talks about philosophers in the great centers who make it all a matter of definition. He finishes:

> How do we become true and good, happy and genuine, joyful and free? Never by magic, never by chance, never by sitting and waiting, but only by getting in touch with good, true, happy, genuine human beings, only by seeking the company of the strong and the free, only by catching spontaneity and freedom from those who are themselves spontaneous and free.

And then Malik makes a promise about "the sharpness of perception" that will help us

> differentiate unerringly between the true and the phony, between the beautiful and the hideous, the noble and the mean. You will also develop the ability to blush, the ability to cry and shed tears, the ability to repent, the ability to fall on your knees and pray, the ability to become a real moral human person.

He encourages the reading of the gospels and the Psalms regularly every day, meeting the deepest and purest saints, faithfully serving your church, and practicing the great art of mental and moral discipline. He says,

> I guarantee you two things: first, that you will experience in your own life and being a taste of what is beautiful and strong and certain and free; and second, you will develop such a sharpness of vision as to distinguish the true from the false whenever you come across them. And both your being and your vision will grant you some knowledge of God.[6]

Speaking Truth

Of speaking the truth, Sir Thomas More and Charles Malik are wonderful examples. There are others. A 13-year-old boy, after a nervous interlocutor approved his spelling of a word in the national finals, returned to his seat and thought it over. Then he went back, tapped the man on the shoulder, and said, "I think I spelled that word wrong, sir." He had, and he lost. Not long ago, the United States golfer of the year marked his score card wrong and was not caught in the act—he did it totally inadvertently. But he thought it over, considered it carefully, and withdrew from a tournament he was leading, and, when somebody tried to congratulate him, just said, "Why you may as well congratulate me for not stealing somebody's wallet or their automobile. It was a mistake, it was an error, and there are rules against it. There is no other answer than to acknowledge that I inadvertently made that mistake and pay the penalty."

An outstanding all-American basketball player at BYU once came to talk to me about going on a mission. He said he would rather not go now, but there were those who told him that if he didn't go now, he would never go. He was halfway in his college career. I asked, "What do you really want to do?"

He answered, "I want to finish, and then go on a mission."

I said, "You know the risks—people have been honorable in trying to help you identify them. You will find a lovely girl—maybe you already have—and you will want to marry. You will probably have a contract to play in the NBA. You will have scholarships through the NCAA. You will have a lot tougher decision to make, so you had better think it over. As far as I am concerned, I would not tell you what to do. You decide. You pray enough and think enough and look ahead enough and, if you think you can make it and must have a mission, then you will make it. Other things will have to wait."

I met him next when he was assistant to the president of a mission in New Zealand, after he had become all-American, received his $1,000 NCAA scholarship, turned down a contract in the NBA, and gone on a mission. I have never heard a missionary voluntarily selected from his peers and spoken of as that young man was, without my ever asking anybody, "What do you think of him?"

But I tell you this not for any of that. He was running an old 16MM movie machine. While he was showing the film, it somehow got caught and tore. The man who was conducting the meeting said something like, "We will just wait for you. Just go ahead, Elder. Those machines have a habit of doing that."

He said, "Maybe they do, President, but, in fact, this was my mistake. I fed this wrong." It was that simple. He didn't have to say that for us; apparently he had to say that for himself. I could give you a hundred other incidents picked up around the earth of people who somehow speak the truth.

A boy was playing in the finals of a Church volleyball tournament in the Deseret Gym in Salt Lake. His dad was in a meeting at the university stake. He kept looking at his watch. I finally said to him, a little bit bemused, "President, where would you rather be than here?" Not knowing that he had been observed in his repeated references to his watch, he said, "Why, no place, Brother Hanks. I'm happy to be here." I said, "C'mon. Something is going to happen in about 10 minutes. We're going to be starting a meeting here. Where would you rather be?" He resisted a little and then said, "Well, to be honest, my two sons are playing in a volleyball championship at the Deseret Gym at seven and I'm kind of concerned." I said, "Your sons are playing in a championship game and you're here? What are you doing here?" He said, "You called the meeting." I said, "For you, I 'uncall' the meeting. Go!" He said, "You mean it?" I said, "Look, we've got a lot of meetings tomorrow if you like meetings. Go, and be with your sons."

He went. He spoke the next morning as a counselor in the stake presidency. He said, "We won last night." He told the little story of our having sent him on his way—he wanted that heard. I believe with all my heart that there was one place more important than the other right then for him. Well, the story he told was of having won the previous night, but he said,

> That really isn't what's important. Last year my same two sons in the finals of the same tournament lost, and we'd been hoping that maybe what happened then would turn out happily in every way for the 15-year-old, who was responsible for his team losing.

> The story in a word: two games each, the score 14–13, our serve. Our side served; they returned it. There were great digs and hard smashes at what looked like hills dug out of the pavement, until finally a big kid on this side jumped way over the net and hit that ball a hundred miles an hour right through the other team and out of bounds. The referee said, "Game. Match. Championship," and all broke loose. Everybody in the stands was yelling and screaming, until the referee climbed down from the net, walked toward our side, and stopped in front of my 15-year-old son. When the sense of what was happening swept that place, it was as quiet as a tomb. The referee said incredulously to my son, "What did you say?" And he said, "Sir, the ball touched me."

> That meant before out of bounds; that meant no point, no game, no match, no championship. The referee climbed back up the ladder, tossed over the towel. We served; they served, made three points, and won it 16–14. Then it happened. I stood with his mother, who had been there watching this event. My son, 15 years old, had just cost his team the championship, when nobody knew that ball had touched him on its way out—only he knew. He stood there with his shoulders squared, his head hanging a little.

> The normal exultation of the winners was muted. The first man to my boy was his brother, a year older, who put his arms around him; then came the four other kids on our team, then those who were on the bench at the moment, and then the six guys playing on the other side of the net and their substitutes and coaches—all surrounding my two sons, with tears and quiet respect.

> I am not exulting because of a won or lost ball game. I had the honor to be the father of a son who at age 15 was that kind of a man.

And when I stood up I said, "President, if I were ever again a mission president, I'd sure love to see that boy coming." If I were ill and needed help and he had become a doctor, I'd know to whom I'd go with confidence. Or if he were to be a lawyer or a farmer or an insurance salesman—this boy would have it already figured out. Speak true.

Righting Wrong

Now let me just finish by noting that third remarkable element in Gareth's projection for his future: "Follow the king." To him this meant not simply living a pure life and speaking the truth, but something else: righting wrongs. And in righting that which is wrong there is frequently a certain amount of trepidation. Let me give you one little, simple example of what is sometimes wrong.

Maxine and I heard and later read the story of a man named Mike Gold. He was head of the Communist Party in the United States of America. Mike Gold was a Jew brought up in a ghetto, not permitted to leave the ghetto because of the circumstances of the world in which he lived. But there came a day when he had to go to school. His people were orthodox Jews and lived a rigorous Jewish life.

When Mike went to school, his parents had their hearts in their throats, I suppose—and justifiably, because one day he came back battered and beaten, his clothes torn, his little face bloodied and cut. His mother took him in her arms and rocked him, and after awhile, when she had cleansed his wounds and comforted him, said, "Mikey, what happened to you?"

He said, "I don't know."

She said, "Well, who did this to you?"

He said, "Some boys."

She said, "Why?"

He said, "I don't know." They rocked awhile and then he looked in her face and said, "Mamma, what's a kike?" She explained that was a not-too-pleasant name for Jewish people. They rocked some more and then he looked up into her face and said, "Mamma, who is Jesus Christ?"

And she said, "Christians believe in him as their savior. Why, Mikey?"

He said, "They all chased me and threw rocks at me and when they caught me all these big boys hit me and knocked me down and kicked me, called me a kike, and said that I had killed Jesus Christ and so I was getting what I deserved. Who is Jesus Christ?" Mike Gold used that little incident to justify the choices he made in the whole course of a lifetime. He didn't like America, and he certainly didn't like Christians, and he abominated the name *kike* and the name *Jesus Christ*. Right wrongs.

I had the honor to listen to a radio broadcast between a man named Thomas Dooley and an older physician. Dooley, sometimes called "the physician of the jungle," was in the hills of Laos, where he had gone to help those poor beleaguered people. Now, after the war, he was over there spending his full time, not in the costly, pretentious, and rewarding ward rooms of the East where he had been brought up, but in the hills of Laos. This interview was to honor his birthday. I think he was no older than 31. He had come back to try to raise funds to help the people by establishing clinics. This is how the interview went:

"Dr Dooley, you are in some serious health trouble yourself. Yet somehow you seem able to overcome that, put it in perspective, and spend your time helping these poor people who are without medical resources. How can you do that? You are living, it is reported, on borrowed time." It was true. He had leukemia.

Dooley's answer was, "You're right sir, I am living on borrowed time. So are you. And so is every other human being. What matters is not how much time, not what I have left, but whether the days, the months, and the years the Almighty has allotted unto me are used in terms of human good. This," he said, "I will do so long as I can continue to borrow time." The phrase that sticks in my heart is his phrase "in terms of human good." That's how he would use his talents, his training, his strength, and, while it lasted, his time. He died, in fact, before his next birthday.

Now I'd like to bear testimony to you that I connect in my own lifetime and in my own discipline with the qualities of which Gareth spoke because the scriptures are full of them—to live pure, to speak true, and to right wrongs. In the practice of law we get plenty of opportunities to make decisions that relate to all of these things.

Whatever else we are, we are sons and daughters of God. We are children with a noble and wonderful heritage. We have life in a land which, with all its problems, is a good and marvelous place, but which can be incalculably better if those who create, apply, administer, and ultimately make judgment on its laws are the kind of people who have that shield to memory that comes only with the recollection that their choices have been right and sincere. I pray for you as earnestly as I know how, with not a lot of fantastic or foolish notions about what you face now and in the future, but with every confidence that there will be among you many who will not only serve the law but shape the law in accordance with your own concepts of integrity and decency and good conscience. May you love and serve with integrity the great, great field of human endeavor called the law, I pray, in the name of Jesus Christ. Amen.

This fireside address was given at the BYU Law School on November 19, 1989. Reprinted from the Clark Memorandum, *Fall 1990, 26–29.*

Marion D. Hanks received his LL.B. from the University of Utah in 1948. He served as a General Authority 1953–92 and was named an emeritus General Authority in 1992.

Notes

1. Ancient Jewish proverb quoted by Rabbi Harold Kushner.

2. Alfred, Lord Tennyson, *The Poetical Works of Alfred Lord Tennyson* (New York: Thomas Y. Crowell, 1851), 210.

3. Robert Rhodes James, ed., *Churchill Speaks: Winston S. Churchill in Peace and War: Collected Speeches, 1897–1963* (New York: Chelsea House, 1980), 734.

4. Robert Bolt, *A Man for All Seasons* (New York: Random House, 1960), 89.

5. *Id.* at 95.

6. Charles Malik, "To Know the True from the False," *Reader's Digest*, August 1972, 84–85 (taken from an address at Oakbrook, Illinois, 1971).

Professional Service as a
Christian Ministry

Carl S. Hawkins

We do not enjoy reminders that we are indebted to others, but sometimes reminders help to sharpen our perspective and increase our resolve. That is why I feel it is appropriate to remind you at the beginning of your legal education that you are indebted to the tithe payers of the Church for more than two-thirds of the cost of your legal education. Your own tuition (often paid in part by others) covers less than one-third of the operating costs of the Law School and makes no contribution to the establishment of this building, our library, and other capital resources.

I offer this reminder to make you think about why the Church has chosen to confer such generous benefits upon you. Surely it is not because you have personally inherited or earned some superior right or claim upon the trust funds of the Kingdom. Neither is it a good enough reason to suppose that the Church wants only to increase your earning capacity so that you can pay more tithing. Sadly enough, that is about as far as some students seem to get in their thinking about the justification of their educational subsidy. In fact, the future tithing on your increased earning capacity might be enough to repay the Church for its investment in your education. But if we are going to reduce this to bare economics, it would be cheaper for the Church, instead of establishing this Law School, to give you tuition grants to attend secular law schools, and it would still get the increased tithing returns on your larger earning capacity as a lawyer.

The Church's reason for subsidizing your preparation for a law career must be based upon some hope that you will get from this school something more than passage into an affluent profession. It must be based upon a hope that you will acquire here not only the necessary legal knowledge and professional skills, but also a commitment to using them not selfishly, but in the service of others. In that belief, I invite you to begin thinking about your law career as an opportunity for a Christian ministry through professional service. This high perspective will not be easy for you to acquire or to maintain. There will be many obstacles.

First, the attempt to idealize your profession as a Christian ministry may appear to conflict with theological disapproval of "paid ministries." Pretensions to a ministry in a paid profession may even suggest the evils of "priestcraft," condemned so often in the Book of Mormon. But priestcraft is the claim to exclusive custody of saving truths and ordinances of the gospel and the pretense of power to dispense them for personal gain. If we make no pretense of selling salvation, there is no priestcraft in accepting pay for professional services anymore than accepting pay for any honest hard work. And if we perform the service with our whole soul, skillfully, and as a witness of our love for God, it can become a kind of ministry to those we serve.

Another difficulty with viewing professional service as a Christian ministry is the irony that it may be easier for active Mormons to segment their lives and to satisfy their religious aspirations in formal church callings. You may feel content to say, "My mission was two years ago in Germany," or "My ministry is my calling as a Relief Society teacher." This may satisfy your need to feel that you are a religious person without having to worry about how your religion applies in the rest of your life. If so, you are deluding yourself.

When the Lord commands that we love him with all of our heart, might, mind and strength, he is not concerned so much with the intensity of our feelings as with the breadth and completeness of our commitment. For the committed Christian, every part of his or her being must become a living witness of love for Christ. Your life must become your ministry. Your roles as husband or wife, parent, friend, church worker, student, and lawyer must all become missions within that ministry, and your whole person, including your religious values, must become engaged in every part of that ministry.

Some of us who have taught at other law schools have observed that Christian law students from other churches who do not have our opportunities to serve in formal church callings unless they become professional ministers seem to feel more than we do the need to pour their religious fervor into their professional calling and to make that their witness for Christ. We should feel the same need no less, even though we have other callings from time to time to serve in other ways.

Another obstacle to viewing law school as preparation for a service ministry will be the daily grind of law school itself. Many of you will have to work harder than you ever have before. There will be stress and anxiety caused by having to learn new ways of thinking, aggravated by a lack of adequate feedback on how you are doing. Your sense of security and, for some of you, even your sense of worth may be threatened temporarily as you seem to be competing in faster company than ever before. And very little that goes on from day to day in the classroom will remind you of the higher aspirations of a Christian ministry. Most of your learning efforts will be spent on acquiring secular knowledge of the law and developing the lawyer's tough-minded skills of analysis and advocacy.

You will have to keep in mind that such knowledge and skill are indispensable preparation for an effective life of professional service, even if they are not enough to fulfill your higher aspirations. Your preparation at this Law School will be no less rigorous than at other good law schools. That sometimes disappoints some of our students, who seem to expect that, because this is a church-sponsored school, and because they are religious persons, their professional development should come easier by some special dispensation without having to work for it, or else they suppose that their religious beliefs will somehow make them superior lawyers without having to acquire all of the tedious knowledge and hard skills that are required of less pious lawyers. That is, of course, a perversion of our religious beliefs.

The Lord has never promised to give us knowledge or skill without effort and pain, and the Ninth Section of the Doctrine and Covenants states explicitly that in seeking to understand a matter, we must first work it out for ourselves. This is not to suggest that spiritual insights have no place in your legal education, but only to remind you that your secular knowledge of the law must be acquired by the same grinding process that applies to everyone else, and only after that may you expect to receive occasional spiritual insights into the higher significance of what you have learned.

Many of you will have difficulty viewing law as a Christian ministry because you harbor ambiguous feelings about the moral character of lawyers. From our larger culture, you have absorbed mixed impressions or images of lawyers as persons of power and prestige and as defenders of sacred rights, on the one hand, and as aggressive manipulators, hired guns, defenders of the guilty, protectors of wealth and special privilege, and moral equivocators, on the other hand. Certainly you cannot aspire to law as a Christian ministry until you are at least tentatively reconciled to the possibility that a lawyer can be professionally effective and still be a morally good person. That process of reconciliation should begin now, with the first day of law school, even if it cannot be completed here.

You can start with the reassurance that the General Authorities of the Church believe that it is possible to be both an effective lawyer and a devout Christian. That is why they have given you J. Reuben Clark, Jr., as a model. Unfortunately, most of your generation know of President Clark only dimly as a great Church leader, counselor to Presidents Heber J. Grant, George Albert Smith, and David O. McKay. But for 27 years before he became a Church official, J. Reuben Clark was a successful, powerful, and prestigious lawyer in government service, in private practice, and in the service of great corporations in Washington, D.C. and on Wall Street. Surely the message implied by establishing this Law School in his honor is not that a lawyer can become a good Christian only by abandoning the legal profession for full-time church service. The message must be that J. Reuben Clark was a good Christian while he was an effective lawyer in the professional service of his country and his private clients. I urge you to begin studying that model by reading Frank Fox's superb biography, *J. Reuben Clark: The Public Years.*

There are two paths you can travel in seeking to accommodate your professional calling and your religious beliefs. One is the path of delusion and segmentation; the other is the path of reconciliation and integration. The path of reconciliation is the harder way, but it is the truthful way. The easy way is the delusion that you can separate your Christian aspirations from that part of yourself that is engaged in earning a living. It is easier because you can then let the secular world define your professional role for you, and you can limit your professional aspirations by the ethics of role. The study of professional ethics for lawyers is a serious and worthwhile part of your legal education. Professional ethics will lift your standards above the daily mores of commerce and politics, but they cannot be substituted for your Christian aspirations if you want to be at a peace with yourself.

That is why I invite you to begin now upon the higher path of reconciliation, to prepare for the legal profession as a Christian ministry. It will be a lifetime process and a highly personal one, for which you must accept individual responsibility. It has to happen within you. We cannot inject it into you. We may be able to help you a little. We are concerned that we may not have tried to help enough. We are resolved to try harder. For those who wish to try it, the Professional Seminar, offered for the first time this year, will provide an intimate forum for explicit discussion of these very concerns.

For those of you who are not Mormons, I hope these remarks about religion and profession will not cause you to feel any less welcome. We recognize that your ideals and aspirations can be just as high as ours. I hope you will interpret my remarks as urging you to make your professional career a ministry in the service of your highest ideals and aspirations. And please feel free to share your beliefs with us. You will make our education richer by doing that, which is part of why we have invited you here.

And for all of you, I hope this somber message has not dampened your enthusiasm for the adventure which you are about to begin. Learning to become lawyers can be exciting and stimulating. It can even be fun. So let's get on with it.

This address was given to the entering class at the BYU Law School on August 22, 1981. Reprinted from the Clark Memorandum, *Fall 1999, 8–11.*

Carl S. Hawkins received his J.D. from Northwestern University School of Law in 1951, clerked for Chief Justice Fred Vinson of the U.S. Supreme Court 1953–53, and served as Dean of the J. Reuben Clark Law School 1981–85. He was named an emeritus professor in 1991. His book, The Founding of the J. Reuben Clark Law School, *was published in 1999.*

Lawyer as Policy Maker

Rex E. Lee

President Romney, President Oaks, President Wilkins, Dean Hawkins, Judge Wallace, members of the faculty, members of the charter class, ladies and gentlemen: I think you know how honored Janet and I are that you asked us to be with you on this occasion. There are few tributes that could please us as much.

Each class that graduates from this Law School will have a place all its own and will make its own distinctive mark. Clearly, there will never be another class like this one—a fact, I might add, that is a source of some solace and comfort to the members of the faculty. Never again will the quantity or the intensity of effort in recruiting and admitting each individual class member be repeated. Nor, for that matter, will it ever need to be, thanks largely to you and the fact that three years ago you were willing to come and share with us the joys and, at that time, the risks, of a new law school.

[A] . . . second thought that I want to leave with you concerns the role of the lawyer as a policy maker. There is no other profession whose members find themselves, as a necessary consequence of the work that they do, so continually involved in important policy-making functions. I believe that for most lawyers this is a plus.

It is equally clear that there are some problems—some of them personal in nature, but more of them institutional. I have no doubt that one of the reasons for the increased interest in law school over the last seven years is that so many law students perceive, and perceive correctly, that law training provides an access to what Dean Hawkins has termed "the levers of power."

It is, I believe, one of life's ironies that those who enter the profession for this reason not only miss the broader satisfactions that the practice of law has to offer but also fail to achieve their immediate objective, the exercise

167

of influence, as fully as those who see the broader service aspects of the lawyer's calling and for whom the exercise of influence is an unsolicited by-product. It is, if you will, another manifestation of the biblical injunction that he who would save his life must lose it.

For some, the role of the lawyer in policy formulation and implementation is direct and predominant. In my view, it is more than coincidence that a disproportionately high percentage of legislators and government administrators come from the members of our profession. I am convinced that the tools that are acquired at a first-rate law school, such as the one that you have attended, qualify the graduate for a direct role in policy formulation and implementation.

But the function of our profession in policy matters is more subtle and of much wider scope than the passage, interpretation, and enforcement of laws. The practicing lawyer who operates in the most traditional lawyering ways—trying lawsuits, drafting contracts, counseling clients—is also a policy maker. Note the choice of verb in the preceding sentence. It is not that he has the opportunity to be a policy maker; he *is* a policy maker. The question is not whether but how well and how consciously. It is on the premise that there is a probable relationship between the consciousness of one's participation in the lawyer policy-making function and the quality of that participation that I have selected this as one of my four points.

The inevitability of the lawyer as a policy maker is rooted in the unique characteristic of our common law system: the pivotal role of the judge. Under our system, the resolution of disputes among private parties not only results in determining who owes whom how much; it is also an important source of law. Unlike his civilian counterpart, the common law judge is not confined to interpreting what some legislative body probably meant. In addition, he has the power and the duty in appropriate cases to make law where there is no law and to fill in the interstices of legislative judgment where they exist.

This, I submit, is the essence of policy making. And it is not restricted to judges. A foundational premise of our adversary system is that we best approach the determination of truth when the facts and the law supporting each opposing position are marshaled and presented by skilled advocates and then leave the ultimate judgment to a neutral arbiter, whether judge or jury. Necessarily, therefore, the trial lawyer, as an officer of the court, plays an integral role in the common law judge's policy-making function.

Similarly, the substance of commercial document drafting and client counseling is determined in large part by the lawyer's anticipation of how the courts probably would decide particular issues if called upon to decide them. This necessarily involves the same basic kind of policy formulation, even though on an anticipatory level, that the courts themselves pursue. This anticipatory policy-making process, when undertaken by skilled craftsmen, in turn has an effect on the decisions of the person whose judgment is anticipated, namely the judge.

So I hope that you will enter the profession conscious of your role as a policy maker. Your entrances come at a time when the profession faces policy issues of great magnitude.

For example, unless some rather bold steps are taken during the course of your professional lifetime, the ability of the American courts to perform their tasks will be seriously jeopardized. An article published last year in the *Stanford Law Review* by Professor John Barton pointed out that if federal appellate cases continue to grow at the same rate as they have grown for the past ten years, then by the year 2010 the United States Circuit Courts of Appeal will be required to decide over 1,000,000 cases each year, which will require 5,000 appellate judges to make the decisions and 1,000 new volumes of the Federal Reporter to report them.

When you consider that for every case that reaches Judge Wallace's level in our system there are ten cases that are filed in the federal district courts, and when you consider further that in one state, California, there are four times as many lawsuits filed each year as in the entire federal system, you begin to develop a feel for the real crisis that currently faces the courts, the place where you will work. Proposals have been advanced, including (1) the identification of certain matters such as probate and divorce that traditionally have been handled by the courts but that might better be solved by simpler and more effective alternative means; (2) exercising some control over the ever-increasing tendency of Congress and state legislatures to impose new burdens on the judiciary without any corresponding increases in judicial resources; and (3) doing away with jury trial in civil cases.

These and other proposals are not without serious costs. Participation in the resolution of these kinds of complex, societal-impacting issues, unlike the policy roles necessarily involved in the lawyer's day-to-day work, is largely optional. It is an option that I hope most of you will take.

Now, as long as we are talking of policy, I would particularly invite your attention to a bill that is now in the hatching stage among some of the most thoughtful people in the Department of Justice. This bill has not yet come to the attention of the attorney general, and, in fact, if it did, there would probably be a few replacements. But it promises to be one of the most far-reaching pieces of legislation in the history of our republic. Title I, Section 1, would initiate the process for partial repeal of that provision of Article I of the Constitution that no title of nobility can be granted by the United States. Section 2 of Title I then provides that any person elected to any House of Congress shall have the option of designating himself to any title of nobility of his own choosing, whether duke, earl, marquis, or whatever, together with all the traditional perquisites of nobility, an annual stipend of $100,000 for life, and the right once each year to select a representative of the Executive Branch to be subjected to the rack, screw, or any other appropriate torture device. The only quid pro quo is the modest undertaking never to exercise any of the powers conferred by Article I of the Constitution.

Title II provides for the appointment of a special president, chosen from the ranks of living presidents or, if there is none, at random from the Manhattan phone book. The function of the special president will be to review the acts of all ex-presidents and conclude without exception that they were within the public interest.

Title III provides for judicial reform. It would require that all judges' opinions prior to publication be submitted to a board consisting of college freshmen logic students and eighth-grade grammarians.

Having perfected only three titles thus far, the architects of this bill are now working on Title IV, which deals with government bureaucrats and still needs some work. Section 1 provides for a resident reasonable man in each department and agency of government. To any first-year law student, the need for such a position is obvious. But since he will function much like an oil filter, he will have to be replaced every six months, and there is a serious problem what to do with him in his clogged-up condition. The most promising suggestions to date have been that he could teach tax or that he could write evidence exams. Section 2 of Title IV requires an embroidered notice to be hung in the office of every government administrator, in letters at least four inches high, stating, "If stupidity is an adequate explanation for what has happened, don't look for any other."

If this bill becomes law, it will obviously solve most of the policy problems facing our nation. If it does not, then you will continue to fill the lawyer's role as policy makers. . . .

I [also] want to discuss the unusual expectations that lawyers and non-lawyers hold concerning the standards of professional conduct to be observed by the members of this class. This involves your relationships with your clients, with your fellow lawyers, and with the community at large.

Of those three groups, the one with which you should be most concerned is your fellow lawyers, because it is they who will be most influential in establishing your reputation for high ethical standards. Whatever the community in which you practice, you will shortly come to an understanding that there are certain members of the bar within that community whose oral assurance is all that you will ever need as a basis for confident reliance. There is no advantage that any lawyer enjoys that compares with that kind of reputation among his brethren at the bar.

In some respects, I think that people are trying too hard to find differences between you and the graduates of other law schools. But with regard to standards of professional conduct, I have no objection to the unusually high expectations of you that I perceive among the members of the profession that you are about to enter. I am convinced that these expectations exist. You should not consider their existence threatening but only supportive of the standards of professional conduct that you should be willing to demonstrate.

Remember that like any great edifice, a lawyer's reputation cannot be quickly built, but it can be quickly destroyed. Remember also that there are enormous opportunities and temptations to trade long-range benefits, including your reputation, for short-term advantages. It is the same kind of trade-off that Jacob proposed to Esau some three millennia past. It was not a good deal then, and it hasn't improved with age.

So I'm hopeful that in your dealings with your fellow lawyers you will always lean a little on the careful side. When those opportunities come, as they surely will, to harvest an advantage in a particular case at the cost of your long-range relationship with your fellow lawyers: Don't do it.

I come now to my final point. In a sense, it is the most important of all in achieving a proper fit of your professional activities within your broader whole existence and interests. It is a subject that we first discussed on that memorable day three years ago when we first met as a class in the Jesse Knight Building. It is a subject that has warranted and has received continual attention, discussion, and dialogue since that time, involving not only you but also your spouses.

The graduation of this class coincides with the centennial of our university and the bicentennial of our nation. I recently finished a novel by James Michener bearing the title *Centennial*. It is a fictional history of a Colorado community and surrounding areas since the beginning of time. A consistent theme that emerges from the events that are the subject of that novel is that at any given time in the development of our country, those who were fortunate enough to be present and participating labored under an assumption that the prevailing way of life and the circumstances that made it possible would last forever.

During the early 19th century, the rivers and streams of the Rocky Mountains abounded with beaver. There were literally millions of them. The trappers and traders who were the only white inhabitants of the area could not conceive of such a vast wilderness ever being useful for anything but a harvest ground for pelts.

A little farther east, and a little later in time, the historic treaty of Fort Laramie in 1851 assumed that the Great Plains would always be inhabited by buffalo. Since the land had no possible utility for any other purpose, the treaty confidently assured that the Great Plains would belong to the Indians for as long as the water flowed and as long as the grass still grew.

The pattern repeated itself as the buffalo gave way to the cattlemen, who in turn saw their great open-range empire broken up by the sod-busting farmer, armed with that curious new invention, barbed wire.

The continuing recurrence of the familiar pattern led me to contemplate how rewarding it would have been to have personally witnessed, for example, the annual gathering of the great northern and southern buffalo herds—sixty million of them—or to have been present at one of the raucous trader/trapper rendezvous during the early 1800s. Inevitably those who were witnesses to such events would have seen them in a different perspective if they had realized that they were part of our American heritage that would one day reach a stopping point and never be repeated.

But the main function of history is to give some guidance to the present and future, not just to satisfy curiosities about the past. In a very real sense, every case that you will work on as lawyers is unique. The savoring of those experiences need not be retrospective only.

The practice of law can be a much richer experience if at the time that you are working on each of these unique cases you will appreciate it at that time for what it is, for the societal and economic environment in which it arises, and for the contribution that it makes to the community in which you live and to your individual development as a lawyer. That kind of approach reaches beyond the professional experience.

I want to show you a picture. Some of you may remember that little face. I do too. The only place you can see that face today is in a picture. It is true that we still have a Wendy. But she's three and a half years older. Never again will there be opportunities to have and to love this Wendy at this stage of her existence, to share her experiences, and to contribute to her happiness. She's nine years old now. Pretty soon she'll be ten, and then when she's twice as old as she is now, she probably will be gone from our home. She also has brothers and sisters, and each new day brings a new opportunity for loving, for sharing, for understanding.

I have no greater hope for this class than that you will fully appreciate not only your professional opportunities at the time that they occur but also the individual, personal, and family opportunities.

Now I'm going to say something that I hadn't really planned to say but that I want to be the last words that you hear as a part of your official law school program. A dominant feature of your law school training has been to instruct you in the skills of skepticism. This has been a necessary part of your training as advocates. But I want you to hear one last time from me that although I value those skills as highly as anyone, and though I feel very strongly that the Law School must continue to give that kind of rigorous, intellectual training, there are absolutes in this world, and just as there is a place for skepticism, there is also a place where skepticism is as inappropriate as it is unnecessary. I have serious doubts concerning the eternal verities of the Rule of Shelley's Case, the doctrine of prior restraint, the law of offer and acceptance, or even, as much as it pains me to say so, the Rule of Reason under the Sherman Act.

But I want you to know, my brothers and sisters, that there are eternal verities. I was not present on the spring day in 1820 when Joseph Smith saw the Father and the Son, nor was I present some nine years later when he and Oliver Cowdery had hands laid upon their heads and the Aaronic Priesthood was restored. But I want you to know with all of the surety of one who was not there at that time that it really happened and that those truths are far more important than anything that you ever learned in Law School, and I leave this with you in the name of Jesus Christ. Amen.

This convocation address was given to the charter class of the BYU Law School on April 23, 1976. Reprinted from the Clark Memorandum, *Fall 1999, 2–7; a fuller version also published "Convocation 1976,"* Utah Bar Journal, *vol. 4, nos. 4–9, 36–42, Summer–Fall 1976 and "Convocation Address 1976," in* Speeches at the 1st Convocation of the J. Reuben Clark Law School, Brigham Young University, April 23, 1976, 3–8.

Rex E. Lee (1935–96) received his J.D. from the University of Chicago in 1963, clerked for Justice Byron R. White of the U.S. Supreme Court 1963–64, served as founding Dean of the J. Reuben Clark Law School 1976–81, Solicitor General of the United States 1981–85, and President of Brigham Young University 1989–95.

The Ethical Professional:
Consecration in the Workplace

Constance K. Lundberg

I am often asked, although there was some respite during President Hunter's term, how can I be a lawyer and be moral, ethical, or raise my head in civilized company. As an environmental lawyer I have been accused, within a single week, of killing children who lived in the same community with one of my "smoke stack" clients and also of killing families who might have accidents on a road the Department of Transportation couldn't expand because I was suing to stop the construction. Clearly, at least in the minds of my self-appointed critics, lawyers do get away with murder.

Believe it or not, when I was in school, the morality of lawyers was not a major issue. Lawyers were the champions who brought German and Japanese war criminals to justice, who stood between innocent blacks and hate-driven lynch mobs, who tried to make corporate America accountable for the essentially unrestrained contamination of our air, water, and soils.

In my high school and college years, questions of morality surrounded other professions:

- Nuclear physics was a morally questionable profession. We agonized over the conflict between J. Robert Oppenheimer and Edward Teller. Was the Hiroshima bombing a morally justifiable act? Was the United States foreign policy of mutually assured destruction viable or a death sentence to the world? The Committee of Concerned Scientists began while I was in high school. I was thrilled that there were scientists that were not, as most seemed to me, moral ciphers.

- Doctors and medical researchers were in the ethical spotlight. Tennessee Williams wrote a play and film script focusing on the immorality of indiscriminate prefrontal lobotomies. Disclosures in the aftermath of World War II raised the specter of human subject experimentation, and we learned that forced sterilization had been an American practice for fifty years.

- State government was the *bete noire* of my generation. It was crabbed, counter productive, and regressive. State and local government meant the Scopes trial and George Corley Wallace stirring hate against the lone black child, Sharlane Hunter, who was escorted to school each day by U.S. marshals to protect her life. Bull Connor, turning the water hoses of Birmingham on civil rights demonstrators was the symbol of states' rights, which meant segregation, Jim Crow, lynching, third-rate education, and economic exploitation of the poor.

Publicly perceived heroes and villains change with varying political currents. You cannot assure yourself morality or an ethical life by category, by associating with an "ethical" discipline or profession. So how can we identify and follow the pathways of righteousness Monday through Saturday? I address the special challenges of morality among the professions since our common challenges are greater than our differences.

J. R. R. Tolkien wrote *The Lord of the Rings*, a trilogy of morality in troubled times in a fantasy feudal world. In *The Two Towers* (volume 2 of the trilogy), Eomer, a warrior of one country, speaks to Aragorn, a stranger, a warrior hero on a quest from another land.

> "The world is all grown strange. . . . How shall a man judge what to do in such times?"
>
> "As he ever has judged," said Aragorn. "Good and ill have not changed since yesteryear; nor are they one thing among Elves and Dwarves and another among Men. It is a man's part to discern them, as much in the Golden Wood as in his own house."[1]

So if we must judge good and ill the same, whether among elves, dwarves, lawyers, physicists, or musicians, how do we judge? What is the hallmark of an ethical professional?

The ethical professional is a servant and a steward, using her knowledge, wealth, power, and position in service of her God and her fellowman. Paraphrasing Moses' farewell sermon to the Israelites, in a speech entitled "How to Get Rich," Hugh Nibley wrote:

> The first rule, and one never to be forgotten, is that everything you have or ever will have, individually and collectively, is a gift from God, something that he blesses you with, has blessed you with, or will bless you with—you owe it all to him. . . . Throughout the book [of Deuteronomy], the refrain is repeated at the end of almost every pronouncement: You must do this in recognition of your dependence to God, because first and foremost he has given you your lives, he rescued you from Egypt, and he redeemed you—that is, he paid the price for you that you could not pay yourself.[2]

As King Benjamin taught, we cannot withhold from one another a portion of all God has given, when he has asked us to give, since all we have is his (Mosiah 4:21). The rich man in the account in Luke did not understand this first rule. He said he kept the commandments from his youth, but Jesus said, "Yet lackest thou one thing: sell all that thou hast, and distribute unto the poor, and thou shalt have treasure in heaven: and come, follow me." The man was "very sorrowful: for he was very rich" (Luke 18:22–23).

In the scriptures, consecration has two forms. One can consecrate himself, his time, talents, and service. King David called the people to build the temple: "And who *then* is willing to consecrate his service this day unto the Lord?" (1 Chronicles 29:5). Or one can consecrate one's wealth, as Christ commanded the rich man, and as saints did in the primitive Church and in the early days of the latter-day Church. Both forms of consecration are partial obedience to the first commandment, as explained by Moses in Deuteronomy. Both forms require both giving and receiving. Again, Dr. Nibley explains the offerings required of the Israelites:

> The great gathering and feasts, whose strict observance makes up such an important part of the old law, all have the same purpose, to remind the Israelites that everything they had was a free gift from God. In holding these solemn conferences "you and yours—sons, daughters, servants, . . . strangers, orphans, widows must all come together and rejoice and be happy," as one big happy family. That is the spirit in which this must be done, and that is the spirit of the law of consecration and the United Order. "Remember that thou wast a bondman in Egypt"—if some are slaves, all are slaves. This is to show where we stand with each other and the Lord.[3]

How does this translate into your lives as professionals? First, you must share your gifts—knowledge, skills, talents—with others in need, whether or not they can pay for your services. Lawyers and doctors have professional obligations to provide service *pro bono publico*—for the good of the public. Does this mean you oppress the poor until four o'clock Friday afternoon and then spend one hour giving nonreimbursed service to a poor person? I think not. Neither do I think it means providing service to the poor only when someone else (Legal Services, Medicare, the Peace Corps) pays you to do so.

You should, of course, pay all your tithes and offerings. Your donations to the Church do not discharge your obligations to support community service organizations, ranging from the food bank to the opera, with your donations, time, and efforts. You have a special obligation, I think, to use your professional skills and income as a stewardship to repay those whose contributions gave you those skills. Whether you graduated from a private school like BYU or a state-supported school, you should replenish, with generous interest, the resources that supported your education—scholarships, income, tuition subsidies, library resources, etc. Those of us with multiple degrees may not be able to support all our alma maters to the same level, but the principle of repaying, for the benefit of the next generation, what we received from past generations is a good starting point.

When I think of our obligation to train future generations in our profession, I think of musicians. I know few musicians unwilling to spend time and energy helping young musicians grow. An example for me is that of a young musician in Utah with a promising career as a concert pianist. He was stricken with a nerve disease that ended his career as a pianist, but not his vocation. He began a chamber music group that has grown and now has several records and tapes and a regular concert season. This year, his third season, Grant Johannesen, the concert pianist and former head of the Cleveland Institute, came to Utah to appear as a guest artist with the group. I thought, as I watched this young man conducting the silver-haired, gracious master musician, how committed Johannesen is to the future of his profession. He drastically reduced his performing career to serve as director of the Institute, because it is the obligation of musicians to help the next generation, and here he was, gently and elegantly, helping a young conductor through the use of his name, his talents, and his subtle, unseen assistance in teaching the conductor how to accompany a soloist. It was the equivalent of a senior litigator from a national firm coming to Utah to sit at counsel table with a young lawyer in a major trial, coaching, but not trying the case himself.

Beyond the obligation to use your skills and position to pay for your own education debts and for the benefit of any in need, there are constraints on how a professional functions. If it is your intent to sell apples or clean streets, your obligation is to work hard, do your job well, and give a full day's work for a full day's pay. A true professional has other obligations. The original professions were the Church, medicine, and law. We have added others, to the irritation of some members of the original three. I define a profession as one where specialized higher education and a specific code of acceptable conduct and responsibilities are recognized by a legal or societal monopoly to give the service for which the professional is trained. I once did research on the chartering of professional licensing organizations. I learned that almost the first thing engineers, social workers, psychologists, librarians, and others did in establishing themselves as professionals was adopt codes of ethics.

What should those ethics include? Thomas L. Shaffer, a legal ethicist, identifies four roles for lawyers. For Shaffer, these are counseling roles. For me, counseling is when the lawyer interacts with his client in the full gamut of their professional relationship. The superficial elements of each of these roles will be used by any lawyer at one time or another. The question is not the facial elements of the roles, but the nature of the relationship underlying them—*that* determines whether the representation is ethical.

The Godfather

[T]he godfather controls the action and serves the interests of his client, the godchild. Don Corleone, as his son Michael says, is a "man who is responsible for other people." Also . . . the godfather acts without regard to the harm his action causes to other people. Godfather lawyers either decide what their clients' interests are, without consulting their clients, or they persuade their clients to accept lawyers' views on what their interests are. They pursue client interests with their own "technical" devices, without much interest in their clients' moral reservations.[4]

In President Ezra Taft Benson's famous conference address on April 1, 1989, he spoke about the sin of pride and how it affects our relationships.

[A] major portion of this . . . sin . . . is enmity toward our fellowmen. We are tempted daily to elevate ourselves above others and diminish them.

The proud make every man their adversary by pitting their intellects, opinions, works, wealth, talents, or any other worldly measuring device against others.[5]

Lawyers in the godfather role use their intellects, opinions, and skills against their opponents in the guise of being an advocate for their clients. In reality, like the lead character in the movie *The Godfather,* the godfather lawyer establishes and maintains her own power, in her case, over both opponents and clients. In the elevated status of godfather, the lawyer no longer needs to interact with her client or her opponents—their concerns are irrelevant. She pretends to serve the interests of the client, whose reality she has denied. This pretense is no less acceptable if she deludes herself as well as others.

The double tragedy of the godfather role is that the professional overrides the client's moral reservations, but can leave her own at the door, arguing that she is merely pursuing the client's agenda, not her own. This is the classic defense of the scientist. "I am not a policy maker, I am a scientist. It is the politician's job to decide what to do with my work." This means there is no moral dialogue at any time in the representation.

Clients do not necessarily want a godfather lawyer. One third of all divorces granted in the United States never become final. Lawyers in my acquaintance comfort themselves with the often repeated observation that clients in family matters really don't know what they want. I suggest that the lawyers don't know what the clients *really* want and, as godfathers, deliver what they know how to deliver without inquiring too closely. If clients in one third of the cases have the determination to extricate themselves from their lawyers' imposed solutions, how many more are divorced because they do not have the will or ability to fight back?

The Hired Gun

The hired gun, or client-centered counselor, focuses on the desires of the client. "The lawyer should not act in ways that would influence the client's choice. The lawyer should be 'neutral' and 'nonjudgmental.'"[6] Shaffer points out the limitations of the hired gun, though literature is replete with examples. One example from recent pulp fiction is John Grisham's *The Firm*. In that book, an entire law firm surrenders moral autonomy to the mob and becomes owned by it. Autonomy is no virtue to be bought. By allowing clients moral autonomy, the right to make moral judgments with no controls and to have those judgments implemented unquestioningly, we are consigning clients to hell—people, as described by C. S. Lewis, "on the outskirts of a city who continually move further and further away from one another."[7]

Our own values and beliefs support the idea that we exist as part of a community. The autonomous model is unacceptable to a Christian, particularly a Mormon Christian, either as client or as lawyer. In addition, the hired gun model requires the professional to accept the moral code dictated by the client. This model is surely as unacceptable to a lawyer. But I think it equally unacceptable to a doctor counseling a pregnant-out-of-wedlock woman or terminally ill patient, a psychologist counseling a suicidal patient, a businessman whose partner wants to engage in predatory pricing, or a government scientist when a general is suggesting testing nuclear weapons in populated areas.

The Guru

Shaffer's lawyer as guru is an appealing role for those of us from a proselyting background. Shaffer quotes Judge Clement Haynsworth in a speech to a law school graduating class:

> [The lawyer] serves his clients without being their servant. He serves to further the lawful and proper objective of the client, but the lawyer must never forget that he is the master. He is not there to do the client's bidding. It is for the lawyer to decide what is morally and legally right, and, as a professional, he cannot give in to a client's attempt to persuade him to take some other stand. . . . During my years of practice, . . . I told [my clients] what would be done and firmly rejected suggestions that I do something else that I felt improper.[8]

Philosopher Martin Buber advocated what he called I-thou relationships. We should approach others as moral human beings capable of moral dialogue. However, he felt that professional relationships were rarely a source for moral counseling. The professional looks at the client and sees, not a *thou*, another person, but an *it*. "The sides are too *unequal*: 'I see you *mean* being on the same plane, but you cannot. . . . [T]he situation . . . may sometimes be tragic, even more terrible than what we call tragic.' Not only tragic, he said, but, for the professional, also morally perilous. Professionalism is an invitation to arrogance."[9]

The guru is arrogant. Here, as in the godfather role, the professional dictates to the client. The difference is that the godfather gets what the client says he wants with no consideration for moral judgments the client might make. He is paternalistic and controlling. The guru makes moral judgments for the client and in essence says to him, "This is what you should do/want." It is another form of paternalism and, like the first, leaves the client out of the equation. This role has the same pitfalls as the godfather, or the father-knows-best model of professional behavior, but this model has one additional problem: By removing the client from the moral dialogue, the professional as guru denies the client his free agency.

The Friend

Shaffer says the godfather wants client victory, the hired gun wants client autonomy, and the guru wants client rectitude. He proposes a fourth model, one more difficult to follow and less likely to achieve its goal: the lawyer as friend. His goal is client goodness.

> The model that we advance for the lawyer who is concerned with the goodness of the client is the lawyer as friend. We are not suggesting that the lawyer can become a friend to every client, but that the lawyer and client should deal with moral issues that arise in representation in the way that friends deal with moral issues. Our point of view here does not turn on friendship as a bit of good luck, but on being like a friend—as a counseling skill. . . . A friend is concerned with the other as a person. In Martin Buber's terms, a friend treats the other as a "thou" rather than an "it." Or, in Kant's terms, perceives the other as an end and not merely as a means to some other end.[10]

By friend, Shaffer means Aristotle's definition of friendship in *Nicomachean Ethics*: "Friends must enjoy one another's company, they must be useful to one another, and they must share a common commitment to the good."[11]

Why is commitment to goodness important? Consider the constellation of professional problems surrounding the family. One in ten women lives in an abusive situation. The statistics for children are similar. Separation of the family may or may not eliminate the abuse—as we all know from news accounts, separated partners often return with violence and devastation. However, regardless of the abuse, twenty percent of children in Utah live below the poverty line, mostly children in single-head-of-household families. National statistics are worse.

If you are a lawyer, doctor, psychologist, nurse, social worker, or teacher representing one of the partners or the children in a troubled family, the model becomes a critical issue. Will you help those children, that family, if you seek victory of one member of the family over the others, or autonomy for your client from the rest of her family? Will externally imposed rectitude alter the internal dynamics of the family or leave the family in as great a distress as ever but give the professional a self-satisfied feeling?

Imagine that you are the lawyer contacted by the husband of a family in town. He is making $1,500/month and has a wife and three children ages 1, 3, and 5. He says he has had it with the marriage. The children have no discipline and are always crying and whining. His wife, of whom he speaks in ugly and derogatory terms, is nagging, he says, and getting uppity. She is turning the kids against him. She does not work—has a high school diploma but no particular skills and is unlikely to get more than minimum wage in any job, unlikely to get enough to pay for child care while she works. Her mother is an interfering old witch. The bishop stuck his nose into things that weren't any of his business. The man wants to be free, to get out of the marriage, to get enough of the $1,500/month to live on (all of it if he can). If you listen carefully, what do you hear from this man? He is poor. His family lives in poverty. Divorce or separation will make it impossible for the family to live without assistance. It seems probable that there is abuse in the home. There may be a support system for the wife—mother, Church leaders—but it is unlikely. It is equally unlikely that there is much support for the husband. How do you become a friend in this case? How do you establish a moral dialogue? The fact that you are handling this case *pro bono* should make it easier, but probably won't. Charity clients are more likely to be defensive and hostile than grateful.

Here is the real challenge of the consecration of a profession. It is so easy to be moral in the abstract; so much harder in the dirty, raging, hate-filled reality that is muttering and swearing a blue streak in your office. Moses didn't get nice, clean, well-educated, upper-middle-class Hebrews. He got illiterate, superstitious slaves. As he reminded them in Deuteronomy, they were not the chosen people because they were more pure, more upright than others. But from these people came the seeds of the people of the covenant—they preserved the scriptures through war and pestilence. Finally, they were the family of the Savior. By the same token, Paul didn't get a nice, clean, well-behaved BYU ward in Corinth. He thanked God he didn't baptize the Corinthians, because they are so quarrelsome (1 Corinthians 1:14–15). He found the Corinthians carnal, envying, and full of strife and division (1 Corinthians 3:3). They were greedy, withholding support for missionary work and for the Church, but providing for themselves (1 Corinthians 4:10–14). What did Paul find in these quarrelsome and sinful Corinthians? He found them epistles from God, written on the fleshy tables of his heart (2 Corinthians 3).

As professionals, you will minister to the needy, the weary, those who are falling by the wayside. The whole do not come to the healer. If you wish to share a common commitment for the good, as described by Shaffer and Bellah, after Aristotle, you will have to look carefully. And it will not be enough to say it is a miracle of God that good could come from such people. They are the children of God, and you have consecrated your time and talents to serve them, to bring them into goodness.

How do you do that? Not as one young LDS associate in my very gentile law firm did. He stayed isolated in his office and increased the isolation by putting a very large painting of Moroni burying the gold plates on the wall in his office. Perhaps he could have created a greater division by putting a sign on his door reading "Desolation of Dragons," but I doubt it. Paul came to know the Corinthians. He listened to their quarrels, their concerns, their contentions. He scolded and upbraided them. But ultimately, he accepted them as God's children and looked for their strengths. Then he saw them as God's recommendation to him.

I spent a lot of time traversing the intellectual no-man's-land between the requirements of my clients and the demands made upon them by government representatives or by opponents in the community. I learned that people often do not know what they want or need. Like children, their demands may be tokens or talismans for other unidentified and misunderstood needs. It takes patient and careful listening to hear the needs behind the demands. What does the young, confused father need?

One of my students, faced with a similar problem in a class assignment, showed his capacity as a representative of Christ, as well as a creative problem solver, when he sought out educational opportunities for the young man. He counseled him about the need to expand his capacities, asking about his willingness to take classes, seek additional training, and enter counseling. He gently explored the problems of dividing a pittance among two households. He explored ways to reduce family tensions, provide greater face with in-laws. He reached out to the young man and found the pain and need within him. From there he was able to suggest meaningful solutions.

Often it also takes the good fortune of a person well prepared to instinctively react to challenges that appear in the process. Atticus Finch is a hero in *To Kill a Mockingbird* because of who he is. He is successful, not in the trial, where he fails, but in his instinctive act of courage and defiance before the lynch mob.[12] You can probe an apparently insoluble problem for months, even years; but you must understand it—and the capacities of your client—to see the light eking through a small crack in the opposition and know it suggests a solution acceptable to both parties. This understanding comes, I suggest, from love. "A good man out of the good treasure of the heart bringeth forth good things: and an evil man out of the evil treasure bringeth forth evil things" (Matthew 12:35).

I came to understand friendship and love in problem-solving from the man who is now my husband. Boyd Erickson was the head of environmental control for U.S. Steel in the western United States. I was his lawyer—outhouse counsel, as we sometimes laughingly called it. He was committed to keeping Geneva Steel open and operating. I do not ask you to agree with him but to understand him. He felt a stewardship for each of the 4,500 employees of the plant. He worried about their families, their homes, their debts, and their children. Those were not institutional concerns in Pittsburgh. The plant operated under a constant shadow of threatened closure.

We were negotiating with EPA for new standards that would allow the plant to operate while meeting EPA established clean air standards. The standards we wanted would work if Geneva employees did every maintenance and repair procedure that was required. Much trust was necessary, however. It was difficult and cumbersome for EPA to enforce the standards. During a discussion with the agency about trust, agency representatives protested that it was difficult to trust the plant when employees were shutting down the pollution control equipment then in place to save the $56,000/month of power bills that came when the equipment operated. This fact was unknown to me and to the Pittsburgh representatives. Pandemonium broke loose. The senior USX official from Pittsburgh threw the EPA representatives out of their own meeting, held in their offices. I sat with my head in my hands saying, "You can go to jail for this. People go to jail for this." The Pittsburgh people were having a contest to see who could come up with the foulest and most profane epithets for the Geneva operators, one of whom was literally backed up against a wall grinding his teeth.

Boyd finally found a small window of quiet in the uproar and said, "You just have to understand . . ." and proceeded to make sure we did. He did not say the operators were right or justified. He just said they were human, doing their best under frightening and trying circumstances. That day I saw that a professional, operating with understanding and love, acts as the Savior's representative on earth. He mediates with the judge. He does not pretend things are other than they are, but places them in their true context. Like Paul, he found a recommendation from God written in the fleshy tables of the heart. He never spoke directly of God, or the Savior, but he brought their spirit into a room that had, moments before, been filled with a spirit of anger and contention.

I believe that is the way consecration figures in our professional lives. It is not an artificial or externally imposed thing. But, by bringing understanding and love to our contacts with others—clients, opponents, judges—we can share those things most sacred to us—the spirit of the Savior, the eternal concepts of Christ's love and the atonement—not through preaching, but through demonstration, not by announcement, but by letting others feel its sweetness and peace. I believe that we cannot perform immoral acts and pursue unethical courses if we remain true to that spirit as we bring it to our daily service.

This Honors Devotional was given at BYU on February 7, 1996. Reprinted from the Clark Memorandum, *Spring 1996, 6–13.*

Constance K. Lundberg received her J.D. from the University of Utah in 1972. She is currently Associate Dean of the BYU Law School and Director of the Howard W. Hunter Law Library in Provo, Utah.

Notes

1. J. R. R. Tolkien, *The Two Towers*, Lord of the Rings 2 (New York: Ballentine, 1965), 15.
2. Hugh Nibley, "How to Get Rich," *Approaching Zion*, The Collected Works of Hugh Nibley 9, ed. Don E. Norton (Salt Lake City: Deseret Book, 1989), 178, 179–180.
3. *Id.* at 181.
4. Thomas L. Shaffer and Robert F. Cochran Jr., *Lawyers, Clients, and Moral Responsibility* (St. Paul: West, 1994), 8. Shaffer originally defined the four lawyer roles in *On Being a Christian and a Lawyer* (Provo, Utah: Brigham Young University Press, 1981).
5. Ezra Taft Benson, "Beware of Pride," *Ensign*, May 1989: 4–6.
6. Shaffer and Cochran, 19.
7. See C. S. Lewis, *The Great Divorce* (New York: Macmillan, 1946), as quoted in Shaffer and Cochran, 28.
8. Shaffer and Cochran, 35–36.
9. See Martin Buber, *The Knowledge of Man*, 171–172, trans. M. Friedman and R. Smith (1965), as quoted in Shaffer and Cochran, 37.
10. Shaffer and Cochran, 45.
11. Robert N. Bellah, et al., *Habits of the Heart: Individualism and Commitment in American Life* (1985), 115, as quoted in Shaffer and Cochran, 45.
12. See Thomas L. Shaffer, "Christian Lawyer Stories and American Legal Ethics," *Mercer Law Review* 33 (1982), 890.

Just Lawyers

Ralph R. Mabey

I'm honored that each of you would come. I am, after all, just a lawyer. Indeed, the title of my comments is "Just Lawyers"! I respect you. I respect you because you would come out on a Sunday evening after a long day. I know it's a sacrifice. I respect you because of your attendance and study of the law at the J. Reuben Clark Law School. I have a vision of great things that will come from you through your studies and your careers. The theme of Discovery Week is "So we, being many, are one body in Christ, and every one members one of another" (Romans 12:5). Now, how might you say that in Latin? *E pluribus unum.*

E Pluribus Unum: the motto of the Great Seal of the United States of America. In other words, I submit to you that the purpose of the laws of this land is to make of many one. This is not just the purpose of the Constitution but the purpose of all of the laws of this land.

Take the example of two parties who are entering into a contract. They've got different interests. One wants to sell high, the other wants to buy low. One wants to sell for cash, the other wants to buy on terms.

The contract laws of this country allow them to be brought together. Their very different interests are brought together in one agreement. They are unified and enabled to work together for their separate interests—unified by the law.

Now suppose they have a dispute and one claims breach of the contract by the other. The law is still there to forge a compromise. It gives them something to compromise around, a chance for them to reunify themselves based upon the principles of the law. Or, if they're unable to reunify themselves, they can reconcile themselves to each other through the enforcement of the law in court—whose purpose is then to reconcile this unhappy seller with this unhappy buyer.

Think about it. There is something profound in the purpose of our laws when seen in this context.

Even the criminal laws are there to unify us in obedience to those laws and, in the event of a breach of the criminal law, to reconcile the offender with the rest of society, to reconcile that offender through enforcement of the law.

Scripture recognizes that this is the purpose of the civil law. By "civil law," I mean the secular law.

Doctrine and Covenants 134:6 says of our laws:

> We believe that every man should be honored in his station, rulers and magistrates as such, being placed for the protection of the innocent and the punishment of the guilty; and that to the laws all men show respect and deference, *as without them peace and harmony would be supplanted by anarchy and terror; human laws being instituted for the express purpose of regulating our interests as individuals and nations, between man and man;* and divine laws given of heaven, prescribing rules on spiritual concerns, for faith and worship, both to be answered by man to his Maker (emphasis added).

What is meant here? Harmonize? Bring peace between human beings? *The purpose of the law,* according to scripture, is to unify us.

So now we come to the next question: If the purpose of the civil law is to unify us, what is the purpose of lawyers? Can it be that the purpose of lawyers is to unify persons? To harmonize my client's interests with your client's interests so that we can do a deal, so that you can go about your business? To reconcile our clients with their adversaries so that they can get on with their lives? Is the purpose of lawyers to unify humankind through adherence to law and/or reconcile humankind through the operation of law?

Perhaps nobody has heard people say that is the duty of lawyers. But it is the divine purpose of our laws—to unify us, separate and different though we are. Then is the divine purpose of lawyers to take us, separate and apart, and unify us under the law or reconcile us with the law?

I submit, brothers and sisters, that that is the purpose of a lawyer: to unify us under the law or reconcile us with the law. And only one of you laughed out loud. I would expect more of you to laugh out loud. It seems counterintuitive to the way we picture lawyers. But I want you to think about this because I submit to you that it is true.

I believe with this purpose in mind—that lawyers are to unify—the Lord said:

> We believe that men should appeal to the civil law for redress of all wrongs and grievances, where personal abuse is inflicted or the right of property or character infringed, where such laws exist as will protect the same [and such appeals are made by lawyers]; but we believe that all men are justified in defending themselves, their friends, and property, and the government, from the unlawful assaults and encroachments of all persons in times of exigency,

where immediate appeal cannot be made to the laws, and relief afforded (Doctrine and Covenants 134:11).

To put it another way, no law enforces itself, no law interprets itself. If the purpose of the law is *e pluribus unum*, then the purpose of a lawyer is to effect *e pluribus unum*.

I submit that it is important even to the salvation of Zion, therefore, that we study the law. Indeed, the Lord said in Doctrine and Covenants 93:53: "And, verily I say unto you, that it is my will that you should hasten to translate my scriptures, and to *obtain a knowledge* of history, and of countries, and of kingdoms, *of laws of God* and *man,* and all this *for the salvation of Zion.* Amen" (emphasis added).

From this I take it the Lord says that for the salvation of Zion we should study the law of man and become lawyers. Now I'm likening this scripture to me and to you. But if Nephi could liken them, perhaps we all can. Out of that, I take a divine call to you and to me to study the law.

I believe then, with the purpose of lawyers in mind, that we must befriend the law. We must seek for wise lawyers and magistrates and persons who will rule on the law. You can tell that I'm referring to scripture. "And that law of the land which is constitutional . . . belongs to all mankind. . . . I . . . justify you . . . in befriending that law." It is lawyers who must befriend the law. "I, the Lord God, make you free, therefore ye are free indeed; and the law also maketh you free." That reference has to be to secular law, I believe.

In their entirety these verses read:

And that law of the land which is constitutional, supporting that principle of freedom in maintaining rights and privileges, belongs to all mankind, and is justifiable before me.

Therefore, I, the Lord, justify you, and your brethren of my church, in befriending that law which is the constitutional law of the land;

And as pertaining to law of man, whatsoever is more or less than this, cometh of evil.

I, the Lord God, make you free, therefore ye are free indeed; and the law also maketh you free.

Nevertheless, when the wicked rule the people mourn.

Wherefore, honest men and wise men should be sought for diligently, and good men and wise men ye should observe to uphold; otherwise whatsoever is less than these cometh of evil (Doctrine and Covenants 98:5–10).

I take out of all of these scriptures that, yes, maybe the Lord recognizes that it is our divine obligation to give effect to the motto of the United States of America.

As we—through lawyers, I submit—gain power to organize our businesses, organize our human transactions and relations, and organize the Church, we will be preserved in and able to keep the laws of God. In other words, now I'm ready to take one further step. The step I'm going to take is to suggest that by lawyers acting in their divine calling to unify people under the law, they are partially fulfilling the divine law stated in Romans, that we should each unify ourselves together under Christ.

You may not want to take that leap with me. But let me read from Doctrine and Covenants 44:1–5:

> Behold, thus saith the Lord unto you my servants, it is expedient in me that the elders of my church should be called together, from the east and from the west, and from the north and from the south, by letter or some other way.
>
> And it shall come to pass, that inasmuch as they are faithful, and exercise faith in me, I will pour out my Spirit upon them in the day that they assemble themselves together.
>
> And it shall come to pass that they shall go forth into the regions round about, and preach repentance unto the people.
>
> And many shall be converted, insomuch that *ye shall obtain power to organize yourselves according to the laws of man.*
>
> That your enemies may not have power over you; that *you may be preserved in all things; that you may be enabled to keep my laws;* that every bond may be broken wherewith the enemy seeketh to destroy my people (emphasis added).

There you have it. I submit that the Lord is saying that if you are going to be enabled to keep that divine law that Paul spoke about in Romans, it will be by organizing yourselves according to the laws of man.

I believe we can see the fulfillment of divine purposes by the unifying action of lawyers under the law. We can see Professor Wardle, who is here tonight, and other professors at this university and other legal powers at work in the world, attempting to unify the world through adherence to just law—and thereby opening the world and her peoples to the gospel.

I submit that there is a logical and scriptural basis for the progression that I've proposed to you this evening. If that's the case, that's all well and good. But I have to make a living practicing law, and some of you may have to, too.

Can we practice law as the Lord has outlined that we should practice the law, by unifying one with another, by reconciling our clients with others? I think that is an important question.

Could we follow the example of Christ? Isn't He our lawyer with the Father? Don't we read in Jacob 3:1 that "He will console you in your afflictions, He will plead your cause, and send down justice"? "But behold, I, Jacob, would speak unto you that are pure in heart. Look unto God with firmness of mind, and pray unto him with exceeding faith, and he will console you in your afflictions, and he will plead your cause, and send down justice upon those who seek your destruction." We can console and plead. We can't send down justice, but we can try to go get justice.

I think that when it comes down to the practice of law, we can be most successful if we fulfill our calling to unify and reconcile people with each other and the law. We need to seek common ground, to narrow differences.

A few years ago I went to a dinner with my legal adversaries. I represented a client who was missing more than a billion dollars and couldn't find it under any rock or under any bed. The bad guys sat across the table at dinner; we had fought for a couple of years. All of a sudden we reached a compromise—and it had a spiritual undertone to it. Opposing counsel spoke later of the occasion as a dramatic, unexpected, and crucial reconciliation and unification.

I submit to you that settlements under the law are part of our duty, our divine duty in unifying and narrowing the ground. If we do that, we reduce the transaction costs greatly. We reduce the psychic costs too, and we allow people to go forward, to move on.

I conducted a mediation in a hard-fought lawsuit a few weeks ago. These parties settled after a day's mediation. They were apart millions at the beginning of the day (several hundreds of percent in magnitude), and both sides expressed mistrust and pessimism. But they settled. One of the parties said to me, "You know, I didn't realize that my adversary was a pretty good guy. I could have picked up the phone three years ago and we could have settled this."

There is power in narrowing issues, in finding common ground. There is great lawyering in that effort.

A few years ago I was involved in a case where hundreds of millions had been lost, rather publicly, by a rather public family. I ended up mediating a dispute between the family and the party who was suing the family and had gone to the trouble of filing RICO charges against them. It was a nasty dustup.

We sat together for three or four days. One night at about eight or nine or ten o'clock, I was thinking, "This is going nowhere. I should have broken things off and gone to the baseball game." But the parties began talking together without me and without lawyers. By 7:00 A.M. the next morning, we had a settlement.

Well, I asked myself, "What are all we lawyers doing?" These parties got together and settled it themselves after years and much acrimony.

You know, there is a force, a power, in narrowing differences, and there's sometimes a religious component in it. It feels right.

Recently a respected trial judge assisted the parties in a large and disputatious case to reach a global settlement. This judge, a devout Catholic, assesses and reassesses his life at the end of each day. In so doing, he concluded that participating in this settlement was probably his finest day on the bench—ever—exceeding the many years of trials and adjudications at which he had presided and which he had decided.

Another way we can unify is by seeking just results, seeking a just reconciliation by enforcing the law. You know, if you've got the power and you've got the money and you've got the people in your law firm, you can pulverize the other guy.

But J. Reuben Clark, Jr., who served decades as an international lawyer before his call to the First Presidency, said, "Even in war, there should be some things that human beings would not do to their fellows." He opposed one-sided settlements or treaties based upon one party's overwhelming firepower.[1] He said, "Guns and bayonets will in the future as in the past bring truces, long or short, but never peace that endures. I believe that moral force is far more potent than physical force in international relations."[2]

Now just a minute here. "I believe that moral force is far more potent than physical force in international relations," said J. Reuben Clark, Jr. The moral force of international law and international opinion may unify people better and forge peace and truces better than guns and bayonets.

There is some truth to this, I submit, in our practice of law. That truth is that if you can reach a fair settlement, that settlement is likely to stick. It's likely to be enforced. Those parties are likely to be able to do business with each other again in the future. They're likely to get on with their lives. Justice is more likely to be done.

If it's just guns and bayonets, then it's going to be expensive. It's going to go on a long time, and any peace achieved may well later fall out of bed.

So I believe also in this principle: Fulfilling a lawyer's divine calling makes good sense in the practice of law.

Now what about respecting diversity, a fundamental precept of Discovery Week?

E pluribus unum. The idea in Romans is not that we are homogenized— the idea is out of many, one. It is that the arm and the ankle and the elbow and the eye can be unified in purpose. So it is in the practice of law: We must work together with diverse peoples in bringing about unity. That is our calling.

You need go no further than the seller and the buyer. They've got very diverse interests. Your job is to allow them to do the business they want to do unified under the umbrella of that law, in their diversity.

Diversity is crucial to entrepreneurial success. It's crucial to the energy of this country. As we unify, we must respect diversity.

As President J. Reuben Clark began his assignment as ambassador to Mexico, he adopted this credo: "There are no questions arising between nations which may not be adjusted peaceably and in good feeling, as well as with reciprocal advantage, if those questions are discussed with kindly candor, with a mutual appreciation of and accommodation to the point of view of each by the other, and with patience and a desire to work out fair and equitable justice."[3]

When he was ambassador to Mexico, President Clark filled one of the most important ambassadorships in the world. There were momentous disputes between the U.S. and Mexico. There were upheavals and internal armed conflicts and boundary disputes with us. There were calls for armed U.S. intervention.

J. Reuben Clark served seven presidents of the United States as their lawyer, as undersecretary of state, as the chief legal officer for the Department of State, and in many other assignments, as well as ambassador to Mexico. He knew the international law, and he said the way to forge agreement is peaceably, with good feeling, through questions discussed with candor, mutual appreciation, and accommodation of each other's point of view, through desire to work out fair and equitable justice.

What happened when he left the ambassadorship? This is what the *Mexico City Excelsior* editorialized: Ambassador Clark had "distinguished himself by a virtue that is not common among diplomats: that of not putting himself forward, of not calling attention to himself, of observing a prudent reserve that has won him the esteem of all social classes in Mexico."[4] He practiced what he intended to practice.

There is, I think, a great lesson in that: have respect for your adversary. How often are we or the other side painted as Satan simply because we play adversarial roles in our judicial system? It makes it very difficult to unify our differing interests.

There has been and is discrimination in this country. A friend told me of a kid who went to work at a great Los Angeles law firm not too many years ago and realized that he was making a thousand dollars less than the others in his class. He went to the senior partner and complained. The senior partner said without apology, "We can pay you less. You're Jewish. Where else are you going to get a job for more?"

A professor friend of mine who is preeminent in her field tells of standing up for a client in court for the first time. The judge looked over his glasses and said to her client, not realizing that she might have a *woman* lawyer, "Don't you have a lawyer?" Well, that judge was very apologetic. But it may have been the first time he had seen a woman lawyer—and it was not many years ago.

A person of color, a student of mine, reminded me that a few years ago, to travel in this great country, his family had to take their food with them and sleep in the car. Discrimination is unfortunately still with us.

There are strong differences among us. Our job is to respect those with whom and against whom and for whom we practice law and to forge unity. That means no ethnic or cultural jokes, brothers and sisters. That means that even if she tells a joke on herself, I will not repeat that joke. If I tell a joke about Mormons, that's fine. If you tell a joke about Mormons, that's not so fine with me. It means not saying things like, "Yeah, some of my best friends are Mormons. I took a Mormon to lunch last week." Do you feel the condescension in that? We have got to be careful about what we say, even when we have good intentions.

The J. Reuben Clark Law Society stands for these principles of J. Reuben Clark, these principles of *e pluribus unum*, of unifying the world under law, whether as graduates of this law school or any other law school, whether as members of this faith or of any other faith.

I was moved when the J. Reuben Clark Law Society in Salt Lake City presented its annual award to Nick Colessides of the Greek community. The Greek Orthodox clergy appeared at that luncheon in the Joseph Smith Building, honoring him and honoring us. Lawyering is building these bridges. That is what the J. Reuben Clark Law Society is all about. That is its mission.

I have one other radical suggestion for you on the practice of law. This time you can all laugh out loud. You will be successful and you will be living the scriptural admonitions for lawyers and the law if you will practice the paradox of humility. You will be smarter, better, and more successful if you are humble. It makes you happier. Someone said, "Too many humble people are proud of it." So I can't speak for myself. But I speak for you, brothers and sisters. (In general priesthood meeting last October, Bishop Richard C. Edgley spoke of the paradox or irony that strength comes from humility.)[5]

The way you become the best trial lawyer you can is with the humility to learn from what that witness tells you, to learn how that other attorney does it.

You may say, "Michael Jordan, he's not humble. He says, 'Give me the ball.'" And that's what a good lawyer says: "Give me the ball."

How did Michael Jordan come to want to get the ball and to know what to do with it? He did it through the humility of working harder than others, of learning everything about his opponents, of learning every move from the other guy and employing it. There is the paradox in humility.

You will be a smarter lawyer, a happier lawyer, and a better lawyer if you—if we—can learn that paradox. Learn to say to the client who says, "You're charging me 500 bucks an hour. What's the answer?" "I don't know the answer." Learn not to take credit for every deal. Just get it done even though you're thinking, "I've got to be out there self-promoting myself or I'll starve to death." Your work and your service will promote you.

I'll close with scriptural proof of this paradox, expressed in Helaman 3:35:

> Nevertheless they did fast and pray oft, and did wax stronger and stronger in their humility, and firmer and firmer in the faith of Christ, unto the filling their souls with joy and consolation, yea, even to the purifying and the sanctification of their hearts, which sanctification cometh because of their yielding their hearts unto God.

Now there's the paradox, and I think it applies to us temporally as well as spiritually.

And in Ether 12:27 we read,

> And if men come unto me I will show unto them their weakness. I give unto men weakness that they may be humble; and my grace is sufficient for all men that humble themselves before me; for if they humble themselves before me, and have faith in me, then will I make weak things become strong unto them.

We become strong through the humility to pray, through the humility to let the Lord know that we're imperfect, and through the humility of repentance. We become strong in the practice of law through the humility to learn from the other person, to listen to others, even to adversaries, and to change ourselves for the better.

In conclusion, I submit this: It isn't that there is a religious life we live and a lawyer's life we live and that we'd better try to reconcile them as best we can. No, I'm proposing something maybe a little more dramatic: that they are the same life, that your calling as a lawyer under *e pluribus unum* is part of your calling as a disciple of Christ under Romans 12:5. I say this in the name of Jesus Christ. Amen.

This Discovery Week fireside was given at the BYU Law School on November 14, 1999. Reprinted from the Clark Memorandum, *Spring 2000, 2–9.*

Ralph B. Mabey received his J.D. from Columbia University in 1972 and served as United States Bankruptcy Judge for the District of Utah 1979–83. He is currently a partner at LeBoeuf, Lamb, Greene & MacRae in Salt Lake City, Utah.

Notes

1. Edwin Brown Firmage and Christopher L. Blakesley, "J. Reuben Clark, Jr.: Law and International Order," 13, no. 3 *BYU Studies* (Spring 1973): 81.

2. *Id.* at 68.

3. Frank W. Fox, *J. Reuben Clark, The Public Years* (Provo, Utah: Brigham Young University Press, 1980), 549.

4. *Id.* at 583.

5. Richard C. Edgley, "Behold the Man," *Ensign*, Nov. 1999, 42–44.

Apostles of Equality

Kenneth R. Wallentine

Despite the infusion of billions of dollars into our cities, innumerable studies and blue-ribbon commissions, and decades of litigation, racial division remains America's most obdurate dilemma. Recent riots in Los Angeles show how pathetically little has changed in race relations in the past 30 years. Social scientists, politicians, and activists spin theories of blame and responsibility, and still the song remains the same. Scholars of the New Left and Neoconservatism alike voice a dismal chorus of failure in the realm of civil rights litigation.

Yet equality, as conceived by mortal law and refined by moral law, is a value intrinsic to the beliefs of a Christian lawyer and an essential objective in an ethical society. How can those schooled in the "knowledge of the laws of man in light of the laws of God,"[1] best pursue the path of equality?

The first step must be that proposed by Critical Legal Scholars: reject legal ideology as the basis of discussion. There is nothing unique or novel in seeking a higher measure of conduct than that of law. Portia, the heroine of Shakespeare's *Merchant of Venice*, reminds us "that in the course of justice, none of us should see salvation: we do pray for mercy."[2] Elder James E. Faust, a member of the Quorum of the Twelve Apostles, explained:

> There is a great risk in justifying what we do individually and professionally on the basis of what is "legal" rather than what is "right." In so doing, we put our very souls at risk. The philosophy that what is "legal" is also "right" will rob us of what is highest and best in our nature. What conduct is actually "legal" is, in many instances, way below the standards of a civilized society and light years below the teachings of the Christ. If you accept what is "legal" as your standard of personal or professional conduct, you will rob yourself of that which is truly noble in your personal dignity and worth.[3]

Ensuring procedural or formal equality is "legal." Achieving equality of condition, in harmony with applicable gospel principles, is "right."

Despite traditions to the contrary, no Latter-day Saint can hold any racial or ethnic bias and declare himself consistent with official theology. Elder Howard W. Hunter, President of the Quorum of the Twelve Apostles, unequivocally repudiated any notion that one race is superior to another:

> The gospel of Jesus Christ transcends nationality and color, crosses cultural lines, and blends distinctiveness into a common brotherhood. . . . All . . . are invited to come unto him and all are alike unto him. Race makes no difference; color makes no difference; nationality makes no difference. . . . As members of the Lord's church, we need to lift our vision beyond personal prejudices. We need to discover the supreme truth that indeed our Father is no respecter of persons.[4]

Speaking bluntly, President Spencer W. Kimball asked: "What did you . . . do that made you superior to your other darker brothers and sisters? . . . Take this message back to your people. . . . Racial prejudice is of the devil. Racial prejudice is of ignorance. There is no place for it in the gospel of Jesus Christ."[5]

Prejudice and inequality have plagued the Church from its foundations. Paul wrote to the Saints in Galatia, a commercial center peopled by a multitude of distinct ethnicities, affirming that all are justified in Christ and rejecting the argument that new converts needed to embrace Jewish practice as well as the gospel. Through the covenants of baptism, "there is neither Jew nor Greek, there is neither bond nor free, there is neither male nor female: for ye are all one in Christ Jesus" (Galatians 3:28). Paul does not call upon the Galatians to abandon their respective cultures and heritages. Rather, he gently reminds that we are defined by our kinship with Christ. Paul firmly instructs the Galatian saints to put off their disputes over conformity, heal the division, and become one.

The Book of Mormon is replete with examples of the consequences of equality and inequality. The people of King Benjamin and his successor son Mosiah aspired to equality and reaped the rewards. King Benjamin told his people:

> And now, for the sake . . . of retaining a remission of your sins from day to day, that ye may walk guiltless before God—I would that ye should impart of your substance to the poor, every man according to that which he hath, such as feeding the hungry, clothing the naked, visiting the sick and administering to their relief, both spiritually and temporally, according to their wants (Mosiah 4:26).

Note King Benjamin's stated grounds for charity—to receive a remission of one's own sins! When Mosiah stepped down, and judges replaced the monarch, he told the people that inequality should be no more in the land (Mosiah 29:32). There must have been notable economic disparity, otherwise Mosiah, Benjamin, and Alma would not have commented on the poor, the needy, and the remedy applied to ease their situation.

The people heeded the counsel and example of Mosiah and his father. A moral law was obeyed and the natural consequence obtained.

> And when the priests left their labor to impart the word of God unto the people, the people also left their labors to hear the word of God. And when the priest had imparted unto them the word of God they all returned again diligently unto their labors; and the priest, not esteeming himself above his hearers, for the preacher was no better than the hearer, neither was the teacher any better than the learner; and thus *they were all equal,* and they did all labor, every man according to his strength.
>
> And they did impart of their substance, every man according to that which he had, to the poor, and the needy, and the sick, and the afflicted; and they did not wear costly apparel, yet they were neat and comely.
>
> And thus they did establish the affairs of the church; and thus they began to have continual peace again, notwithstanding all their persecutions.
>
> And now, because of the steadiness of the church they began to be exceedingly rich, having abundance of all things whatsoever they stood in need—an abundance of flocks and herds, and fatlings of every kind, and also abundance of grain, and of gold, and of silver, and of precious things, and abundance of silk and fine-twined linen, and all manner of good homely cloth.
>
> And thus, in their prosperous circumstances, they did not send away any who were naked, or that were hungry, or that where athirst, or that were sick, or that had not been nourished; and they did not set their hearts upon riches; therefore they were liberal to all, both old and young, both bond and free, both male and female, whether out of the church or in the church, having no respect to persons as to those who stood in need (Alma 1:26-30; emphasis added).

As the people pursued equality, peace and prosperity followed, and for a season untold riches and commercial success resulted. Yet it was not an invulnerable bliss and could be sustained only as long as equality survived as a living principle.

As the surplus swelled, so did the people's pride, and the heritage of Benjamin and Mosiah was about to be undone. Alma saw it coming; he raised a warning cry. But class division was too enticing to those who had a little more. By segregating themselves and hoarding their possessions, they raised their worldly station a notch or two. It hadn't taken long; a scant eight years had passed from the time Mosiah had warned them to eliminate inequality. Even the elect, the people of the church, "began to wax proud, because of their exceeding riches, and their fine silks, and their fine-twined linen, and because of their many flocks and herds, and their gold and their silver, and all manner of precious things" (Alma 4:6).

The pattern was to be repeated nearly 120 years later, although equality was then to endure as a social condition for four generations. Shortly before his crucifixion and subsequent visit to the American continent, Christ established the one fundamental criterion to be worthy of his name:

> For I was an hungred, and ye gave me meat: I was thirsty, and ye gave me drink: I was a stranger, and ye took me in:
>
> Naked and ye clothed me: I was sick, and ye visited me: I was in prison, and ye came unto me....
>
> ... Verily I say unto you, Inasmuch as ye have done it unto one of the least of these my brethren, ye have done it unto me (Matthew 25:35-36, 40).

"Equality among the Lord's covenant people constitutes the measure of their righteousness."[6] It has been so from the beginning. While establishing Zion among his people, the prophet Enoch warned of the consequences of inequality: "man hates his neighbor" and "covetousness" reigned as the order of the day, for the people had "trusted in [their] riches."[7] The Book of Mormon peoples knew well the warnings of Enoch; shortly before the birth of the Savior, Samuel disdained the class divisions embraced by those infatuated with their riches, quoting Enoch.[8] The Lord's law of equality is no less explicit in modern scripture. In a revelation describing the function of the bishop's storehouse, the Lord cautioned that "if ye are not equal in earthly things ye cannot be equal in obtaining heavenly things" (D&C 78:6). A few months earlier, the Lord had proclaimed the essential role equality played in promoting the spiritual health of the Church: "Nevertheless, in your temporal things you shall be equal, and this not grudgingly, otherwise the abundance of the manifestations of the Spirit shall be withheld" (D&C 70:14).

Much of the scripture condemning inequality or establishing the law of equality is stated in the context of economic equality. The sin of esteeming oneself as greater than one's sister or brother is no less pernicious when the bias is based on external, immutable characteristics of appearance rather than on relative economic condition. It is the self-aggrandizement that is privative of the Lord's spirit, for such suggests that Father prefers one child, or group, over another. This is false, for the Lord "inviteth ... all to come unto him and partake of his goodness; and he denieth none that come unto him, black and white, bond and free, male and female, and he remembereth the heathen; and all are alike unto God, both Jew and Gentile" (2 Nephi 26:33). Joseph Smith taught that our responsibility is to lift up our kindred, whether "black or white, bond or free; for the best of books says, 'God hath made of one blood all nations of men, for to dwell on all the face of the earth.'"[9]

Today, as the dogma of "political correctness" has crept into our consciousness, we have learned a new vernacular of code words. For example, when one hears a politician belittling welfare recipients, or members of the underclass,[10] can the audience hold any doubt as to the race and social status and perhaps even the gender of the subject? No modern lawyer would dare publicly remark in a fashion that might be construed as racist, or perhaps even sexist. Any employment lawyer would shrink at the thought of a client asking a prospective employee how she would perform in light of her obligations to husband and children, or how an applicant would perform as the first minority employee in the shop. Yet few have any such compunctions about revealing class bias. As long as one speaks in code, no one is discomforted. Ruth Sidel, an eminent sociologist specializing in family issues, notes that "when people disparage 'welfare mothers,' it's really [the] code words for the black poor. The term 'underclass' is really a code word for black people. . . . It's very hard to separate our hatred of the poor from racism."[11]

Sometimes, for instance, we readily distinguish between the local Wasatch Front poor—those who are experiencing temporary hardship due to a loss of employment, death of a provider, divorce, or some other fate entirely beyond their control—and the teeming masses whose poverty frankly frightens us, or so it should. We are comfortable with the former. We believe that they are safe within the clutches of bishops and ministers, Deseret Industries, and various community charities. They carry themselves in worn, but not tattered vestments, with a noble humility to which we give our approbation. There is no shame imposed thereon by the comfortable in Zion.

It is the latter group that slightly troubles us. We don't openly admit it, but our charity and compassion are generally limited by membership in the Church, or at least persons perceived to be roughly equal in social position. It is a short step from concluding that the poor—or at least most of them— are undeserving. Because the fault for their poverty lies with them, they have no claim on tax funds or charity and have forfeited their right to equality. This conclusion is bolstered by a conviction of poverty's inevitability. Believing that there will always be poor assuages our concerns. Mosiah's people were infected by this attitude, and he cautioned them appropriately:

> And if ye judge the man who putteth up his petition to you for your substance that he perish not, and condemn him, how much more just will be your condemnation for withholding your substance, which doth not belong to you but to God, to whom also your life belongeth; and yet ye put up no petition, nor repent of the thing which thou hast done.

> I say unto you, wo be unto that man. For his substance shall perish with him; and now, I say these things unto those who are rich as pertaining to the things of this world (Mosiah 4:22-23).

Inequality and poverty are not inevitable in our society. Several Western European countries have virtually eliminated poverty. Family Self-Sufficiency, a Charlotte, North Carolina, cooperative, has helped twenty-four families buy single-family homes. The program includes home management and career development training. Three years after inception, all twenty-four heads of household are still employed and living in their homes.[12] A small group of activists has raised nearly a hundred people from poverty to a state of self-sufficiency beyond mere survival. The scriptures stand before us as powerful witnesses that inequality need not afflict even large and complex societies. What, then, is required, and how may a Christian attorney contribute to the effort?

One must first ask God for an abiding conviction of the essential unity of humankind. Reverend Martin Luther King, Jr., taught: "We are tied together in the single garment of destiny, caught in an inescapable network of mutuality."[13] Not long ago, I heard Maya Angelou preach a wonderful sermon. She explained that once she obtained comprehension of her divine parentage, she was constrained to admit that each man and woman is also a child of God, and hence her brother and sister in the truest sense. As we seek the Father, we, too, will gain a richer understanding of our familial ties.

Since attorneys are key elements in the structuring and ordering of government and commerce, the Christian attorney must "bring her values into the workplace."[14] Lawyers often counsel and lead their clients or agencies in significant decisions. Leadership toward equality cannot long survive without a spiritual dimension; the countervailing forces of pride, greed, and esteeming oneself as higher than one's sister are potent. The force of litigation should be reserved for the most recalcitrant inequalities, in general deference to persuasion and negotiation. Litigation to achieve equality is seldom desirable, often being the aftermath of un-Christian behavior and presaging more of the same. "Mankind's history has proved from one era to the next that the true criterion of leadership is spiritual. Men are attracted by spirit. By power, men are forced. Love is engendered by spirit. By power, anxieties are created."[15] True leaders, says Hugh Nibley, have a "passion for equality."[16]

Many developing, equality-promoting concepts hold great promise. Most cannot be facilitated without attorneys. The Family Self-Sufficiency housing and employment project required many hours from real-estate attorneys. Corporate attorneys must assist in the formation of private undertakings. The business acumen and steady hand of veteran attorneys can be invaluable on boards of directors.

One of the most promising Neoconservative initiatives, the concept of enterprise zones, is utterly worthless without the services of those skilled in redevelopment and taxation law. Individual small businesses, the sort most likely to employ neighborhood workers, created in those zones need low-cost, start-up legal counsel.

One committed individual can alleviate much suffering. Charles Ballard was alarmed at the number of single mothers in his community. He foresaw the consequences of hundreds of children maturing without the guidance of a father in the home. Benevolently bold, he launched Teen Fathers of Cleveland, Ohio. Over the past four years, he has persuaded more than two hundred fathers to marry and stay with the mothers of their children—creating a legacy of hundreds of children who now live in two-parent homes.[17] In Salt Lake City, Utah, Reverend France Davis of the Calvary Baptist Church ministered to many elderly who lived in inadequate housing. Mustering his congregation, and securing government financing, he spearheaded the construction of Calvary Tower, a safe and comfortable home for many low-income elderly persons. Reverend Earl Lee, of the Twelfth Street Baptist Church in Detroit, used church funds to buy up crack houses one by one. As the drug dealers were evicted, Lee employed church members to rehabilitate the houses, creating local jobs. The church extended mortgages to poor, but earnest, church members. In nine years, Reverend Lee and his parishioners have rolled over the funds many times, buying up more dilapidated drug dens. Crime near the church has dropped 37 percent. As Bishop Glenn Pace gently reminds us, we cannot be the salt of the earth if we are lumped together in the cultural hall.[18]

We must allow equality to inform our counsel and choices, professional and personal. Viewing clients' circumstances and needs through the lens of the equality pronounced by the gospel will help inoculate clients from litigation and elevate the profession to its traditional position of respect. For example, a lawyer guided by the ethic of equality while counseling her client in an employment situation may suggest multicultural awareness programs as a tool to smooth employment relations and increase morale as well as productivity. Is it not more profitable to teach employees about each other than to defend against a discrimination or harassment action? An extended outlook on a client's needs might result in a recommendation that the client actively participate in community education programs, boosting individual employability and strengthening the client's prospective labor pool.

We can be saved from the repercussions of inequality. Parallel to the velocity with which many of the world's totalitarian regimes are crumbling is the immediacy with which the gospel takes hold in those lands as they gain new stability. Is it any less likely that a surge in racial harmony and economic prosperity, obtained through the pursuit of equality, will be accompanied by an outpouring of the Lord's spirit? Mosiah's subjects transformed their society from Zion to one not unlike our present society in eight short years. Hitler steered an entire nation into perverse prejudice and destructive hate in one brief generation. Disaster may yet attend our society if we fail in the struggle for equality.

As we form new circles in our communities, we must be mindful of diverse cultural heritages. Whites must struggle to become conscious of behaviors that minorities may perceive as racist. Minorities should welcome efforts to establish new bonds and strive to eliminate their own racist thinking. We must leave behind the political fray—both the right and the left, and even the middle, have room for "equality activists." Certainly, there will be risks and fears. Risks are inherent in any worthwhile venture. The Great Emancipator, Abraham Lincoln, implored all Americans to extend "charity toward all." This was his prescription to "bind up the wounds" inflicted in the course of the Civil War.[19] It is a timeless prescription, first recorded in ancient scripture. Paul described the awful circumstance of one not possessing charity (1 Corinthians 13:3). True charity conducts one to an abiding belief in equality. Steeling ourselves with compassion and charity will ease the growth pains.

> It may well be that the survival of the species will depend on the capacity to foster a boundless capacity for compassion. In the alchemy of man's soul, almost all noble attributes—courage, love, hope, faith, beauty, loyalty—can be transmuted into ruthlessness. Compassion alone stands apart form the continuous traffic between good and evil proceeding within us. Compassion is the antitoxin of the soul. Where there is compassion, even the poisonous impulses remain relatively harmless.[20]

Counselors at law ought to be "apostles of equality."[21] Equality must become a beatitude of personal and professional life. "Behold, this I have given unto you as a parable, and it is even as I am. I say unto you, be one; and if ye are not one ye are not mine" (D&C 38:27).

Reprinted from the Clark Memorandum, *Fall 1992, 2–4, 6–9.*

Kenneth R. Wallentine received his J.D. from Brigham Young University in 1990 and served as Editor-In-Chief of the BYU Law Review. He is currently Administrative Counsel at the Utah Department of Safety in Salt Lake City, Utah.

Notes

1. Marion G. Romney, "Becoming J. Reuben Clark's Law School," *Clark Memorandum*, Fall 1993, 7; published also in *Addresses at the Ceremony Opening the J. Reuben Clark Law School, August 27, 1973* (Provo, Utah: Brigham Young University, 1973), 17–27.

2. *The Merchant of Venice*, 4:1:200.

3. James E. Faust, "The Study and Practice of the Laws of Men in Light of the Laws of God," *Clark Memorandum* (Fall 1988): 20; also reprinted in this volume on page 40.

4. Howard W. Hunter, "All Are Alike unto God," *Ensign* (June 1979): 72, 74.

5. *The Teachings of Spencer W. Kimball,* ed. Edward Kimball (Salt Lake City: Bookcraft, 1982), 236–237.

6. Avraham Gileadi, *The Last Days,* 2d rev. ed. (Salt Lake City: Deseret Book, 1991), 200.

7. James H. Charlesworth, ed., *The Old Testament Pseudepigrapha: Apocalyptic Literature & Testaments,* vol. 1 (New York: Doubleday & Company, Inc., 1983), 1 Enoch 84:8, 2 Enoch 34:1–2.

8. *Cf.* Helaman 13:21–22, with 1 Enoch 84:8; see Hugh Nibley, *Enoch the Prophet* (Salt Lake City: Deseret Book Co.; Provo, Utah: Foundation for Ancient Research and Mormon Studies, 1986), 71, 86.

9. See Joseph Smith Jr., *Times and Seasons* (Nauvoo, IL: Times and Seasons, 1971), 5:28–33 (citing Acts 17:26); quoted in Martin B. Hickman, "The Political Legacy of Joseph Smith," *Dialogue* 3 (Autumn 1968): 22, 29.

10. Gunnar Myrdal, *Challenge to Affluence* (New York: Pantheon Books, 1963), 34. Swedish social commentator Gunnar Myrdal coined the term "underclass" to represent the lower economic strata of society, that group believed to be destined for permanent poverty.

11. "Bigotry Shifts Its Emphasis: Poor Are the New Target," [Minneapolis] *Star Tribune,* 28 Dec. 1991, sec. 1E. Ruth Sidel is the author of *Women and Children Last: The Plight of Poor Women in Affluent America* (New York: Viking, 1986).

12. *Id.*

13. Martin Luther King Jr., "Nobel Prize Acceptance Speech," in *Negro History Bulletin* (May 1968): 22.

14. Joseph Allegretti, "Christ and the Code," *Clark Memorandum* (Fall 1990): 16, 23.

15. *The Autobiography of Malcom X* (New York: Grove Press, 1965), 424.

16. Hugh Nibley, "Leaders and Managers," Commencement Address at Brigham Young University, 19 August 1983, *Speeches of the Year* 1982-83 (1983): 184, 186.

17. "What We Can Do Now," *Fortune,* 1 June 1992, 41.

18. Glenn L. Pace, "A Thousand Times," *Ensign* (Nov. 1990): 10.

19. Abraham Lincoln, Second Inaugural Address, reprinted in Diane Ravitch, ed., *The American Reader: Words That Moved a Nation,* 1st ed. (New York: HarperCollins, 1990), 153.

20. Eric Hoffer, "Beware the Intellectual," *The National Review* 28 (Sept. 1979): 11.

21. Matthew Arnold, *Essays in Criticism* (London: MacMillan and Co., 1865), ii.

WHAT THINK YE OF CHRIST?

While the Pharisees were gathered together,
Jesus asked them, Saying,
What think ye of Christ? whose son is he?
They say unto him, The Son of David.
(Matthew 22:41–42)

How Do Justice and Mercy Relate to the Atonement?

Tad R. Callister

The Immutable Laws of the Universe

Justice and mercy are difficult concepts to explore, not because there is an absence of scriptural references, but because these concepts exhaust our intellectual resources long before divulging all the answers. Elder McConkie wrote, "We know that in some way, incomprehensible to us, his suffering satisfied the demands of justice."[1]

The scriptures frequently refer to "justice" and the demand for its satisfaction. What, then, is justice, and who requires it? Dictionary definitions are many—"fairness," "righteousness," and "the administration of that which is right." These are only a few. But who determines what justice is? Who demands it? What are the consequences of violating or complying with that which is just?

There are certain laws of the universe that are immutable, that are without beginning of days or end of years. They are not created by an intelligent being, nor are they the product of moral thought, rather they are eternal, co-existent realities with the intelligences of the universe. These laws are immutable in that they cannot be altered or modified in any form. They are unchangeable from eternity to eternity. They are self-existing, self-perpetuating laws to which even God himself is subject. B. H. Roberts spoke of the "eternal existences" that govern even Gods:

> [There] are things that limit even God's omnipotence. What then, is meant by the ascription of the attribute omnipotence to God? Simply that all that may or can be done by power conditioned by other eternal existences—duration, space, matter, truth, justice, reign of law, God can do. But even he may not act out of harmony with the other eternal existences which condition or limit even him.[2]

Brigham Young taught the same truth: "Our religion is nothing more nor less than the true order of heaven—the system of laws by which the

Gods and the angels are governed. Are they governed by law? Certainly. There is no being in all the eternities but what is governed by law."[3]

Certain of these immutable laws affect the physical or natural world. For example, the Prophet Joseph taught that the "pure principles of element . . . can never be destroyed: they may be organized and re-organized but not destroyed. They had no beginning, and can have no end."[4] Likewise, the Doctrine and Covenants teaches, "The elements are eternal" (D&C 93:33). In other words, the universe contains basic, elemental matter that cannot be created or destroyed, or as Brigham Young said, "[It] cannot be annihilated."[5] There is no exception to this natural law. Even God is not exempt. The Prophet Joseph confirmed this when he taught, "Intelligence . . . was not created or made, *neither indeed can be*" (D&C 93:29; emphasis added).

In and of themselves, the laws of the physical or natural world seem to have no moral implications. They do not affect our spiritual growth. We cannot sin by breaking these laws, because it is not possible to break them. We would not drop a ball from a tower and deduce, "This ball will always fall in this way, because the laws of gravity are just." Justice and mercy have no meaning in these circumstances; fairness or rightness are not issues when it comes to the physical, natural laws; they do not allow for obedience by choice, but rather require uncompromising, involuntary compliance.

There appear to be other immutable laws in the universe, however, that offer both a choice and a consequence, and hence, in this sense, they are spiritual laws. These spiritual laws govern all intelligent beings in the universe—and also govern their progress. For these purposes, progress means an increase in eternal power. In other words, there seem to exist certain immutable laws that will bring power if they are followed or "obeyed," but if they are neglected or "disobeyed" they may trigger the opposite result. For example, it may be that an individual cannot progress without acquiring knowledge. President John Taylor noted that even the gods submit to these immutable laws: "There are certain eternal laws by which the Gods in the eternal worlds are governed and which they cannot violate, and do not want to violate. These eternal principles must be kept, and one principle is, that no unclean thing can enter into the Kingdom of God."[6]

Thus certain laws govern even the gods. President Taylor does not seem to be suggesting that these laws cannot be violated or broken under any set of circumstances, but rather that they cannot be violated by gods who desire to remain as such.

The Savior observed every spiritual law with undeviating exactness. Apparently because of his compliance with each one, he received power upon power until he acquired the attributes of God, even in premortal times. Such progress was a natural consequence of his exacting compliance. His godhood thus seemed to result not from a creation of these laws, but rather from compliance with them. But what of the rest of us, who do not comply with each and every immutable law? Could we not just try and try and try again until we finally got it right, and then become gods, even though it might be on a delayed timetable? The answer is no. Evidently these immutable spiritual laws offer no leniency or mercy or second chances. If we do not comply, we have lost forever that opportunity for increased power that naturally flows from compliance. Aaron taught that once "man had fallen he could not merit anything of himself" (Alma 22:14). In other words, he could not pull himself up by his own bootstraps, regardless of how much time he had to try to do so. The Savior taught the Nephites the same principle: "While ye are in prison can ye pay even one senine? Verily, verily, I say unto you, Nay" (3 Nephi 12:26). The message is clear—once we sinned, violating the laws of eternity, there was no means of escape without outside help.

If someone falls from an airplane, he will plummet to the ground. The law of gravity will not change to accommodate his dire circumstances. There will be no slowing of the descent or softening of the earth to cushion the fall, however good a fellow he may be. He cannot say just before impact, "Let me take that last step one more time." No, there is only the automatic application of the law, hard and fast and uncompromising. Why does it work this way? There is no answer to that question. It is like asking, "Why does matter exist?' or "Why is the sky endless?" "Why" is not a question that can be asked of something that was never created. It exists because it exists.

The Justice of God

One might refer to these immutable spiritual laws that govern our progression as justice. Yet such "justice" as this is simply the natural conse-quence that flows from uncreated law. It exists co-eternally with and independent of the uncreated intelligences of the universe. In this regard, one might ask, "Do these laws constitute or determine justice? Does justice, as a concept of fairness and righteousness, exist only as determined and created by a moral being?" If the answer is yes, then justice would not be a self-existing law, but rather a principle of morality that is the product of intelligent thought. If this is the case, then what being or beings determine and demand justice? Is it God alone? Mankind? The intelligences of the universe? All or part of the above?

The scriptures make it clear that God has a system of justice. It is often referred to as "the justice of God" (Alma 41:3; 42:14, 30; D&C 10:28) or "his justice" (2 Nephi 9:26) or "divine justice" (Mosiah 2:38); but clearly the prophets confirm that God provides a moral system by which man is governed. But how does this moral system relate to the immutable, uncreated laws of which we have just spoken? God understood that our failure to comply with these immutable laws would forever bar us from godhood unless there was another source of power that could be available to man—not because he earned it, not because he had a right to it through worthiness, but because another being with more power was so loving and kind that he was willing, even anxious, to propose and implement a plan that would provide the necessary power to exalt man. God instituted such a plan, known as the "plan of the great Creator" (2 Nephi 9:6), he rejoiced with exclamation, "O how great the plan of our God!" (2 Nephi 9:13). Joseph Smith spoke of the purpose of this plan:

> God himself, finding he was in the midst of spirits and glory, because he was more intelligent, saw proper to institute laws whereby the rest could have a privilege to advance like himself... He has power to institute laws to instruct the weaker intelligences, that they may be exalted with himself, so that they might have one glory upon another.[7]

These laws "to instruct the weaker intelligences" are referred to as "his law" (2 Nephi 9:17) or "the laws of God" (D&C 107:84).

Elder Erastus Snow wrote of the immutable laws of the universe: "I understand that what has exalted to life and salvation our Father in heaven and all the Gods of eternity will also exalt us, their children[.] And what causes Lucifer and his followers to descend to the regions of death and perdition will also lead us in the same direction; *and no atonement of our Lord and Saviour Jesus Christ can alter that eternal law,* any more than he can make two and two to mean sixteen."[8]

That "eternal law" of which he spoke is the immutable law that governs the path to godhood. God's law can never violate it, circumvent it, or "short-change" it, but it can complement and supplement it. Perhaps it is not unlike the conditions under which Nephihah operated as chief judge. He was given "power to enact laws according to the laws which had been given" (Alma 4:16). In other words, he could create "smaller" laws, provided they did not violate the principles of any existing "larger" laws. It is a well-known legal principle that individual states may create any law that is not expressly prohibited by the federal constitution. This gives each state wide latitude in determining a system of justice that will govern its citizens, provided such laws never violate our charter. Perhaps, in a similar way, God may establish any law he desires, provided it does not violate one of the immutable laws of the universe. These laws established by God, if obeyed, will endow his children with added power, even that power necessary to become gods.

By the way of illustration, God might not be able to rob a man of his agency to jump from a plane (i.e., to prevent him from sinning), but he might be able to put a parachute on the man's back before he leaps (i.e., provide a means to repent). As the dire consequences of this man's foolish decision quickly unfold, he still has a chance to land safely: He can pull the rip cord. In such a circumstance no law is violated or circumvented.

The law of gravity is still in full force and effect. No justice is robbed; yet the sinner is given power to land safely if he will just pull the rip cord (i.e., repent and rely on the protective life-preserving power of the Atonement). Nephi spoke of those who relied on the "tender mercies of the Lord" as those who were "mighty even unto the power of deliverance" (1 Nephi 1:20).

What constitutes the basis, the underlying rationale, for God's laws? God has certain inherent, eternal qualities that never change. He can never act inconsistent with or contrary to those qualities, not because he lacks the power to do so, but he has no desire to do so. Perhaps the brother of Jared was alluding to this fact when he said, "O Lord, . . . thou hast all power, *and can do whatsoever thou wilt*" (Ether 3:4; emphasis added). God's consistent compliance with these inherent qualities is a form of justice (i.e., the administration of that which he deems to be fair and right) because his own moral sense demands compliance. This leads to the next question: Is it possible that God demands justice not only to satisfy his own inherent moral sense, but also to satisfy all the other moral beings in the universe who have a similar standard of morality? In other words, could it be that God has in common with every man who has chosen to be a citizen of his kingdom a set of moral values by which they are desirous of being governed?

The People Also Desire Justice

Justice in the secular sense is the administration of those laws that are established and consented to by the citizens of a nation or a kingdom. Such justice is demanded by the people. Without this form of justice, chaos rather than order would reign. Likewise, justice in the divine dimension is the administration of those laws that are established and consented to by the people who comprise the kingdom of God. No doubt, in the great primeval council such divine laws were discussed and eventually agreed to. The Prophet Joseph explained, "It has been a doctrine taught by this church that we were in the Grand Council amongst the Gods when the organization of this world was contemplated and that *the laws of government were all made and sanctioned by all present*."[9] We the people, who would be subject to such laws, had a voice in their adoption.

No doubt the Grand Council in Heaven consisted of far more than a divine proposal immediately followed by a sustaining vote. More likely such a council (or perhaps councils) would have included ample time for discussion, debate, questions, the exchange of feelings, and the sharing of testimonies. This is not to suggest that the plan of salvation was in any way altered or refined, for the Father's plan, as presented, would have been perfect in every way. But the participants, other than the Father and Son, were not perfect. No doubt many of us had an anxious desire to explore every facet of the plan, to understand the consequences of moral agency and the risks inherent with mortal birth. All knew there would be pitfalls, crossroads, high roads, low roads, and sometimes seemingly no road at all. Surely we did not receive the plan in a spirit of casualness. No doubt this was a time of rapt attention and intense inquiry. We were profoundly interested and concerned, for our eternal destinies were at stake. Elder Joseph F. Smith taught:

> [We] were in the councils of the heavens before the foundations of the earth were laid. . . . We were, no doubt, there, and took a part in all those scenes; we were vitally concerned in the carrying out of these great plans and purposes; we understood them, and it was for our sakes they were decreed and are to be consummated.[10]

At some point Satan and his followers must have raised objections and competing issues. God certainly had the power to silence such opposing arguments and suppress every contrary thought with his compelling logic and commanding spiritual presence, but he seemed to have temporarily withheld—perhaps for the sake of agency he allowed the events to run their course. If the Grand Council was similar to councils today, each man who so desired would have had the opportunity, the "equal privilege" (D&C 88:122), to discharge the honest feelings of his heart. The noble and great ones probably stepped forward to courageously and boldly defend the plan. Just as the Gods "counseled among themselves" (Abraham 5:3), so too the members of this council may have counseled with each other, not to improve the plan, but to more fully understand and embrace it. Then, after all questions had been answered and testimonies borne, the decisive question was most likely put to a vote.

Among the most basic of all gospel principles is the law of common consent. Mosiah taught this law to his people: "It is not common that the voice of the people desireth anything contrary to that which is right; but it is common for the lesser part of the people to desire that which is not right; therefore *this shall ye observe and make it your law—to do your business by the voice of the people*" (Mosiah 29:26; emphasis added; see also Alma 1:14; Mosiah 22:1).

This fundamental principle of governance by consent was announced upon the formation of the Church in the latter days, and similar counsel was repeated twice thereafter within the short space of six months. Each time the message was similar; "And all things shall be done by common consent in the church" (D&C 26:2; see also D&C 28:13).

This law is fundamental not only in mortality, but in all spheres of our existence. Brigham Young taught: "The eternal laws by which he [God] and all others exist in the eternities of the Gods, decree that *the consent of the creature must be obtained before the Creator can rule perfectly.*"[11] Even when the voice of the people goes contrary to God's will, he has respected their agency. Israel desired an earthly king in lieu of their heavenly king. God told

Samuel to explain to the people the consequences of a king, so there would be no misunderstanding about their political future. Then he instructed Samuel to "hearken unto their voice" (1 Samuel 8:9), and make them a king.

Would it seem reasonable that God would violate this basic principle of common consent, so emphasized by him, and impose upon his subjects laws not approved by the voice of the people? To the contrary, it seems no one was more anxious and more willing to promote and foster an environment of agency and common consent than God himself. Unfortunately, "the lesser part of the people" (i.e., Satan and a third part of the host of heaven) desired "that which is not right" (Mosiah 29:26) and therefore were cast out of God's presence. This seemed an appropriate consequence, since they chose not to be bound by the laws that would govern God's kingdom. Unbelievably, they chose chaos over order, contention over harmony, war over peace. By rejecting the Father's plan, they could not become the beneficiaries of those very laws that had the power to exalt them. Why they chose Satan over the Savior is the great enigma of the ages. Was it a lack of faith in the Savior's ability to undergo the atoning sacrifice? Was it lack of faith in their own ability to keep the terms and conditions of God's law? Was it pride, ambition, selfishness—all of these weaknesses combined? Whatever the cause, the heavens wept over their wickedness—but honored each person's right to be disobedient.

The two-thirds who remained accepted the laws given us by the Father. "The voice of the people" (Mosiah 29:26) sanctioned the divine laws he proposed through the Son. That is what the Prophet Joseph taught: "At the first organization in heaven we were all present, and saw the Savior chosen and appointed and the plan of salvation made, and we sanctioned it."[12]

If we sanctioned the laws by which we would be governed, it seems that we did so with full understanding of their corresponding blessings and punishments. These laws, with their attendant consequences, were considered just. No one forced us to consent. We voluntarily chose to accept these laws that would govern our spiritual lives so that order rather than chaos would reign.

Who Administers the Laws?

The administration, supervision, and execution of these laws, punishments, and blessings by which we chose to be bound is what we know to be "justice." The person responsible for administering these laws is the judge. Mosiah urged his people to "appoint wise men to be judges, that will judge this people according to the commandments of God" (Mosiah 29:11). Those in the great primeval council consented that the wisest of all the Father's children—the Savior—should be judge. We did so with the comforting assurance that he would be absolutely fair and just and merciful in the administration of the law. Enoch called him the "righteous Judge, who shall come in the meridian of time" (Moses 6:57). Not only could the Savior sympathize with our cause, but he could empathize. He would suffer the full spectrum of mortality. No one would know the laws better than he who had been our lawgiver. No one was wiser, for he was "more intelligent than they all" (Abraham 3:19). And no one was more merciful, more kind, more loving or concerned than the Savior himself.

The Savior possessed all the qualifications needed and desired in a perfect judge. The "voice of the people" (Mosiah 29:26) wanted him and approved him and rejoiced in him as their judge. No one at a later date could claim exemption from his decrees. No one could claim he did not understand. No one could claim he was unacceptable, for he had our approval, our consent, our vote in advance of the final judgment. David recognized this; "God is the judge" (Psalm 75:7). Isaiah knew it: "The Lord is our judge" (Isaiah 33:22). And Moroni spoke of the Savior as "the Eternal Judge of both quick and dead" (Moroni 10:34). Jesus also testified of this truth: "The Father judgeth no man, but hath committed all judgment unto the Son" (John 5:22).

Mercy and Grace—Gifts from God

As crucial as are the laws of justice, they cannot save us. Lehi spoke of man's fate if justice alone were the governing scepter: "By the law men are cut off" (2 Nephi 2:5). Jacob, a son of Lehi, knew there was only one spiritual remedy that could prevent a permanent separation from God: "It is only in and through the grace of God that ye are saved" (2 Nephi 10:24; see also 2 Nephi 2:8). Paul taught the same; "According to [God's] mercy he saved us" (Titus 3:5). There are no exceptions—without mercy and grace there is neither salvation nor exaltation. With his usual insight Shakespeare wrote of that spiritual truth:

> Though justice be thy plea, consider this,
> That in the course of justice none of us
> Should see salvation. We do pray for mercy.[13]

Mercy and grace are gifts from God. In essence, they are companion doctrines. The LDS Bible Dictionary defines grace as a "divine means of help or strength, given through the bounteous mercy and love of Jesus Christ."[14] In other words, the merciful nature of God prompts him to lovingly provide us with gifts and powers (i.e., his grace) that will enhance our godly nature.

Sometimes we have a tendency to shy away from the word *grace* and instead to emphasize works (while certain others take the opposite approach)—but in truth, these two concepts go hand in hand. When the lifeguard stretches out a pole to the drowning swimmer, the swimmer must reach out and hold on if he desires to be rescued. Both the lifeguard and the swimmer must fully participate if the swimmer's life is to be saved. Likewise, works and grace are not opposing doctrines, as is so often portrayed. To the contrary, they are indispensable partners in the process of exaltation.

The word *grace* occurs 252 times in the standard works, while the word *mercy* occurs 396 times. It is apparent that these words are not descriptive of fringe gospel principles. They lie at the core of LDS doctrine, flowing directly from the Atonement of Jesus Christ. Elder McConkie taught; "As justice is the child of the fall, so mercy is the offspring of the atonement."[15] We might further add that grace is the offspring of mercy.

Grace, which denotes divine help or gifts from God, is, as the LDS Bible Dictionary tells us, "made possible by [Jesus'] atoning sacrifice."[16] Each of these gifts is a form of "enabling power"[17] designed to strengthen or assist us in our pursuit of godhood. The terms mercy and grace describe both God's loving nature and the actual gifts endowed upon us by God. By definition, these gifts are unearned by the recipient. Paul referred to grace as "the free gift" (Romans 5:15). Lehi made it clear that "salvation is free" (2 Nephi 2:4), and Nephi echoed the sentiments of his father when he preached that salvation was "free for all men" (2 Nephi 26:27). In certain circumstances these gifts are bestowed without any required action on the part of the recipient; in other circumstances the beneficiary must satisfy certain conditions, not as a means of earning the gift, for there is no equal *quid pro quo*, but because the giver will not bestow the gift until certain minimum conditions are satisfied.

Stephen E. Robinson tells of his little daughter, who anxiously pled for a bicycle. He promised her that if she saved all her pennies, she could one day have one. Motivated by her father's promise, she anxiously engaged in chores around the house, carefully saving every penny she earned. One day she returned to him with a jar full of pennies, anxious to now buy her bicycle. Good to his word, Brother Robinson took his elated daughter to the store where she soon found the perfect bike. Then came the moment of truth—the price tag was more than one hundred dollars. Despondent, she counted her sixty-one pennies. She quickly realized that at this rate she would never have enough to buy her dream. Then Brother Robinson lovingly came to the rescue. "I'll tell you what, dear. Let's try a different arrangement. You give me everything you've got, the whole sixty-one cents, and a hug and a kiss, and this bike is yours."[18]

The bicycle was certainly not totally earned by the young girl, but nonetheless, it was gladly given by a father who recognized she had given her all.

This is the spirit in which Nephi counseled, "For we know that it is by grace that we are saved, after all we can do" (2 Nephi 25:23). In other words, we contribute to our salvation, but we do not earn it. That was also the spirit of Paul's message: "For by grace are ye saved through faith; and that not of yourselves: it is the gift of God: not of works, lest any man should boast" (Ephesians 2:8–9). Thus works alone cannot save us; grace is an absolute prerequisite. But a certain amount of works (i.e., the best we have to offer) are necessary to trigger God's grace and mercy. No matter how hard we work, how diligently we serve, or how righteously we live, we will never deserve more than we receive. We will never be too qualified for our kingdom of glory. Brigham Young taught this principle with his usual brevity: "There never was any person over-saved; all who have been saved, and that ever will be in the future, are only just saved, and then it is not without a struggle to overcome, that calls into exercise every energy of the soul."[19]

Alma revealed that only the repentant, meaning those who have given of their spiritual best, "have claim on mercy through mine Only Begotten Son" (Alma 12:34). In this way, works and grace are complementary companions. In fact, they are inseparable partners in our pursuit of perfection. While discussing the superiority of faith or works, C. S. Lewis responded in his characteristically pragmatic fashion, "It does seem to me like asking which blade in a pair of scissors is most necessary."[20] Perhaps Brigham Young summarized the relationship between grace and works as well as it can be said: "It requires all the atonement of Christ, the mercy of the Father, the pity of angels and the grace of the Lord Jesus Christ to be with us always, and then to do the very best we possibly can, to get rid of this sin within us."[21]

God's mercy, both conditional and unconditional, is manifest in abundant fashion. It was demonstrated by our spirit birth, by our physical birth, and by the creation of the world. These outpourings of mercy seem to be independent of the Atonement, yet each of them added power to our lives. Certain other acts of mercy or grace flow directly from the atoning sacrifice. In each instance they are manifestations of gifts or enabling powers conferred upon man.

Mercy—Compassion and Leniency

In one sense mercy is the father of grace (and all the powers that flow therefrom), as discussed above. In another sense, mercy means leniency and clemency; it is compassion shown to an offender. In its highest form, it is love and compassion and wisdom all mixed in divine proportion. Portia pled with an earthly tribunal to exercise this quality that is so quintessentially godlike in nature:

> The quality of mercy is not strain'd,
> It droppeth as the gentle rain from heaven
> Upon the place beneath. It is twice blest:

It blesseth him that gives and him that takes.
'Tis mightiest in the mightiest; it becomes
The throned monarch better than his crown. . . .
It is an attribute to God himself.[22]

That attribute was fully operative in the Savior at all times. He could have called upon his vast reservoir of celestial power, removed himself from the cross, and avenged himself of his persecutors with fiery indignation; to this he was justly entitled—but mercy, not retribution, was his governing scepter.

Nehemiah spoke of this boundless benevolence of God: "Thou art a God ready to pardon, gracious and merciful" (Nehemiah 9:17). David used the same imagery: "Thou, Lord, art good, and ready to forgive; and plenteous in mercy" (Psalm 86:5). One can almost visualize the imagery of those scriptures—God, anxiously and tenderly watching over his creations, so as to detect every righteous act or benevolent thought that he might reward in abundant measure. He is constantly seeking for the good—"his bowels of mercy are over all the earth" (Alma 26:37; see also D&C 101:9). It is he who "delight[s] to bless with the greatest of all blessings" (D&C 41:1). To the tender Saints of the newly restored Church, the Savior said, "I will have compassion upon you. . . . [F]or mine own glory, and for the salvation of souls, I have forgiven you your sins" (D&C 64:2-3). Even in God's day of wrath, he has said, "with everlasting kindness will I have mercy on thee" (Isaiah 54:8; see also D&C 101:9). All of God's faculties, all of his inclinations are poised and bent on blessing at the slightest provocation. Oh, how God loves to be merciful and bless his children! Perhaps that is his greatest joy. It is that inherent quality that drives him with tireless vigilance to save his children. Lehi so observed: "Because thou art merciful, thou wilt not suffer those who come unto thee that they shall perish!" (1 Nephi 1:14). Indeed, our God "is mighty to save" (Alma 34:18).

Mercy was an attribute that Abraham Lincoln possessed in magnificent measure. Robert Ingersoll penned this tribute of him:

> Nothing discloses real character like the use of power. It is easy for the weak to be gentle. Most people can bear adversity. But if you wish to know what a man really is, give him power. This is the supreme test. It is the glory of Lincoln that, having almost absolute power, he never abused it, except on the side of mercy.[23]

Lincoln was entitled to this tribute—Christ infinitely more so.

How Does Justice Relate to Mercy?

At one end of the law is mercy in all its compassionate splendor, at the other is justice in all its stern reality. The Atonement is the one act in recorded history that demonstrated the maximum mercy, yet never robbed justice of one ounce of payment. The Atonement ran the full gamut of the law, end to end, mercy to justice. It was all-inclusive, infinite, so to speak, in its compliance with the law. Lehi explained this doctrine: "He offereth himself a sacrifice for sin, to answer the ends of the law, unto all those who have a broken heart and a contrite spirit; and unto none else can the ends of the law be answered" (2 Nephi 2:7; see also 2 Nephi 2:10).

Those who do not repent will suffer everything, Brigham Young said, that "justice can require of them; and when they have suffered the wrath of God till the utmost farthing is paid, they will be brought out of prison."[24] Elder Marion G. Romney also spoke of the awful consequences of those who fail to repent: "Without complying with these requirements and the other principles and the ordinances of the gospel, one is left beyond the reach of the plan of mercy, to rely upon the law of justice, which will require that he suffer for his own sins, even as Jesus suffered."[25] Justice will exact its full penalty, every ounce of its crushing weight, upon the unrepentant; from this there is no escape.

But what of the repentant? Is there any leniency on their behalf? Elder Bruce R. McConkie gave the answer: "It is through repentance and righteousness that men are freed from the grasp of that justice which otherwise would impose upon them the full penalty for their sins."[26] Amulek taught that the unrepentant are "exposed to the whole law of the demands of justice" (Alma 34:16), thus implying that the repentant suffer something less. In pursuing this thought Amulek concludes, "Only unto him that has faith unto repentance is brought about the great and eternal plan of redemption" (Alma 34:16). Alma taught of this sequential relationship between repentance and mercy: "Whosoever repenteth, and hardeneth not his heart, he shall have claim on mercy through mine Only Begotten Son, unto a remission of his sins; and these shall enter into my rest" (Alma 12:34).

The unrepentant person is like the criminal who is forced to serve every year, every month, every day of his ten-year term. On the other hand, the repentant person is like the prisoner who is released for good behavior after five years of his ten-year term. Both paid the legal price; both satisfied the laws of justice; but one received a "reduced sentence" by availing himself of the laws of mercy.

In the process of leniency, the Lord has not exempted the repentant from all suffering. Orson F. Whitney taught, "Men and women still suffer, notwithstanding Christ's suffering and atonement but not to the extent that they would have to suffer if such an atonement had not been made."[27]

Repentance still requires remorse of conscience and godly sorrow, but the Lord does allow the repentant to escape the type and depth of suffering he experienced. Thus, mercy has its claim and the repentant are not "exposed to the whole law." Leniency and clemency are extended to their fullest, but no further, and by so doing are able "to appease the demands of justice, that God might be a perfect, just God, and a merciful God also" (Alma 42:15).

This principle is beautifully illustrated in a parable shared by Elder Boyd K. Packer. He tells of a man who incurred substantial debt in order to acquire some coveted goods. The man was warned against incurring the debt, but he felt he could not wait for the luxuries of life. He must have them now. He signed a contract to pay the obligation in what then seemed to be the distant future. The date of payment seemed to be a long time off, but as the days passed the thought of the creditor loomed in the back of the debtor's mind. Eventually, as it always does, the day of reckoning came. The debtor did not have the means to pay. The creditor threatened foreclosure on the debtor's goods if payment were not made. The debtor pled for mercy, but to no avail. The creditor demanded justice—stern, unflinching justice, to which he was entitled. The creditor reminded the debtor that he had signed the contract and agreed to the consequences. The debtor responded that he had no means of repayment and begged for forgiveness. The creditor was not swayed. There would be no justice if the debt were forgiven. Just at the moment when all apparent avenues of escape had vanished, a deliverer appeared on the scene. Elder Packer continues the parable as follows:

> The debtor had a friend. He came to help. He knew the debtor well. He knew him to be shortsighted. He thought him foolish to have gotten himself into such a predicament. Nevertheless, he wanted to help because he loved him. He stepped between them, faced the creditor, and made this offer.
>
> "I will pay the debt if you will free the debtor from his contract so that he may keep his possessions and not go to prison."
>
> As the creditor was pondering the offer, the mediator added, "You demanded justice. Though he cannot pay you, I will do so. You will have been justly dealt with and can ask no more. It would not be just."
>
> And so the creditor agreed.
>
> The mediator turned then to the debtor. "If I pay your debt, will you accept me as your creditor?"
>
> "Oh yes, yes," cried the debtor. "You save me from prison and show mercy to me."
>
> "Then," said the benefactor, "you will pay the debt to me and I will set the terms. It will not be easy, but it will be possible. I will provide a way. You need not go to prison."
>
> And so it was that the creditor was paid in full. He had been justly dealt with. No contract had been broken.
>
> The debtor, in turn, had been extended mercy. Both laws stood fulfilled. Because there was a mediator, justice had claimed its full share, and mercy was fully satisfied.[28]

The debtor of this story was not fully forgiven of his debt, but through the intercession of the friend, the terms of payment were made more palatable, and when those terms were satisfied the debt was erased. Likewise, the Savior made it possible for us to pay our debt on more merciful terms through the divine principle of repentance. He is always offering the maximum mercy without ever encroaching on the demands of justice.

President John Taylor spoke of the engaging relationship between justice and mercy in the gospel setting: "Justice, judgment, mercy and truth all harmonize as the attributes of Deity. 'Justice and truth have met together, righteousness and peace have kissed each other.'"[29] Eliza R. Snow has taught in lyric form that same celestial truth:

> How great, how glorious, how complete,
>
> Redemption's grand design,
>
> Where justice, love, and mercy meet
>
> In harmony divine![30]

Christ Becomes Our Advocate

The Savior pleads our case for mercy. He is our advocate.[31] He is the champion of our cause as no other can be. We have seen advocates of law before earthly tribunals—mere mortals who have argued their cases with spellbinding suspense, whose logic was flawless, mastery of the laws disarming, and powerful petitions compelling. Before such mortals, juries have sat in awe, almost with breathless wonder, moved and swayed by every glance, every crafted word, every passionate plea. Yet such advocates, almost Herculean heroes to their patrons, are no match to Him who pleads our case on high. He is the perfect proponent "to appear in the presence of God for us" (Hebrews 9:24). How fortunate we are that he is our "advocate with the Father" (1 John 2:1).

On more than one occasion, a devoted mother pleaded with Abraham Lincoln for the life of a son who had committed a serious offense while serving in the Union forces. Often, touched by that mother's own sacrifice for her country, Lincoln granted the pardon. Perhaps he thought, "Not for your son's sake, but for your sake I will pardon him." Likewise, God the Father must have been deeply moved by the incomparable sacrifice of the Savior. Like the mother who pleaded for the life of her son, the Savior pleads for the spiritual lives of his spiritual children. Not because of their own worthiness, but because of the Savior's sacrifice, they will be spared. This is the Son's plea to the Father:

> Listen to him who is the advocate with the Father, who is pleading your cause before him—
>
> Saying: Father, behold the sufferings and death of him who did no sin, in whom thou wast well pleased; behold the blood of thy Son which was shed, the blood of him whom thou gavest that thyself might be glorified;

Wherefore, Father, spare these my brethren that believe on my name, that they may come unto me and have everlasting life (D&C 45:3-5; see also Hebrews 7:25; D&C 38:4; 110:4).

For the Savior's sake, the Father of us all granted the necessary pardon. Zenos readily acknowledged this truth: "Thou hast turned thy judgments away from me, because of thy Son" (Alma 33:11).

The Prophet Joseph noted these influential powers of the Savior. While offering the inspired dedicatory prayer at the Kirtland Temple, he made reference to the Savior's power to influence the Father: "Thou . . . wilt turn away thy wrath when thou lookest upon the face of thine Anointed" (D&C 109:53). It seems that there was something so noble in the Savior's countenance, so moving and powerful in reflection upon his sacrifice, that it profoundly affects the Father.

Christ's advocacy was not meant to change the nature of an already perfect God, any more than Moses' plea to save Israel (Deuteronomy 9:13–29; Exodus 32:10–14) or Abraham's "bargaining" with the Lord to spare Sodom (Genesis 18:23-33) transformed God into a more merciful or compassionate being. The scriptures plainly state, "Notwithstanding their sins, my bowels are filled with compassion towards them" (D&C 101:9; see also Isaiah 54:8). Regardless of man's wickedness, God's bowels are *already filled* with compassion, *before* any pleading or advocacy commences.

If God's nature is not altered by such actions, then why does Christ advocate and plead our case? Such pleading may open doors for God that would otherwise be closed under the laws of justice. For example, faith opens the door to miracles. Moroni declared, "For if there be no faith among the children of men *God can do no miracle*" (Ether 12:12; emphasis added; see also Mark 6:5–6; 3 Nephi 19:35). Asking opens the door to revelation: "If thou shalt ask, thou shall receive revelation upon revelation" (D&C 42:61). In a similar manner, perhaps advocacy, when combined with the Savior's sacrifice, opens the door to divine pardons. It may be that under the laws of justice, advocacy is a necessary prerequisite to invoking God's mercy—a manifestation of that eternal principle that all available resources must be exhausted before harnessing the powers of heaven.[32] In other words, it may be that man, or his divine advocate, must plead his best case before divine pardons are dispensed.

Thus it may be that the ardor of the Savior's request for mercy—coupled with his infinite sacrifice—permits the God of heaven, under the laws of justice, to respond in like fashion. It is a fulfillment of the scriptural truth that "mercy hath compassion on mercy" (D&C 88:40). Faith precedes miracles, asking precipitates revelation, and pleading prompts pardons.

There may be yet another reason for advocacy, particularly Christ's: it brings about a spiritual bonding between Christ and his children that cannot be achieved in any other way. It is the thread that knits our hearts and souls together. Who among us could watch him plead our case with fervent passion, listen to him rehearse the grueling events of Gethsemane, hear his expressions of unbridled love, and not feel a spiritual kinship with him?

As a result of the Savior's Atonement and advocacy, at the judgment day, when the eternal fate of all hangs in the balance, the Savior will stand "betwixt them and justice" (Mosiah 15:9). He will then "make intercession for the children of men" (Mosiah 15:8). He will plead the perfect balance between mercy and justice. He will be each man's advocate and hope for salvation.

Reprinted with permission from The Infinite Atonement *(Salt Lake City: Deseret Book, 2000), 299–321.*

Tad R. Callister received his J.D. from the University of California, Los Angeles in 1971 and his LL.M. in Taxation from New York University in 1972. He is currently a partner at Callister and Callister in Glendale, California and serves as an Area Authority Seventy.

Notes

1. Bruce R. McConkie, "The Purifying Power of Gethsemane," *Ensign*, May 1985, 9.

2. B. H. Roberts, *The Truth, The Way, The Life*, edited by John W. Welch (Provo, Utah: BYU Studies, 1996), 418.

3. *Journal of Discourses*, 14:280.

4. Joseph Smith, *Teachings of the Prophet Joseph Smith*, selected and arranged by Joseph Fielding Smith (Salt Lake City: Deseret Book, 1977), 351–52.

5. *Journal of Discourses*, 3:356.

6. *Journal of Discourses*, 25:165–66.

7. Smith, *Teachings of the Prophet Joseph Smith*, 354.

8. *Journal of Discourses*, 7:354 (emphasis added).

9. Joseph Smith, *The Words of Joseph Smith*, compiled and edited by Andrew F. Ehat and Lyndon W. Cook (Salt Lake City: Bookcraft, 1981), 84 (emphasis added).

10. *Journal of Discourses*, 25:57.

11. *Journal of Discourses*, 15:134 (emphasis added).

12. Smith, *Teachings of the Prophet Joseph Smith*, 181.

13. William Shakespeare, *Merchant of Venice*, in *Complete Works*, edited by G.B. Harrison (New York: Harcourt, Brace & World, 1952), 4.1.198–200.

14. LDS Bible Dictionary, in Holy Bible, Authorized King James Version (Salt Lake City: The Church of Jesus Christ of Latter-day Saints, 1979), 697.

15. Bruce R. McConkie, *The Promised Messiah* (Salt Lake City, Utah: Deseret Book, 1978), 245.

16. LDS Bible Dictionary, 697.

17. *Id.* at 697.

18. Stephen E. Robinson, *Believing Christ* (Salt Lake City: Deseret Book, 1992), 30–32.

19. Brigham Young, *The Discourses of Brigham Young*, selected and arranged by John A. Widtsoe (Salt Lake City: Deseret Book, 1961), 387.

20. C. S. Lewis, *Mere Christianity* (New York: Simon & Schuster, 1996), 131.

21. *Journal of Discourses*, 11:301.

22. Shakespeare, *Merchant of Venice*, 4:1.184–89, 195.

23. Robert G. Ingersoll, *The Works of Robert G. Ingersoll* (New York: The Ingersoll League, 1929), 3:172.

24. Young, *Discourses of Brigham Young*, 382.

25. Marion G. Romney, "The Resurrection of Jesus," *Ensign*, May 1982, 9.

26. McConkie, *Promised Messiah*, 326.

27. Orson F. Whitney, *Baptism, the Birth of Water and of the Spirit* (Salt Lake City: Deseret News Press, 1927), 4.

28. Boyd K. Packer, *That All May Be Edified* (Salt Lake City: Bookcraft, 1982), 319.

29. John Taylor, *The Mediation and Atonement* (Salt Lake City: Deseret News Company, 1977), 171–72.

30. Eliza R. Snow, "How Great the Wisdom and the Love," in *Hymns* (1985), no. 195.

31. We have previously discussed that Christ is our judge. If that is the case, one might wonder how he can also be our advocate. Does it make sense that he would plead with himself for leniency on our behalf? The scriptures are clear that the Savior is not pleading with himself, but rather is our "advocate *with the Father*" (D&C 45:3; emphasis added; see also 1 John 2:1; D&C 38:4; 110:4). If that be the case, then the Father must also be a judge. The Doctrine and Covenants confirms this assertion: "God and Christ are the judge of all" (D&C 76:68; see also 2 Timothy 4:1). This is consistent with John's observation that the Father "hath given [the Son] authority to execute judgment *also*" (John 5:27; emphasis added). Evidently, the Father is somewhat like a "presiding judge"—the other judges, the trial judges (i.e., the Savior and his apostles), hear the evidence and render the verdict, but each such trial judge is ultimately accountable to the presiding judge for his actions. The Father delegated judicial powers to his Son (who delegated certain powers to his apostles), but the Son still accounts to the Father. John helps us understand the role of each in the judgment process: "As I [the Son] hear, I judge: and my judgment is just; because I seek not mine own will, but the will of the Father which hath sent me" (John 5:30). In the process of advocating, the Father's will is made manifest in the most favorable circumstance to man, which will the Son then carries out through his judgments.

32. This principle is taught by the Lord in Section 101 of the Doctrine and Covenants. Mobs had driven many of the Saints from their homes in Missouri;

they had threatened and persecuted many others. The Lord instructed the Prophet Joseph as to the order of redress the Saints should take. First they should importune the judge, and then the governor, and then the president. If none of those worked "then will the Lord arise and come forth out of his hiding place, and in his fury vex the nation" (D&C 101:89).

Jesus the Christ,
the Resurrected Son of God

J. Reuben Clark, Jr.

Nineteen and a half centuries ago this morning, as men have counted it, a lone woman, love-driven, moved hurriedly, but carefully, over the rough cobblestones of the streets leading to Golgotha and the newly hewed tomb of Joseph of Arimathaea in the garden, where they had laid the Master. In the deep stillness of the morning air, listening, she might have heard the priests in the Temple court calling to the lookout, peering southward from the topmost pinnacle of the Temple wall: "Is the sky lit up as far as Hebron?" for then the morning sacrifice began. But the lookout would not answer back, for it was still dark.

Reaching the tomb and finding the great sealing stone rolled back and the guard of the high priests gone, Mary Magdalene, for she it was, ran back to Peter and John, telling them the body was gone; she knew not where it was laid. Hastening to the tomb, John outrunning Peter, they found the tomb empty, the burial clothes lying about. They returned, Peter wondering and John seeing and believing (John 20:1–10).

Mary Magdalene, out of whom he had cast seven devils, stood weeping without the sepulchre. Stooping down and looking in, she saw two angels sitting, one at the head, the other at the feet of where Jesus had lain. "Why weepest thou?" said they, and she answering, said, "Because they have taken away my Lord, and I know not where they have laid him" (John 20:11–13).

And there stood a man beside her, who asked, "Why weepest thou? Whom seekest thou?" Thinking it was the gardener, she answered, "Sir, if thou have borne him hence, tell me where thou hast laid him, and I will take him away." Then Jesus, for it was he, saith unto her, "Mary," and she, recognizing him, overwhelmed with emotion, turned and saith unto him, "Rabboni," Master. As she would have touched him he, gently, affectionately, forbade her, saying: "Touch me not; for I am not yet ascended to my Father: but go to my brethren, and say unto them, I ascend unto my Father, and your Father; and to my God, and your God." Returning, she told the disciples all that had happened, but they believed not (John 20:14–18).

Mary saw, talked with, and would have touched, but that she was withheld, the resurrected Christ.

At sunrise, Mary, the Mother of James, and Salome, and other women came to the tomb with spices to prepare the body for final burial, wondering who would roll back the heavy stone sealing the tomb that they might enter. But the tomb was open. Two men stood before them in shining garments, declaring: "Ye seek Jesus of Nazareth. Why seek ye the living among the dead? He is not here, but is risen. Tell his disciples and Peter that he goeth before you into Galilee: there shall ye see him, as he said unto you" (Luke 24:1–6: Mark 16:6–7).

As they quickly fled from the sepulchre, with fear and great joy, to tell the disciples, "Jesus met them, saying, All hail. And they came and held him by the feet, and worshipped him. Then said Jesus unto them, Be not afraid: go tell my brethren that they go into Galilee, and there shall they see me" (Matthew 28:9–10).

So telling no man on the way, they, with Mary Magdalene, returned and told all "unto the eleven, and to all the rest. . . . And their words seemed to them as idle tales, and they believed them not" (Luke 24:9–11).

The Marys and Salome and the other women saw and talked with and touched the risen Christ.

As this first day grew older, Jesus lingered about, seemingly loath to leave the scenes of his mortal ministry and his beloved disciples, he knowing how much they needed his help, being bereft of his presence.

So as Cleopas and another sadly journeyed to Emmaus, Jesus drew near and went with them. But their "eyes were holden that they should not know him." He asked of what they talked. They told him of Jesus and of their trust "that it had been he which should have redeemed Israel"; they told him of the death, the burial, the empty tomb, of the angels who had been seen by the women. And Jesus, trying to teach them to walk in the strength of the spirit, said to them, "O fools, and slow of heart to believe all that the prophets have spoken." He then explained to them, beginning at Moses, the teachings of the prophets about the Christ. Journeying on towards the village, he made as though he would go on, but they asked him to tarry with them, for the day was far spent. So he went in and sat down with them at meat. He took bread and blessed and brake it, and gave to them; then their eyes were opened; they knew him; and he vanished from their sight (Luke 24:13–31).

"They said one to another, Did not our heart burn within us, while he talked with us by the way, and while he opened to us the scriptures?" (Luke 24:32).

They sensed it not, but they had the testimony of the spirit before there came to them the witness of the eyes.

Returning to Jerusalem they found gathered together in a chamber the disciples, who told them, "The Lord is risen indeed, and hath appeared to Simon." They told the disciples of how they themselves had walked and talked and sat at meat with Jesus (Luke 24:33–35).

And even as they spoke one with another, Jesus suddenly stood amongst them in the chamber. Terrified and affrighted they "supposed that they had seen a spirit." Asking why they were troubled, why thoughts arose in their hearts, he said: "Behold my hands and my feet, that it is I myself: handle me, and see; for a spirit hath not flesh and bones, as ye see me have" (Luke 24:36–40).

While "they yet believed not for joy, and wondered," he asked for food; they gave him a piece of fish and honeycomb, and he ate before them (Luke 24:41–43). The Christ, the creator of all things whatsoever that were made, the second member of the Godhead, himself created in the express image of the Father, now returning to sit on the right hand of God, his Father, was a tangible person in human form, that talked and walked and ate, doing what he had seen his Father do. Then he taught them as he taught the two on the way to Emmaus, and they were glad. He saith to them, "Receive ye the Holy Ghost" and the power to remit and retain sins (John 20:22–23).

These all talked and touched and ate with the risen Lord.

But Thomas was not with them. When told of Jesus' visit he believed not, saying he, too, must see, and adding, unless I "put my finger into the print of the nails, and thrust my hand into his side, I will not believe" (John 20:24–25).

At the end of the week they were all again gathered together in a chamber; the doors were shut. Suddenly Jesus stood amongst them, asking Thomas to touch him, saying, "be not faithless, but believing. And Thomas answered and said unto him, My Lord and my God. Jesus saith unto him, Thomas, because thou hast seen me, thou hast believed: blessed are they that have not seen, and yet have believed" (John 20:26–29).

Once more the disciples had talked with the resurrected Christ, and touched his body.

But the disciples yet knew not their calling and their work. Peter said to Thomas, and Nathanael, and the sons of Zebedee, and two others, "I go a fishing." And they said, "We also go with thee." Hieing themselves to the Sea of Tiberias, they went fishing, the work from which he had called them into his service. They fished the night through; they caught nothing. In the early morning, drawing near the shore, they saw standing there a man who, calling to them, asked if they had any meat. They answering no, he called back, "Cast the net on the right side of the ship, and ye shall find," and doing so, they filled their net (John 21:1–6). This was the sign which, three years before, Jesus had given to Simon Peter, and Andrew and James and John, when he called them to his service, saying: "Follow me, and I will make you fishers of men" (Matthew 4:19).

This memory must have surged into the mind of John, for he said to Peter: "It is the Lord," and Peter, girding his fisher's coat about him, for he was naked and would not so come unto the Lord, cast himself into the sea, and went to the Master. Then, again in mild reproof, this time because they had so soon left his service, going back to the old ways, he, "when they had dined," thrice questioned, "Simon, son of Jonas, lovest thou me?"; thrice Peter answered, "Yea, Lord; thou knowest that I love thee"; and thrice the Christ instructed, "Feed my sheep" (John 21:7–17).

Again they talked, sat at meat, and were instructed by the risen Lord.

Thereafter Jesus was seen of James, of above five hundred brethren at once, and of Paul, "as of one born out of due time" (1 Corinthians 15:6–8).

He shewed himself again to his Apostles, on the mount in Galilee to which he had called them, and while they worshipped him, some yet doubted. Declaring all power was given unto him in heaven and earth, he gave them their charge and commission to teach all nations, baptizing, and instructing in the principles he had taught them (Matthew 28:16-20).

Finally, having instructed them to tarry in Jerusalem "until ye be endued with power from on high," he lifted up his hands and blessed them (Luke 24:49–51), then "he was taken up; and a cloud received him out of their sight," heaven-bound to sit on the right hand of God (Acts 1:4, 8–9).

As the disciples stood gazing after him, two men in white apparel stood by them, saying:

"Ye men of Galilee, why stand ye gazing up into heaven? This same Jesus, which is taken up from you into heaven, shall so come in like manner as ye have seen him go into heaven" (Acts 1:10–11).

Thus for forty days after the morning Mary had first seen him at the tomb's mouth, Jesus had moved among his disciples. They saw him, heard him, walked with him, talked with him, sat at meat with him, touched him— they fearing him as a spirit, he said to them, "a spirit hath not flesh and bones, as ye see me have" (Luke 24:39). He was risen indeed, a resurrected being of flesh and bone, and man made in the express image of the Father, a perfect soul, the first fruits of the resurrection, the only Begotten of the Father, the second member of the Godhead.

The Christ came also to this hemisphere, to the other sheep of whom he spoke to the Jews in Jerusalem (John 10:16; 3 Nephi 15:11–24), and ministered among their multitudes for three glorious days. With these other sheep he talked, he blessed their little children, he fed them, he administered the Sacrament to them, he called other disciples to whom also he gave divine commissions (3 Nephi 11–28).

Yet while Jesus still moved and ministered in mortality in Palestine, there came two great occasions when he was called the Christ.

The first came as he and the disciples paused in their great Galilean Mission for a needed momentary respite from their labors. They were in the coasts of Caesarea Philippi. As they rested Jesus asked, "Whom do men say that I the Son of man am?" They answered, some say John the Baptist, some Elias, some Jeremias, or one of the prophets. Then plumbing their own knowledge and testimony, Jesus asked, "Whom say ye that I am?" And Simon Peter answered: "Thou art the Christ, the Son of the living God." Saith the Savior, "Blessed art thou, Simon Barjona: for flesh and blood hath not revealed it unto thee, but my Father which is in heaven" (Matthew 16:13–17). So Peter for an instant glimpsed the full truth.

So also the humble Martha, gently chiding Jesus:

If thou hadst been here, my brother had not died. . . .

Jesus saith unto her, Thy brother shall rise again.

Martha saith unto him, I know that he shall rise again in the resurrection at the last day.

Jesus said unto her, I am the resurrection, and the life: he that believeth in me, thought he were dead, yet shall he live:

And whosoever liveth and believeth in me shall never die. Believest thou this?

She saith unto him, Yea, Lord: I believe that thou art the Christ, the Son of God, which should come into the world (John 11:21, 23–27).

Thus while he lived amongst them, there came to the humblest of them—Peter, the fisherman, and Martha, the good housewife "cumbered about much serving" (Luke 10:40)—the testimony for which men since have devoutly lived and gloriously died—that Jesus was the Christ, the Son of God.

At the beginning and ushering-in of this Last Dispensation, the Father and Son appeared in person, in the form in which Jesus returned to the Father, to the boy Joseph in the woods, in the most glorious vision vouched to man in all time (Joseph Smith—History 1:17–20).

And thereafter, Joseph and Sidney together declared:

And now, after the many testimonies which have been given of him, this is the testimony, last of all which we give of him: That he lives!

For we saw him, even on the right hand of God; and we heard the voice bearing record that he is the Only Begotten of the Father—

That by him, and through him, and of him, the worlds are and were created, and the inhabitants thereof are begotten sons and daughters unto God (D&C 76:22–24).

And now may I, of the lowliest of the lowly who seek to serve him, and fully acknowledging my own weaknesses and imperfections, bear in deep humility my own testimony, born of the Spirit, that Jesus is the Christ, the Son of the Living God, the Only Begotten in the flesh, chosen before the foundations of the earth were laid to be the Redeemer of the World, the First Fruits of the Resurrection, through and by whom the spirits and bodies of all men will, in the due time of the Lord, be reunited and resurrected from the grave, "they who have done good, in the resurrection of the just; and they who have done evil, in the resurrection of the unjust" (D&C 76:17).

May I be preserved in this testimony till I lay down my body in my last sleep, I pray, in the Lord's name. Amen.

This Easter radio broadcast was given over KSL in Salt Lake City, Utah on March 28, 1948. Reprinted with permission from On the Way to Immortality and Eternal Life *(Salt Lake City: Deseret Book, 1950), 69–78.*

J. Reuben Clark, Jr. (1871–1961) received his LL.B. from Columbia University in 1906, served as editor of the Columbia Law Review, *Assistant Solicitor and then Solicitor for the U.S. Department of State 1906–13, author of* Memorandum on the Monroe Doctrine *1928, and U.S. Ambassador to Mexico 1930–33. He served as a counselor in the First Presidency of The Church of Jesus Christ of Latter-day Saints 1933–61.*

Lawyers and the Atonement

Thomas B. Griffith

Aloha. I am honored to be here today to speak to students, faculty, and staff at Brigham Young University—Hawaii. As was mentioned, I am a graduate of the College of Humanities at the "other" BYU, and I must say that the decision to attend BYU and participate actively in the unique blend of the life of the mind and the life of the spirit offered at Church schools is among the most important decisions I have made in my life. I congratulate you on your choice of school, and I encourage you to take full advantage of that which is uniquely offered at a university that has at its core purpose the worship and adoration of the Risen Lord Jesus Christ and the commitment to making of its students disciples who will actively prepare themselves, their families, and their communities for his return.

There was a time when most universities shared a common purpose. The pursuit of an education was not seen simply as a means to enter the workforce; rather, education was a component of discipleship: the acknowledgment that God was sovereign and that the pursuit of knowledge was the pursuit of the Divine. As a student at BYU more than 20 years ago, I heard a great rabbi-scholar, Jacob Neusner, lecture on a common trait of Judaism and Mormonism, the idea captured in the phrase "the glory of God is intelligence" (D&C 93:36). Dr. Neusner said of Judaism that which hopefully can be said of your experience here at BYU—Hawaii:

> The most distinctive and paramount trait of Judaism as it has been known for the past two thousand years is the conviction that the primary mode of the service of God (not the sole mode, but the paramount one) is the study of Torah. Torah is revelation. Torah, by its content and its nature, encompasses all of God-given knowledge.... It is Torah which reveals the mind of God, the principles by which He shaped reality. So studying Torah is not merely imitating God ... but is a way to the apprehension of God and the attainment of the sacred.[1]

Earlier this week, I confronted a negative view not just of my profession in general, but—more troubling—of my personal role as a lawyer. Nine months ago the governor of Virginia, Jim Gilmore, asked me to serve as general counsel to the Advisory Commission on Electronic Commerce, a commission created by Congress to study and make proposals on how Congress should approach the thorny issue of whether a person should have to pay taxes on goods purchased over the Internet. The commission comprised 19 distinguished individuals including three governors, the chairman of AT&T, the president of American Online, the president of MCI-WorldCom, the president of Time-Warner, the president of Charles Schwab, and the president of Gateway. The commission held its last meetings earlier this week in Dallas, Texas, and as was reported in the national media, it was contentious. As general counsel, I was called upon to offer my opinion on a divisive topic. The opinion I offered gave support to a position that Governor Gilmore had pursued and that was vigorously opposed by a minority on the commission. I came under some heavy public criticism by some of those commission members. The controversy was reported widely in the media, and my name was mentioned in a *New York Times* article in a way that I thought unfairly characterized what took place.[2] The day the article appeared, I went and spoke with the reporter. I explained what had taken place and tried to place it in a larger context that would help him see the error of what he had written. He listened respectfully and said, "Tom, it isn't anything personal. I know what you were doing. Lawyers are hired guns, and you were doing what was necessary so that your client, Governor Gilmore, could do what he wanted to do."

Without boring you with the details of the matter, you'll need to trust me that this assessment was flat-out wrong. I tried to explain to him why he was wrong, but I had the distinct impression that he was not persuaded. In his mind I was a "hired gun" willing to do anything to help the client do what he wanted.

Now, I didn't have this problem with my prior career. I was a director in the Church Educational System's Department of Seminaries and Institutes. I was responsible for delivering weekday religious education to LDS high school and college-age students in the Baltimore, Maryland area. Yet, I left that wonderful vocation to pursue a career in the law. What you will hear today are my musings about that decision.

The inspiration for my remarks came several years ago while I was sitting in a priesthood lesson on "building Zion." The next day I was to speak at the "other" BYU about being Senate legal counsel, the chief legal officer of the United States Senate. Talks at BYU should be different than talks at other universities, because you have a freedom here to explore how the Atonement affects every aspect of life. That priesthood lesson got me thinking about the relationship between being a lawyer and the Atonement of Christ.

Let us go back to March 1830. The 24-year-old Prophet Joseph Smith has culminated a 10-year period of divine tutoring by publishing to the world the Book of Mormon, another testament of Jesus Christ, and restoring the Church of Jesus Christ. He and his band of followers number a few hundred. His primary daily activity is organizing the fledgling Church according to a biblical model revealed to him from the Lord. He is engaged in an intensive study of the Bible. The Lord wants Joseph to be immersed in that holy record so that he will be open to receive the revelation he needs to found and direct the Church on correct principles. Sometime during that first year of the infancy of the Church, while studying, pondering, and praying over the Book of Genesis, the Lord reveals to Joseph Smith the remarkable story of a major prophet who is mentioned only briefly in the current version of Genesis. The prophet is Enoch, and his story is to become a model for the infant Church. What Enoch created among his people became the goal for these early Latter-day Saints:

> The fear of the Lord was upon all nations, so great was the glory of the Lord, which was upon his people. And the Lord blessed the land, and they were blessed upon the mountains, and upon the high places, and did flourish.
>
> And the Lord called his people Zion, because they were of one heart and one mind, and dwelt in righteousness; and there was no poor among them.
>
> And Enoch continued his preaching in righteousness unto the people of God. And it came to pass in his days, that he built a city that was called the City of Holiness, even Zion (Moses 7:17–19).

From what we can tell, what Enoch and his people achieved has never been duplicated. The Saints at Jerusalem in the days of the Apostles came close.[3] Those Book of Mormon people who witnessed the post-Resurrection visit to ancient America of the Risen Lord Jesus laid the foundation for a Christ-centered culture that endured for 200 years.[4]

But it was Enoch and his people that captivated the mind and soul of Joseph. Following their example became the rallying cry. Preparing a people who were ready to meet the Lord became the watchword. And what was it about the people of Enoch that allowed them to model for us perfectly what it means to prepare to meet the Lord? The key, I believe, is in verse 18.

> And the Lord called his people Zion, because they were of one heart and one mind, and dwelt in righteousness; and there was no poor among them (Moses 7:18).

The people of Enoch achieved "at-one-ment" with God, with themselves, with their families, and with their community. They set the mark for true spirituality. Spirituality begins with allowing the effects of Christ's atoning sacrifice and his awe-inspiring grace to heal the wounds that sin has inflicted upon our broken hearts. Spirituality begins with uniting us with God from whom we have been separated by sin. But from Enoch and his people we learn—and the powerful symbolism of the Sacrament of the Lord's Supper and the temple endowment confirms this—the highest form of spirituality is when we work to make the effects of the Atonement radiate beyond ourselves and our families to unite our communities. The work of community building is, I believe, the most important spiritual work to which we are called. All other work is preparatory.

Here is the insight I offer for you to consider. To build a community that extends beyond your family or congregation—and I believe we are compelled by our understanding of the Atonement of our Savior to do just that—involves the law. Properly understood, the highest and most noble role of a lawyer, then, is to help build communities founded on the rule of law. By doing so, lawyers are participating in the redeeming work of the atoning power of the Savior at its zenith. To be sure, the working out of the power of the Atonement occurs initially at the intimate level of a sinner realizing her individual need for God's grace. But it must also ultimately include creating a community based on the rule of law.

The rule of law is the idea, of staggering importance in the progress of humankind, that a community should not be organized according to the principle that might makes right. Rather, a community and its laws should reflect the reality that each person is a son or daughter of God and by virtue of that fact alone is entitled to be treated with dignity, respect, and fairness. The most famous and influential expression of this radical idea came from the pen of Thomas Jefferson, Virginia's greatest son and the founder of my other alma mater:

> We hold these truths to be self-evident, that all men are created equal, that they are endowed by their Creator with certain unalienable Rights, that among these are Life, Liberty, and the pursuit of Happiness.
>
> That to secure these rights, Governments are instituted among Men, deriving their just powers from the consent of the governed.[5]

Jefferson was correct to ground the rule of law in the fact that there is a God who has created and endowed each human with rights. But as Christians we know there is more to it than that. We know that each human has dignity not only because he has been created by God, but because he has also been redeemed by God. The Lord Jesus Christ suffered, bled, and died for each member of the human family so that everyone who accepts his act of gracious love would have access to the power of his redemption. As Latter-day Saint Christians, we have significant insights into Christ's redemptive love that must be at the core of who we are as a people and what we are doing in our lives and in the world.

Let's return again to the year 1830. Joseph Smith has spoken with the Father and the Son. He has, by the gift and power of God, translated the Book of Mormon, a powerful second witness to the Bible of the power of Christ's atoning sacrifice. He has received priesthood authority under the hands of angelic messengers, John the Baptist, Peter, James, and John. He stands ready to restore to the earth The Church of Jesus Christ—the vessel that will become the primary means by which the Lord will prepare the world for his Second Coming and millennial reign. And yet there is a final lesson the young Prophet must learn. In many ways, I believe it to be the most important lesson he needed to hear—the capstone of his divine tutoring. Before Joseph Smith could organize anew Christ's Church, he needed to understand that every activity of that church must be done with one thing in mind. The stage for this final lesson had been set a year before in a revelation from the Lord:

> Remember the worth of souls is great in the sight of God;
>
> For, behold, the Lord your Redeemer suffered death in the flesh; wherefore he suffered the pain of all men, that all men might repent and come unto him (D&C 18:10–11).

Joseph knew, as all of Christendom knew, that God's love for his children was manifest in the life and death of his Son. He knew that "God so loved the world, that he gave his only begotten Son" (John 3:16). He knew, as did all who loved and treasured the Bible, that Christ suffered for us in Gethsemane and on the cross at Calvary.

But what Joseph did not know, what no one in the world knew, is the extent of the Savior's personal suffering for us. That knowledge, indispensable to one who would deign to act in the name of the Lord, came to Joseph Smith in a revelation now found in the Doctrine and Covenants, section 19. It was the last recorded revelation Joseph Smith received before he organized the Church in April 1830. It was the final, indispensable lesson for him. It is an indispensable lesson for us. In my view, this revelation and the insight it afford into the breadth and depth of the Savior's gracious love for all humankind is the most significant lesson of the restored gospel. If all we had from the Restoration was this knowledge alone, I would say, as our Jewish brothers and sisters say at Passover when recounting each act of God's message, "Dayenu" ("It is enough.").

In section 19, the Lord takes Joseph Smith (and us) with him back to the Garden of Gethsemane, the scene of some of his most agonizing moments:

> For behold, I, God, have suffered these things for all, that they might not suffer if they would repent;
>
> But if they would not repent they must suffer even as I;
>
> Which suffering caused myself, even God, the greatest of all, to tremble because of pain, and to bleed at every pore, and to suffer both body and spirit—and would that I might not drink the bitter cup, and shrink—
>
> Nevertheless, glory be to the Father, and I partook and finished my preparations unto the children of men (D&C 19:16–19).

For this next thought I rely upon the insight of Eugene England, who notes that the Lord's description of his suffering in verse 18 is incomplete.[6] The dash at the end of the phrase leads me to believe that the Lord could not describe to the Prophet Joseph the full extent of his agony and suffering for us, even some 1,800 years after it took place. It was just too painful for him to recount, even after all those years.

As Latter-day Saints, we, of all people, should value the worth of souls, because we have resources that teach us the depth of the Lord's love for each member of the human race. If our Savior has been willing to endure such suffering for our fellowmen, how can we do anything but exert all our efforts to serve them, too.

It was the great C. S. Lewis who, with an uncommon understanding of the Lord's love for his children, wrote:

> The load, or weight, or burden of my neighbour's glory should be laid on my back, a load so heavy that only humility can carry it. . . . It is a serious thing to live in a society of possible gods and goddesses, to remember that the dullest and most uninteresting person you can talk to may one day be a creature which, if you saw it now, you would be strongly tempted to worship. . . . It is in the light of these overwhelming possibilities, it is with the awe and circumspection proper to them, that we should conduct all our dealings with one another, all friendships, all loves, all play, all politics. There are no ordinary people. You have never talked to a mere mortal. . . . Next to the Blessed Sacrament itself, your neighbour is the holiest object presented to your senses.[7]

The rule of law, the idea that each human being is entitled to the protection of the law, is most firmly rooted and grounded when we approach an understanding of what the Savior has done for each human being. Thus, the calling of lawyers is to build communities based on the rule of law, communities that reach us in the direction of a Zion society, a place where the power of the Atonement unites us.

At this point I should have persuaded each of you to change your plans and go to law school and to believe that together we will change the world. But before you do, let me issue you a warning. I hope when you hear this warning you will see that I realize that the picture of lawyering I have just painted is, shall we say, idealized. I am well aware of the fact that most lawyers are hardly the primary emissaries of the Atonement.

To deliver this warning, I turn to a play written by Robert Bolt, *A Man for All Seasons*. The play is based on the last years of the life of Sir Thomas More, the patron saint of lawyers. More lived in 16th-century England and was lord chancellor, an aide to King Henry VIII, like today's prime minister. After the king, More was the most powerful person in England. He was also the most widely respected, because of his piety and erudition. He was a leader of the "new learning" that was the hallmark of the Renaissance. More was a devoted family man and a father who was actively involved in the education of his children—most remarkably for his time, that of his daughters. He was also a passionate churchman, a devout Roman Catholic, who, although he saw much in the church that needed reform, was committed to the church that he believed was founded by the Lord.

More found himself caught between his allegiance to the crown and the church when Henry declared himself head of the English church and renounced the authority of the pope. To secure his position, Henry required each of his subjects to swear an oath of allegiance recognizing him as supreme head of the Church of England. More refused, resigned his office, and was eventually imprisoned for his recalcitrance.

The climatic scene of the play is the trial of Thomas More. The charge is treason. The penalty is death. More's nemesis, Thomas Cromwell, is his chief prosecutor. Lord Norfolk, More's good friend, is his reluctant judge. Cromwell knows that More has done nothing worthy of the charge of treason. Although he has refused to swear to the oath, More has been silent as to his reasons, knowing that under the law his silence should protect him.

Cromwell's ruse is to find a witness who will perjure himself and accuse More of speaking out against the king. He finds a willing witness in one Richard Rich. Early on in the play we meet Rich as an aspiring young man who frequents the household of Thomas More. He is hoping to gain More's favor and win an appointment to government office. More, however, sees in Rich a weakness of character that would make him ill-suited to hold a position of power where he would be the target of bribes. More tells Rich that he will not help him find an office in government and counsels him instead to "go where he won't be tempted."[8] In disappointment, Rich turns to Thomas Cromwell, who rewards Rich with government posts in exchange for Rich's increasingly diabolic participation in a conspiracy to bring down More.

The stage is now set for the finale: More, the accused, beaten down from months of imprisonment in the Tower of London, sits alone in the court dressed in a simple monk-like tattered gown. Rich, decked out in the finery of a dandy, is called as the witness. He takes an oath to tell the truth and then perjures himself by falsely testifying that More made treasonous statements to him.

More, knowing that this perjured testimony will lead to his death, speaks:

More: In good faith, Rich, I am sorrier for your perjury than my peril.

Norfolk: Do you deny this?

More: Yes! My lords, if I were a man who heeded not the taking of an oath, you know well I need not be here. Now I will take an oath! If what Master Rich had said is true, then I pray I may never see God in the face! Which I would not say were it otherwise for anything on earth. . . . Is it probable—is it probable—that after so long a silence on this, the very point so urgently sought of me, I should open my mind to such a man as that?[9]

Cromwell excuses Rich from the stand. As Rich steps down and proceeds to exit, More says to Cromwell:

> More: I *have* one question to ask the witness. (Rich stops.) That's a chain of office you are wearing. (Reluctantly Rich faces him.) May I see it? (Norfolk motions him to approach. More examines the medallion.) The red dragon. (To Cromwell) What's this?
>
> Cromwell: Sir Richard is appointed Attorney-General for Wales.
>
> More: (Looking into Rich's face, with pain and amusement) For Wales? Why, Richard, it profits a man nothing to give his soul for the whole world . . . but for Wales![10]

Now, my ancestors are from Wales, but I get the point. What is it that we are willing to gain in this world at the price of the loss of our souls?

The Savior warns us of one category of activity that almost always is pursued and gained at the cost of our souls, and it is a warning that each of us would do well to heed, living as we do in such affluent and materialistic times. Remember the words of the Savior to his disciples after they had seen the rich young man who turned down a call from the Savior to join them because he was unwilling to sell his many possessions, give the proceeds to the poor, and follow Jesus and the disciples:

> . . . "I tell you the truth [said Jesus], it is hard for a rich man to enter the kingdom of heaven.
>
> Again I tell you, it is easier for a camel to go through the eye of a needle than for a rich man to enter the kingdom of God."
>
> When the disciples heard this, they were greatly astonished and asked, "Who then can be saved?"
>
> Jesus looked at them and said, "With man this is impossible, but with God all things are possible" (Matthew 19:23–26 NIV).

It is C. S. Lewis' view that the "riches" referred to by the Lord here cover more than riches in the ordinary sense. He believes "it really covers riches in every sense—good fortune, health, popularity, and all the things one wants to have."[11] If Lewis is right (and C. S. Lewis is almost always right when it comes to matters of discipleship),[12] each of us stands in peril to the extent that our trust, our desire, and our passions are motivated by anything other than a profound sense of gratitude to the Savior for his atoning sacrifice. President Spencer W. Kimball had strong words for us on this point. He said that if we are motivated by riches, we are latter-day idolaters.[13]

In his mercy, where the Lord provides such an ominous warning, he always provides a sure means of escape, although it is rarely an easy way out. Let us return to Moses 7:18. If the people of Enoch are to be our role models for how we should work to carry out the effects of the Atonement in society, we find in this verse a description of what we should be doing.

There were four characteristics of their Zion society. They were of "one heart" and "one mind," qualities that underscore the process of at-one-ment at work. I am not exactly certain what these traits mean. They are susceptible to many interpretations. So, too, with the third trait, that they "dwelt in righteousness." But as to the fourth trait, I think the mark is clear: "There was no poor among them." To be sure, poverty can occur at many levels.[14] But I think there is no question that in addition to a poverty of love, the Lord is concerned about a poverty of means. One of the most consistent themes of the revelations the Lord gave to the Prophet in the founding days of the Restoration is the message that we are the "look to the poor and the needy, and administer to their relief that they shall not suffer" (D&C 38:35). We are to get involved in community building. We extend the effects of the Atonement to their farthest reaches by creating a society that has as its goal helping those who have been left behind.

As President Kimball taught us so pointedly, we live in a culture that is saturated by the unhealthy pursuit to acquire wealth for excessive consumption. I recognize that lawyers are at the forefront of that charge. They are always a step or two behind the investment bankers and the entrepreneurs, but, nevertheless, they are there, comrades-in-arms. Let me make clear, so that I am not misunderstood, there is nothing wrong, indeed there is much good, about the creation of wealth. The issue is the purpose for which the wealth is sought and the ends to which acquired wealth is put.

Remember the counsel of Jacob, the brother of Nephi, in the Book of Mormon: "Think of your brethren like unto yourselves, and be familiar with all and free with your substance, that they may be rich like unto you. But before ye seek for riches, seek ye for the kingdom of God. And after ye have obtained a hope in Christ ye shall obtain riches, if ye seek them" (Jacob 2:17–19). Now that is a great promise. The Lord promises us the very material wealth we spend so much of our lives pursuing. But, as you might have guessed, there is a catch, and, upon closer examination of what Jacob said, it is a significant condition. This promise is only to those who seek riches (and I am using the C. S. Lewis view that riches includes wealth, power, and popularity) "for the intent to do good." But what does that mean? Isn't "doing good" so vague that it allows too much room to maneuver? I think Jacob must have been a very good lawyer, because in the very next phase he closed that loophole by defining what the Lord means by "doing good" with riches: "to clothe the naked, and to feed the hungry, and to liberate the captive, and administer relief to the sick and the afflicted" (Jacob 2:19).

Are those our goals as a people? Are those your goals in pursuing your vocation? They must be. Our participation in society, something we are called to do by our understanding of the Savior's love for all humankind, must have as its primary purpose this definition of doing good.

In conclusion, allow me to share with you the words that inspired me to become a lawyer. They come from my boyhood hero, Robert F. Kennedy. As I read them to you today, they remind me of how far short of the mark I have fallen in my discipleship as a lawyer, but I hope they remain a lodestar.

[The Gross National Product] counts air pollution and cigarette advertising, and ambulances to clear our highways of carnage. It counts special locks for our doors and the jails for those who break them. . . . Yet the gross national product does not allow for the health of our children or the joy of their play. It does not include the beauty of our poetry or the strength of our marriages, the intelligence of our public debate or the integrity of our public officials. It measures neither our wit nor our courage, neither our wisdom nor our learning, neither our compassion nor our devotion to our country; it measures everything, in short, except that which makes life worthwhile. And it can tell us everything about America except why we are proud that we are Americans.[15]

There is discrimination in New York, apartheid in South Africa, and serfdom in the mountains of Peru. People starve in the streets of India; intellectuals go to jail in Russia; thousands are slaughtered in Indonesia; wealth is lavished on armaments everywhere. These are differing evils, but they are the common works of man. They reflect the imperfection of human justice, the inadequacy of human compassion, the defectiveness of our sensibility towards the sufferings of our fellows; they mark the limit of our ability to use knowledge for the well-being of others. And, therefore, they call upon common qualities of conscience and indignation, a shared determination to wipe away the unnecessary sufferings of our fellow human beings at home and around the world.[16]

[Let no one be discouraged by] the belief there is nothing one man or one woman can do against the enormous array of the world's ills—against misery and ignorance, injustice and violence. . . . Few will have the greatness to bend history itself; but each of us can work to change a small portion of events, and in the total of all those acts will be written the history of this generation. It is from numberless diverse acts of courage and belief that human history is shaped. Each time a man stands up for an ideal, or acts to improve the lot of others, or strikes out against injustice, he send a tiny ripple of hope, and crossing each other from a million different centers of energy and daring, those ripples build a current which can sweep down the mightiest walls of oppression and resistance.[17]

The reason we must get involved in our society is to help those who have been left out or behind. We have a robust debate about the best way to do that. As a political conservative, I am certain that I would strongly disagree with my boyhood hero's views about how to get there. But I believe that the aim must be the same.

When the boy Joseph Smith went into the grove of trees "on the morning of [that] beautiful, clear day, early in the spring of eighteen hundred and twenty" (Joseph Smith—History 1:14), he was driven there by two related purposes. The first, which he stressed in his earliest known account of the First Vision, was to repair his relationship with God, a relationship that had been strained by the withering effects of sin.[18] The second purpose, featured more prominently in the 1838 account of the First Vision canonized in our scripture (see Joseph Smith—History 1:1–20), involved community building: which church should he join?

Those two questions are intertwined and inseparable. Our discipleship must involve both. How do we become at one with God? How do we become at one with our fellow travelers? The answer to both is the same, even and especially for lawyers: by participating in the atoning sacrifice of our Lord and Savior Jesus Christ and making that ongoing act of mercy and grace the foundation for all we do.

I bear you my witness that the Savior lives, that he stands at the head of his Church today, and I encourage all of us to give our best efforts to the work of extending the effects of his Atonement throughout our society. I say these things in the name of our advocate with the Father, the Lord Jesus Christ. Amen.

This BYU–Hawaii Presidential Lecture was given in Laie, Hawaii on March 23, 2000. Reprinted from the Clark Memorandum, *Spring 2001, 8–15.*

Thomas B. Griffith received his J.D. from the University of Virginia in 1985 and served as Senate Legal Counsel of the United States 1995–99. He is currently Assistant to the President and General Counsel of Brigham Young University in Provo, Utah.

Notes

1. Jacob Neusner, *The Glory of God Is Intelligence: Four Lectures on the Role of Intellect in Judaism* (Provo, Utah: BYU Religious Studies Center, 1978) 2, 7.

2. David Cay Johnston, "Agreement on Internet Taxes Eludes Deeply Divided Commission," *New York Times*, 21 March 2000, sec. C, p. 1, col. 2, late edition.

3. "They devoted themselves to the apostles' teaching and fellowship, to the breaking of bread and the prayers. Awe came upon everyone, because many wonders and signs were being done by the apostles. All who believed were together and had all things in common; they would sell their possessions and goods and distribute the proceeds to all, as any had need. Day by day, as they spent much time together in the temple, they broke bread at home and ate their food with glad and generous hearts, praising God and having the good-will of all people" (Acts 2:42–47 NRSV).

4. "And they had all things common among them; therefore there were not rich and poor, bond and free, but they were all made free, and partakers of the heavenly gift. . . . And it came to pass that there was no contention in the land, because of the love of God which did dwell in the hearts of the people. And there were no envyings, nor strifes, nor tumults, nor whoredoms, nor lyings, nor murders, nor any manner of lasciviousness; and surely there could not be a happier people among all the people who had been created by the hand of God. . . . [T]hey were in one, the children of Christ, and heirs to the kingdom of God" (4 Nephi 1:3, 15–17).

5. Declaration of Independence, pars. 2–3.

6. See Eugene England, *The Quality of Mercy* (Salt Lake City: Bookcraft, 1992), 52.

7. C. S. Lewis, *The Weight of Glory and Other Addresses* (New York: Macmillan, 1980), 18–19.

8. Robert Bolt, *A Man for All Seasons* (New York: Random House, 1962), 5.

9. *Id.* at 90–91.

10. *Id.* at 91–92, emphasis in original.

11. C. S. Lewis, *God in the Dock: Essays on Theology and Ethics* (Grand Rapids, MI: Eerdmans, 1970), 51–52.

12. "I have chosen to talk about the insights and contributions of C. S. Lewis concerning how exacting Christian discipleship really is. . . . [W]hile it is not doctrine for which I look to Lewis, I find his *depiction* of discipleship especially articulate and helpful. The yield from Lewis in this respect is abundant." Neal A. Maxwell, "C. S. Lewis: Insights on Discipleship" in *C. S. Lewis: the Man and His Message*, eds. Andrew C. Skinner and Robert L. Millet (Salt Lake City: Bookcraft, 1999), 8–9.

13. Spencer W. Kimball, "The False Gods We Worship," *Ensign*, June 1976, 4.

14. Mother Teresa, she who gave her life in service to "the poorest of the poor," reminds us: "Where is that hunger? There is a hunger for love. We must have the courage to recognize the poor you may have right in your own families. Find them, love them, put your love for them in a living action. For in loving them, you are loving God Himself." *Mother Teresa: A Film by Ann and Jeanette Petrie* (1986).

15. Robert F. Kennedy, "Recapturing America's Moral Vision" (18 March 1969, Kansas State University) in *Make Gentle the Life of The World: The Vision of Robert F. Kennedy*, ed. Maxwell Taylor Kennedy (New York: Harcourt Brace, 1998), 21.

16. Robert F. Kennedy, "Day of Affirmation Address" (6 June 1966, University of Capetown) in William J. Vanden Heuvel and Milton Gwirtzman, *On His Own: Robert F. Kennedy, 1964–1968* (Garden City, NY: Doubleday, 1970), 156.

17. Arthur M. Schlesinger, Jr., *Robert Kennedy and His Times* (Boston: Houghton Mifflin, 1978), 745–56.

18. See Milton V. Backman, Jr., "Joseph Smith's Recitals of the First Vision," *Ensign*, January 1985, 11–13.

A Christ-Like Attitude

Marion G. Romney

On April 3, 1836, the Savior appeared to the Prophet Joseph Smith and his companion, Oliver Cowdery, in the Kirtland Temple. The record of this vision is found in section 110 of the Doctrine and Covenants. In verse 4, the Savior declares:

> I am the first and the last; I am he who liveth, I am he who was slain; I am your advocate with the Father.

Jesus is our advocate with the Father. You young people who have completed three years of legal training are about to embark on a life as advocates. Be the best earthly advocates you can be. Do no overlook the fact, however, that there is a spiritual, an eternal dimension to advocacy. As we honor you tonight at your commencement, I challenge you to become Christ-like advocates.

When the Board of Trustees announced ten years ago this month there would be a Law School at the Brigham Young University, many wondered about the purposes behind our action. I understand that question is still asked from time to time, and that many of you would be interested in hearing my views concerning the purposes of this Law School. I am not sure it would be worthwhile or even possible for me to give you a complete catalogue of those purposes. Nor is it necessary. Much more important than a list of the Law School's purposes is this fact: whatever they are (and I assure you they exist) the best way to achieve them is for you and those who have graduated before you and those who will graduate after you to respond to the challenge I have laid before you to become Christ-like advocates.

What are the characteristics of the Christ-like advocate? I would like to describe three of these characteristics and illustrate them by using examples from the life of the Savior and from the life of the man for whom this Law

245

School is named, J. Reuben Clark. I knew President Clark personally. I was his disciple. I learned from him as a lawyer, as a child of God, and as one who is convinced of the reality of the Restoration. I would urge each of you to become familiar with his life, his ideals, and his principles. You can gain such a familiarity by reading his writings—principally *Stand Fast By Our Constitution*—and also by reading his biography.

The first characteristic of a Christ-like advocate is integrity. I speak of integrity in its broadest sense. No characteristic is more highly prized by members of the legal profession.

Integrity certainly means honesty, but I believe it includes more than honesty. It includes that cornerstone principle of the Savior's life and teachings, a concern for other people. The reason I give such a broad meaning to integrity is that the word means "completeness" or "wholeness." I can think of no better formula for the complete person than the one the Savior gave: to love our Heavenly Father and to love other people as ourselves.

But how, you may ask, can concern, respect, and even love for other people be reconciled with a lawyer's duty to vigorously represent his client? I recognize that there is a potential tension between a lawyer's duty to represent his client and his obligations to other lawyers and to society as a whole. There are times when this tension will present some difficult problems. (Those kinds of problems are outside the scope of this evening's discussion, though I would urge, parenthetically, that when those problems arise, you not hesitate to discuss them with more experienced members of the bar. You will find your professional colleagues more willing to be helpful in that respect than you might have anticipated.)

For present purposes, I would like to make only three observations. First, neither your obligation to your client nor any other professional obligation should ever require you to be dishonest or in any other respect to compromise your integrity. Your professional responsibilities neither require nor permit you to deal in overt falsehood or misrepresentation, and if your client insists that you do, get another client.

I doubt that any of you will ever have a harder choice to make in this respect than President Clark had on one occasion. I hope that you will make it the same way he did. After many years of struggling, it finally appeared that his chances for success might be realized when he became legal counsel to the first of this country's multi-national corporations. The corporation changed presidents, however, and the new president insisted on taking some steps that were beyond the bounds of what integrity would permit. President Clark had to choose between his conscience and financial success. In the words of the biographer of his law school and professional years, Brother Frank Fox, Reuben let "the dream [of financial success] go glimmering."[1]

Second, even beyond the requirements of truth-telling, service to the client and his interests seldom requires the lawyer to sacrifice the kind of civility that is consistent with the Savior's instruction that we should love all people, including our enemies. All too often, practicing lawyers confuse the pursuit of their clients' interests with lack of courtesy and thoughtfulness toward the opposing lawyer. Most of the time, the two are unrelated. Rarely, if ever, will a client's interests be advanced by rudeness or discourtesy. Do not discard, as a lawyer, those basic attitudes of concern for other people that you have come to regard as the foundation stone of virtue in general.

Third, integrity means being prepared to say or do what must be said or done, regardless of the consequences. After the Savior fed the 5,000, many of those who had been fed followed Him to Capernaum. The Savior knew that they followed Him because He had fed them and would be offended if He declared Himself to be the promised Messiah. Nevertheless, He declared:

> I am the bread of life: he that cometh to me shall never hunger; and he that believeth on me shall never thirst (John 6:35).

Not only those who had followed Him after having been fed but also His own disciples found this declaration troubling. In the Gospel of John, we read that "from that time many of his disciples went back, and walked no more with him" (John 6:66).

A second characteristic of the Christ-like advocate is compassion. In response to the question of "a certain lawyer, ... who is my neighbour?", the Savior reminded us of the importance of compassion by relating the Parable of the Good Samaritan (see Luke 10:30–37). The Savior was compassionate to all. He reached out to touch the lives of those who were despised because of their race, their social condition, or their physical or mental imperfection. We ought to be aware of the needs of individuals beyond our inner circle of family and friends. As advocates, you should be prepared to assist a client who is downtrodden, destitute, or unpopular.

We should not overlook, however, the needs of those who are closest to us. Compassion should begin in our own homes. In the course of your career as advocates, there will be a continuing temptation to spend long hours away from your spouse and children. President Clark struggled with this problem throughout the early years of his career. In October 1909, his wife, Luacine, suffered an allergic reaction to morphine and hovered for two hours between life and death. His biographer, Frank Fox, indicates that this episode had a profound effect on his life:

> He seemed to see life through new eyes. His days at the office grew perceptibly shorter, while evenings at home lengthened. He learned, in fact, to do much of his work in a private study upstairs, his books and notes piled around him and his infant son propped on the desk beyond the lamplight. And when the children came down with chicken pox in December, he let his work go entirely and became a full-time nurse.[2]

I hope that you will be perceptive to the needs—temporal and spiritual—of your spouse and children and remember that the most important service we render in this life is in our own homes.

A third characteristic of the Christ-like advocate is teachability. I speak of teachability as a learning process that encompasses not only an awareness of our lack of knowledge, but also a desire to learn and improve.

The Savior was teachable. The Apostle Paul tells us about the Savior's learning process in Hebrews:

> Though he were a Son, yet learned he obedience by the things which he suffered;
>
> And being made perfect, he became the author of eternal salvation unto all them that obey Him (Hebrews 5:8–9).

As a result of this learning process, the scriptures tell us that "all that heard him [when He was but twelve years of age] were astonished at his understanding and answers" (Luke 2:47). This learning process continued throughout the Savior's life.

You must not regard your legal education as consisting of the three years that you have spent in this Law School. This is part of what I mean when I counsel that you should be "teachable." These three years have only been the beginning. The label "commencement" is particularly appropriate for a lawyer's training. The great lawyers are the ones for whom the legal education process never ends. The longer they practice the more proficient they become.

With your graduation from law school, you will move from one phase of your legal education to another. The emphasis will also change. The principal emphasis of your law school years has been legal analysis, and to a lesser extent learning substantive rules of law. If you are the kind of lawyer you should be, you will continue to improve those legal analysis skills and to acquire additional learning about the rules of law. But those will no longer be the focal points of your continuing legal education. Probably the single time in your professional career when you will know the most about the largest number of rules of law will be the day before you take the bar exam. It should not be the point at which you are the best lawyer. The main focus will now shift to the development of practical application of the analytical abilities and the rules that you have learned in law school. You should always approach those tasks with the same enthusiasm and the same concern as you approached your first semester of law school. I can think of no higher compliment that could be paid to any lawyer than that at any given time in his life, he was a better lawyer than he had ever been before.

Some of you may have heard a talk given by Francis Kirkham at the Law School two years ago this spring on the occasion of the annual Board of Visitors meeting. During the time that Mr. Kirkham served as a law clerk to

Chief Justice Charles Evans Hughes of the United States Supreme Court, he heard an oral argument delivered by John W. Davis, who was then in the late stages of his career. Mr. Kirkham commented to the Chief Justice how impressed he was that a man of aging years could perform so brilliantly. Hughes response was: "That's because he's a lawyer."

I think that Chief Justice Hughes was partially right. Certainly he was right as to John W. Davis. Unfortunately, not all lawyers are like that. Some effectively stop their learning processes once they leave law school. They remain for long periods of time on the same plateau, or even begin a gradual, continuing slide downward. But the great ones are like John W. Davis and J. Reuben Clark. The longer they live, the longer they practice, the better lawyers they become. I know of no better example of this characteristic than J. Reuben Clark. His mind was never satisfied. He was always striving to gain new knowledge and to reach new and higher levels of understanding. In the foreword to the biography of President Clark's law school and professional years, I described him as "a man who was, at times, unsure of himself, a man who altered his decisions, a man who made mistakes and repented of them . . . a soul who struggled harder than most and who faced numerous obstacles, trying temptations, and severe challenges."[3]

You, too, will have decisions to make. In the process of decisions you, too, will make mistakes. Those mistakes, and the willingness to recognize them and learn from them, constitute an important part of the continual learning process that is characteristic of every good lawyer. They will contribute to making you the complete lawyer, the whole lawyer, the lawyer of integrity in the broadest sense of that word. In his continual striving to grow and improve, J. Reuben Clark became a Christ-like advocate in both the earthly and spiritual sense. He also became a Christ-like person. May God bless you to achieve what J. Reuben Clark achieved is my prayer in the name of Jesus Christ. Amen.

This convocation address was given at the BYU Law School on April 24, 1981. Reprinted from Speeches at the Sixth Convocation of the J. Reuben Clark Law School, Brigham Young University, April 24, 1981, 1–3.

Marion G. Romney (1897–1988) received his LL.B. from the University of Utah in 1932. He served as a General Authority 1941–88, member of the Quorum of Twelve Apostles 1951–88, and counselor in the First Presidency 1972–85.

Notes

1. Frank W. Fox, *J. Reuben Clark: The Public Years*, (Provo, Utah: Brigham Young University Press, 1980), 360.

2. *Id.* at 375.

3. *Id.* at xi.

Duty to Rescue: The Case of the Good-Enough Samaritan

Tessa Meyer Santiago

I don't know if you've ever noticed this particular man. He lives among us. Moves around Provo with his sleeping bag, two carry-ons, his stereo, and a pillow. His favorite spot right now is the bus bench just south of the Missionary Training Center. He likes bus benches. I've seen him sitting on them day after day waiting for the bus that never comes. He sat all through the summer and through last winter and the winter before that. That's when I met him.

Two winters ago I looked up from ordering a plate of teriyaki chicken at Teriyaki Bowl and saw him sitting on the bus bench outside Hogi Yogi. It was 32 degrees outside, and this man was sitting quietly like he was listening to prelude music only he could hear. I watched him through the window while I ate. He didn't move during my entire meal. Just sat, almost daintily, with his feet crossed and his arms protecting his life next to him on the bench.

I went outside and asked him whether he had eaten. Could I buy dinner for him? "No, thank you. I've eaten. And I have these if I get hungry." He held up a bag of fruit.

My family and I got into the car and drove up the street. Then I made my husband flip a U-turn in Winchell's parking lot. "Do you have anywhere to stay tonight?" "Not yet." "I can't take you home with us, because our house is too small, but I can get you a hotel room." "Thank you. Motel 6 in East Bay is where I prefer to stay."

So I climbed into the backseat with the kids. He took the front with his belongings. When he signed the motel register, I couldn't help but notice he had the most beautiful handwriting—an almost elegant paradox coming from the hand of somebody who spends his days waiting for the local buses.

His name is Anthony or Andrew or Michael, I recall—something of the Episcopalian saint variety. I think he's from Atlanta or somewhere in Georgia. When he lost his job about four years ago, he gathered his things together and started traveling. He likes Provo. The people are friendly. The police don't bother him too much.

251

As Anthony/Andrew/Michael left to find his room at the motel, the manager turned to me. "Do you mind if I ask you a question?" "No." "Where did you find him?" "Just sitting out in the freezing cold on a bus bench." "You know, you're not the first person to bring him here. He's had people book him into the motel for a week before. He's really just using you guys." "I figured that. He knew exactly where he wanted to stay. As long as he's warm. Nobody should have to sleep outside in the cold like this."

That was two years ago—long ago enough that I can't quite remember his name, not so long ago that I no longer recognize him. When I drive by the MTC and see him sitting quietly in the winter afternoon sun, I cannot help wondering, "Was that all I had to do? Just $71.68 of mercy on the Discover Card and my duty to Provo's homeless is done?" His very presence on that bench unnerves me. I want to turn my head, to pass by on the other side. You see, I don't quite know if that was enough. I have the sense I am still that brother's keeper.

The discussion was particularly heated the day Ms. Augustine-Adams brought in the casino case to our torts class in law school. The facts were brutal: Two young men from California went to visit the casinos in southern Nevada. On some strange, sadistic whim, one of the young men, Jeremy Strohmeyer, abducted a seven-year-old girl outside the casino. He took her into the men's bathroom, locked the two of them in a stall, and proceeded. The other young man, the friend, walked into the middle of a nightmare, as far as he could tell from the sounds coming from the other side of the closed stall. He must have stood there for a moment—the record's not really clear. Then he walked out of the bathroom as quietly as he had entered. He told no one, not a soul. He didn't raise the alarm, didn't rush to the security guard, didn't break down the door to rescue that poor little girl, didn't even tell the police when Strohmeyer confided in him what he had done. He just walked on by.

They tried to find some charge to hang on the friend. Not manslaughter, not murder: he took no physical part of the action. Not depraved indifference to human life: he didn't do anything criminal. Not assault: he didn't threaten to harm the poor girl, didn't even have an intent to harm her. Not an accomplice: he didn't know what the other guy was planning. Not even negligence: he had no duty that he could breach. "But, but, but, . . ." we all stammered. "Surely he had to do something once he heard and knew what was happening." "Didn't have to," said the Nevada law. "Didn't have to do a darn thing."

The legal concept's a difficult one to stomach. It's called "duty to rescue." It should really be called "no duty to rescue." Essentially, the law says: If you had no part in creating the circumstances in which people needing to be rescued find themselves, you have no duty to rescue them. So, if you see a woman in the middle of a rainstorm stranded on I-15 with three children in her car, drive on by. If you see a man caught in the middle of a raging torrent, obviously going to drown, stay right there on the bank. You could even wave as he drifts away. If you walk into a bathroom and hear your friend doing unthinkable acts in a stall, walk out. The law is on your side.

However, if you choose to intervene or attempt a rescue, you have a duty to continue that rescue until your life is threatened. Then you can pull out, and nobody will hold you liable. In fact, you can pull out at any time, as long as you don't leave the person in a worse position than the one you found him in. So, say you jump into that raging torrent to save that man. After battling to get to him, you hold him up and strike for shore. You fight uprooted trees, swirling currents, and floating cats, and 10 feet from the shore you can't hold on any longer. It's either you or him. In an agonizing decision you see your family, your husband, your children, the mortgage on the house, and your very small insurance policy, and you let the man go. He drowns a little while later. No one in his right mind or heart would find you liable for the man's death. Certainly not the law.

Say you jump into that river to save the same drowning man. You battle out to him, fighting uprooted trees, swirling currents, and floating cows. You grab hold of his collar and strike for shore. Just then you remember, "Hey, the 49ers' game is on in a couple of minutes!" You couldn't possibly effect the rescue and be home in time for the kickoff. So you let go of the collar, swim for shore, load up the fishing gear, and head for home. You make the kickoff. The man drowns five minutes into the first quarter. Are you liable for his death? No. He would have drowned anyway. What's the harm in a little false hope?

What actual, quantifiable harm did the friend do to the little girl who heard the door swing open and thought she was about to be saved? What harm more than the harm she was already suffering did the friend inflict on her little soul? Not enough harm to hold him liable, says the American law. Our friend had no duty toward this girl, nothing that could bind him to act toward her in a certain way. Therefore, in the quintessential equation of tort law, if there is no duty to act, then whatever harm comes about cannot be attributed to our friend's failure to do his duty. Thus there is no liability (the civil law's counterpart to guilt). My mind raced to find a duty I could pin on that friend: a special relationship like that of a doctor/patient or a teacher/student or guardianship, because she was so young. I couldn't find one. He didn't even know her. She was a stranger to him. He didn't have to take her in.

When I was 12 years old, I learned the meaning of despair. It was the Christmas holidays in South Africa—a six-week stretch of summer days we filled with beaches, movies, and selecting two-dollar Christmas gifts for the nine members of my family. The closest shopping center was two suburbs away, about two miles along Main Road in Claremont. We walked there and back. It took about half an hour at a brisk pace, weaving in and out of the oak trees planted in a soldierly row along the sidewalk.

One afternoon I set off for home from Claremont. I'm not sure why I was alone. Normally Kim was with me wherever I went. But no matter. I actually enjoyed walking alone. I conjured up the lives of the people who lived in the houses I walked by. I wondered who put up the shawl in the window, who drank all the beer in the bottles piled outside a gate, and why in the world anybody would own a Pekingese.

The walk that day took me over the bridge and past Newlands Cricket Club, where I caught a glimpse of the wicket as I went by the turnstile. Suddenly, just as I started running my hands against the bars of the wrought-iron fence that encircled Kelvin Country Club, I stopped dead in my tracks. I couldn't move. I felt like somebody had tied my insides to a stick and was slowly turning them—like I had seen Indian dyers doing to sheets of cotton streaked with indigo—twisting, turning, wrapping my intestines round and round until it was all I could do to breathe. I sank to the ground, leaning against and gripping the bars with my hands and squatting there under the trees. (I would later become familiar with, although not in the least accustomed to, menstrual cramps, but this was my first severe attack. Perhaps my young body couldn't quite figure out the genteel way to slough the womb. After all, it was only my fifth or sixth time.)

Hindsight was scant comfort to me as I crouched there and waited for the pain to pass. It didn't. I made myself walk 10 steps. I crossed the road, reached the traffic island, and sank to the ground. I started to pray, to plead, to beg anybody who would listen or could hear—my mother, who I knew was at home; the people driving by in the street not 20 feet away; or God, who could pluck me up and transport me home if He really wanted to. I'm not sure what I looked like to the people driving by in those cars. Did they see the curly-headed young girl, fists doubled into her abdomen, rocking as she lay curled on the grass in the middle of a traffic island?

I must not have looked desperate enough. Nobody stopped. I must not have sounded desperate enough either. My mother never came. She didn't hear my cries, as I was certain she would. Every moment of those two hours it took me to creep my way home, I expected the red-and-white VW bus to pull up to the curb and my mother to rush out, saying, "My darling, I heard you. I knew you needed me. I'm here." Even God didn't seem to see me, bent over double, hanging on to fences and walls as I tried so very hard not to cry out loud. All I wanted was the pain to subside so that I could run home. That didn't seem so very much to ask.

I have often wondered why I had to crawl home when I was 12. Why couldn't God have made the pain subside? Why couldn't my mother have heard my urgent pleas sent on those otherworldly mind waves I thought existed between mother and child? Why couldn't somebody have stopped and taken me home? Was the sight of a young girl doubled over on the grass in the middle of a traffic island so common a sight that they thought nothing of it? Or were they so intent on going and getting that they didn't notice me?

I have a mother-in-law with a gift for noticing. I don't believe she has ever passed by on the other side. Ella always knows "a dear, little family" who needs, or a "sweet young couple" who have nothing, or one of her many "young friends" who have been parented by people with no interest in the vocation. Her garage is the cosmic opposite of a black hole. Furniture, clothing, and last-minute birthday and baby-shower gifts pour out of the double doors and take up lodging elsewhere. The supply never seems to diminish. Her neighbors know she knows. They come to her with bags full of clothes, pickups full of furniture. "Where do you find these people?" they ask my mother-in-law. Ella just smiles and makes up a sweet reply that won't hurt their feelings. Later she will take their food and their furniture to her dear little families and to her poor young friends who live only about a mile away on the other side of town.

I don't think Ella's neighbors are cruel or unkind. I know them. They're generous, compassionate, kind people who live very busy lives and who, if you asked, would drop what they were doing to help you. But if you didn't ask, if you were just hungry, needy, naked, sick, or afflicted, they wouldn't know where to find you.

I, on the other hand, was lying the middle of a traffic island. That's about the equivalent of sitting in the middle of the traffic circle at the entrance to Utah Valley State College, or waiting outside the MTC for buses that never come. It's about the equivalent of a man, stripped naked, lying on the side of the road.

In Luke 10:30–35 we read that when a "certain priest" came down that way and saw that half-naked man, "he passed by on the other side." Likewise, a Levite, a minister in the sacred temple sanctuary, came and looked on that naked man. And seeing him where and how he lay injured, the Levite "passed by on the other side." But a Samaritan, a foreigner and a heathen, came where this naked man was, saw him, and did not look away. He looked straight at this man, this naked stranger, and took "compassion on him."

Gathering him in his arms, this heathen "bound up [the stranger's] wounds, . . . set him on his own beast," and, steadying him while they walked, "brought him to an inn, and took care of him." This foreign heathen told the innkeeper when he left the next morning, "Take care of him. When I return I will repay you whatever you have spent to heal my friend."

I recently heard an enlightening interpretation of this parable of the good Samaritan. Most religions teach the parable as the ideal of neighborliness. After all, Christ does ask the question at the end of the parable "Which now of these three, thinkest thou, was neighbour unto him that fell among thieves?" (Luke 10:36). But, gazing up at a stained-glass window in a European cathedral, Jack Welch realized that the parable has not always been taught this way. He saw, in perfect jewel-toned symmetry, a depiction of the Savior's life and the parable of the good Samaritan in an arched window. Wondering about the significance, he asked the curate who worked in the cathedral.

The curate replied that in the early days of the Christian church, the parable of the good Samaritan was taught as an allegory of the Savior's mission: The man Adam went down into the world, where he fell among thieves, who stripped him naked and left him lying there. Two religious men ignored his pitiful state and "passed by on the other side." But Jesus the Christ, who had nowhere to lay His head, saw the man Adam as he lay injured and had compassion for him. This Jesus gathered the man Adam and all his posterity in His arms, bound his wounds with the balm of Gethsemane, and took him to the church. He told the innkeeper of the church to watch over Adam's soul, to take good care of this man. When Jesus came this way again, He would repay the debt he owed for the man Adam's soul.[1]

The day we learned the (no-)duty-to-rescue rule, we also learned about the good Samaritan laws. In some states the legislatures have enacted laws that require passersby to intervene if they see a crime being committed. The same laws also protect from liability those people who decide to help an injured person, should the injured person decide to sue them for making things worse. I suppose these are good laws. They force people to do good things, to help those in their community. I can't help thinking that whoever named the law missed the point completely.

The Good Samaritan did not act because he feared punishment. He acted because he had kindness in his soul, because his bowels were filled with compassion, and his whole soul was bent on mercy. He literally could not have acted another way. To call a law that forces people to be good after the title of the original being whose goodness needed no compulsion is ironic and only serves to perpetuate the myth of the austere Christ, the God of justice, the One who watched to see me fall.

I have learned, though, that there is another Savior, the other Jesus whom I seldom encountered in my Protestant Bible-study classes—the Christ of mercy, of compassion; the Christ who, though not bound by any eternal duty, chose to come to my rescue.

After class the day we read the casino case and studied the good Samaritan laws, I exited the Law School and sat down on the ledge that runs around the building. My gaze was filled with the rise of Squaw Peak and Y Mountain, not a half mile away. Above them the sky was that brilliant, brittle blue of late fall. I don't think I was thinking coherently; I was thinking a feeling. All I could feel was a profound sense of awe, of inexpressible, bone-deep gratitude that He descended below all things to rescue me in my fallen state that I had brought upon myself "because of [my] own disobedience" (Alma 42:12) and that He stayed, despite His own suffering, to complete the act.

Paradoxically, after learning that one young man turned his back on a seven-year-old girl struggling for her life, my thoughts were lifted to the Savior (perhaps in despair, perhaps in hope that the angels came to be with her when no earthly being would volunteer), to His unspeakable sacrifice, His indescribable bravery.

You see, according to American law, He didn't have to do a thing to help me—or you, for that matter. We've brought upon ourselves our own misery. We've lied, coveted, rationalized, committed, and omitted ourselves into our current state: cut off from the presence of God, subject to the demands of justice. According to tort law, the Savior has no duty to rescue us. He had nothing to do with putting us where we are.

"But He volunteered," the first-year law student objects. Yes, He did. And knowing what I know now about volunteers and rescues, I am even more moved by Christ's simple statement: "Here am I, send me" (Abraham 3:27). I don't know whether He knew just exactly what Gethsemane would be. I don't know whether one ever really is prepared for the nails and the crown of thorns. I don't know whether Christ knew He, legally, could turn back. If He had shrunk to drink the bitter cup that lonely night, we could not have held Him liable. Justice would still have been served. If, despite the fervent prayer, despite the angel to strengthen Him, the Redeemer had decided to abandon His eternal rescue mission, no law in this land would have held Him liable. Those whom He intended to rescue are in no worse state than when He started: we are still severed by sin from the presence of God. We'd be no worse off because He tried and failed or even tried and got tired.

But, thanks be to God, our Rescuer "has kindnesses in [His] nature."[2] Thanks be to God that "mercy claimeth all which is her own" (Alma 42:24), which "mercy cometh because of the atonement" (Alma 42:23). Thanks be to God, the Rescuer drank the bitter cup. Thanks be to God, our Good Samaritan looked upon us and looked not away. From the very first council, He noticed us and our predicament. He never passed by on the other side. He traveled from on high to find those who needed rescuing. He saw me on the side of the road, lying injured, unable to save myself. He picked me up, bound my wounds with the balm of Gethsemane, and took me to His church, where he gave the bishop strict instructions to take care of me and my wounded soul until He could return to claim me and take me home. And return He will, because He always was, and is forever willing to be, my Keeper.

Reprinted from The Restored Gospel and Applied Christianity: Student Essays in Honor of President David O. McKay, *1999, 71–81 and the* Clark Memorandum, *Spring 2001, 26–31.*

Tessa Meyer Santiago is an award-winning writer who received her M.A. in English in 1992 and her J.D. in 2001 from Brigham Young University.

Notes

1. See John W. Welch, "The Good Samaritan: A Type and Shadow of the Plan of Salvation," *BYU Studies* 38, no. 2 (1999): 50–115.

2. Jeremy Glastein, "Evil Actions Compel Us to Respond with Good," *San Francisco Chronicle,* 22 September 1998, A21.

Index

Aaron
  denied responsibility for golden calf, 75
  on repentance, 211
abortion, 115–17
Abraham, covenant of, 4–5
actions, 5, 216–17
Adam
  asked where he was, 1, 6
  blamed Eve, 6
  hid from God, 6
  as man who fell among thieves, 256
Advisory Commission on Electronic Commerce, 234
agency, 75, 114–17, 181, 212–13, 213–14
Alma, counsel of, 19
  and lawyers, 134
  on mercy and repentance, 218, 220
Amulek
  and lawyers, 135
  on the unrepentant, 220
Angelou, Maya, on result of divine parentage, 202
answer, best, is how we live, 3
Aristotle, on friendship, 181
arrogance, 134–37. *See also* pride
arson, 62–65
Asay, Carlos E., on virtue, 139
Ashton, Marvin J., on treating others, 6
athletes, 5, 24–25, 56, 157–59
Atonement. *See also* Jesus Christ
  and balance between mercy and justice,
    219–20, 224
  belief in, 6
  and building Zion, 235–36, 243
  makes mercy possible, 217, 219–20
  possible through Jesus' integrity, 86
attorneys. *See* lawyers

Bagehot, Walter, on example of Robert E. Lee,
  81

balance
  mentally, physically, spiritually, and
    socially, 12–21, 32–33
  between responsibilities, 30, 38–39, 43
  between rules and initiative, 49, 57
Baldwin, Stanley, pride of, 84
Ballard, Charles, founded Teen Fathers of
  Cleveland, Ohio, 203
Barton, John, on growth of appellate court, 169
Benson, Ezra Taft, on pride, 179
bill, on policy problems, 169–70
brother of Jared, on God's compliance with
  law, 213
Brown v. the Board of Education, 129
Buber, Martin, on I-thou relationships, 180–81
burden, imposed on covenant people, 4
Burke, Edmund, on adversity, 99

Cameron, William J., on covenant people's
  burden, 4–5
career management, 28–30
casino case, 252–53
Chamberlain, Neville, policies of, 83
charity, 6–7, 16–17, 125, 159–61, 183–85, 198, 204
choice, 114–17
Christians, defined by behavior, 5–6
Church callings, 31, 32, 44–45, 104–5, 123–29,
  133–34, 164
Churchill, Winston
  on conscience, 83, 155
  felt prepared, 92
  on opportunities to serve, 92
Clark, J. Reuben, Jr.
  credo of, 192
  on ethics, 72–73
  example of, 165–66, 192–93, 246–47, 249
  importance of family to, 247
  testimony of, 232
Clark, Luacine, illness of, 247

259

Acknowledgments

William F. Atkin

"But where are the nine?" (Luke 17:17)

On behalf of the J. Reuben Clark Law Society, I want to thank a long list of individuals who have helped this publication move from wonderful musings to reality. *Life in the Law* began some time ago as we recognized the quality and staying power of talks given and articles written for LDS attorneys and law students. Over the years, these pieces have brought perspective, balance and peace to busy professionals. To extend that positive effect, we wanted to bring a collection of them together, under one cover, as a ready reference and a thoughtful addition to personal libraries.

Any good project requires many contributions, and this one has been blessed with many fine ones. I want to express our appreciation to Scott Cameron who, together with me and others, dreamed of such a publication and to Galen L. Fletcher for being the chief historian and researcher. The meaningful content is thanks to the authors of each chapter and to Ron Millett at Deseret Book for allowing the reprint of portions of previous publications.

I am especially grateful for the encouragement and financial support of Dean H. Reese Hansen, Associate Dean Kathy Pullins and Assistant Dean Mary Hoagland at the J. Reuben Clark Law School. I extend many thanks to the members of our tireless selection committee, James M. Dester, Matthew Kennington, Ted D. Lewis, Stephen R. Marsh, Cory H. Maxwell, R. Marshall Tanner and John W. Welch. I also appreciate the BYU Studies staff, who assisted with the book, and Bjorn Pendleton, who designed the book cover.

I offer sincere appreciation to Galen L. Fletcher and Jane H. Wise who led our editing/compiling team with their clear vision of this project and their best efforts. Other contributors to *Life in the Law* include: K. Haybron Adams, Paul Angerhofer, Jeff Belliston, Edward Carter, Carolynn Clark, Lisa Cope, Lyle Fletcher, Bonnie Geldmacher, Justin Hunter, Carl Johnson, GaeLynn Kuchar, Marcene Mason, Jennifer McCall, Kimberly Chen Pace, Marny K. Parkin, Mireya Redd, Carolyn Stewart, Susannah Thomas, Laurie Urquiaga, Lee Warthen and Deborah Wright.

William F. Atkin received his J.D. from Arizona State University College of Law in 1972 and his LL.M. from Columbia University in 1979. He is currently Chair of the J. Reuben Clark Law Society (2001–2002) and Associate General Counsel for The Church of Jesus Christ of Latter-day Saints.